THE *Complete* ROCKING HORSE MAKER

REGULATIONS 1974

THE *Complete* ROCKING HORSE MAKER

by

Anthony Dew

Dedicated to my son Sam

ISBN 0-9545388-1-1 (hardback edition)
ISBN 0-9545388-0-3 (softback edition)

Designed and published by
The Rocking Horse Shop Ltd, Fangfoss, York, YO41 5JH England.

Printed and bound in Spain by Perfils.

Foreword

by Robert Nathan, Toymaker and Manager of The British Toymakers Guild

Of all traditional toys the Rocking Horse is without doubt king of the nursery. Anthony Dew's own beautiful hand-crafted rocking horses have been happily trotting out of his Yorkshire workshops ever since he started up his company back in the mid 1970s. His success as a rocking horse maker and above all his enthusiasm for rocking horses in general have certainly been instrumental in re-establishing with the public an awareness of the rocking horse as a 'must have' toy for the lucky child.

But success in business or even the possession of skill in a chosen craft are not necessarily all that one should look for in a craftsperson. For me the mark of a truly accomplished craftsperson is one who is sufficiently confident of their own talents that they are not afraid to share their knowledge with others, and Anthony Dew fulfils the criteria perfectly. He has succeeded in distilling the skills and knowledge acquired over the past twenty five years as one of this country's foremost rocking horse makers into a wonderfully concise and easy-to-follow book that will assuredly provide you with all the information you will ever need to create your very own rocking horse. With this book you will be able to create not only a wonderful plaything, but one that may well become a family heirloom as it is handed down through the generations.

Author's Note

This book contains all the designs from my previous work, 'The Rocking Horse Maker', which it supersedes, and a lot more. There are several new designs, and many additions and improvements to the existing ones, with lots of new line drawings and colour pictures. Some of my previously published tried and tested designs are reproduced here, with revised or re-written text and many new photographs. Please note that since I have given up the need to try to look like an ageing country craftsman, because I am one now, the chap with the beard in some of the pictures is the younger me.

I hope this book conveys to you something of my love for this wonderful craft and plaything, and inspires you to make a rocking horse. Whichever way you look at it, it is an absorbing, worthwhile and satisfying way to spend your time. What more could you want?

CONTENTS

A great little rocker! Straightforward construction set off by carved head and upper body.

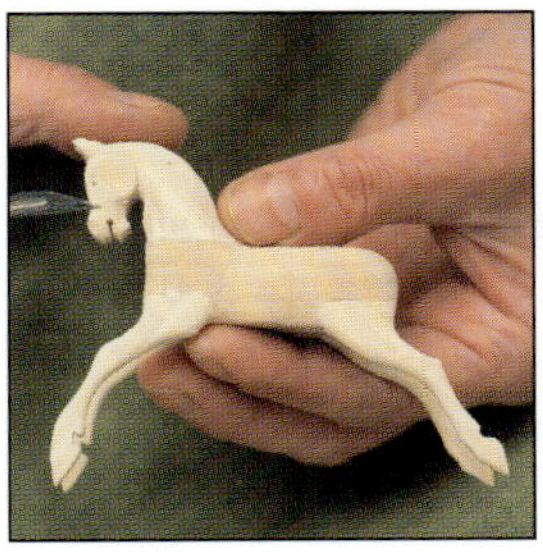

Twelfth scale carved traditional rocking horse.

A proper fully carved Victorian style rocking horse made just like the full size ones, for dolls to ride.

Fully carved Victorian style rocking horse for children aged up to about 5 years.

Fully carved traditional Victorian style rocking horses for children of any age. The real thing & you can make it!

How to make swing iron safety stands for Half Size, Small, Medium & Large carved rocking horses.

How to make traditional bow rockers for Half Size, Small & Medium carved rocking horses

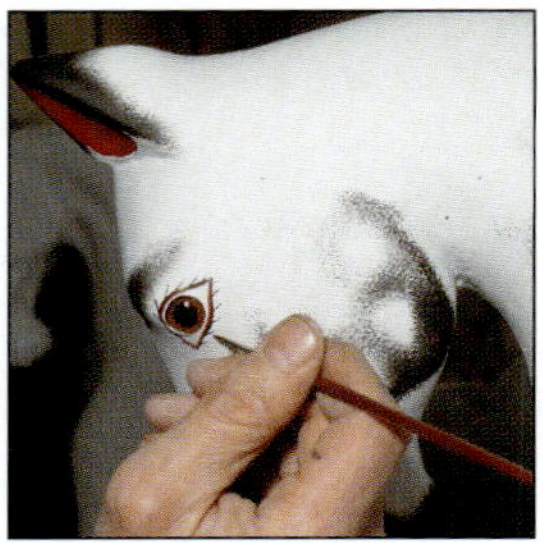

The Guild of Rocking Horse Makers

FINISHED SIZES - WHO IS IT FOR? - HOW EASY IS IT REALLY?

Rocking Horse Project	Finished Sizes*	Suitability**	Can I do It?
Chapter 3 - Chair Horse:	$35\frac{1}{2}$" long x $19\frac{1}{2}$" high x 13" wide [905 x 495 x 330 mm]	1 to 3 years	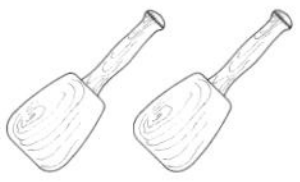
Chapter 4 - Toddler's:	$35\frac{1}{2}$" long x 22" high x $15\frac{1}{2}$" wide [905 x 560 x 395 mm]	1 to 3 years	
Chapter 5 - Swinger:	42" long x 31" high x 16" wide [1067 x 788 x 406 mm]	2 to 6 years	
Chapter 6 - Little Red Rocker:	42" long x 30" high x 16" wide [1067 x 762 x 406 mm]	2 to 6 years	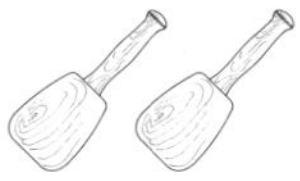
Chapter 7 - Miniature Carved horse on Stand:	5" long x $4\frac{1}{8}$" high x $1\frac{3}{4}$" wide [127 x 45 x 105 mm]	miniature dolls	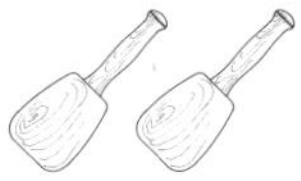
Chapter 8 - Half Size Carved horse on Stand:	$26\frac{1}{2}$" long x 9" high x $21\frac{1}{2}$" wide [674 x 230 x 540 mm]	dolls	
Chapter 9 - Small Carved horse on Stand:	42" long x 33" high x 16" wide [1067 x 838 x 407 mm]	3 to 5 years	
Chapter 10 - Medium Carved horse on Stand:	53" long x 41" high x 18" wide [1346 x 1041 x 457 mm]	3 to 8+ years	
Chapter 10 - Large Carved horse on Stand:	60" long x 49" high x 20" wide [1524 x 1245 x 508 mm]	3 to adult!	
Chapter 12 - Half Size Carved horse on Bow Rockers:	$35\frac{1}{2}$" long x $8\frac{5}{8}$" high x $21\frac{1}{4}$" wide [902 x 220 x 540 mm]	dolls	
Chapter 12 - Small Carved horse on Bow Rockers:	55" long x 32" high x 12" wide [1410 x 813 x 305 mm]	3 to 5 years	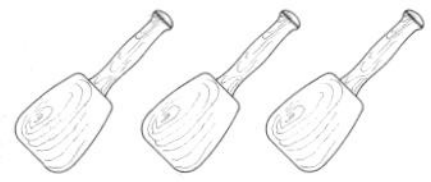
Chapter 12 - Medium Size Carved horse on Bow Rockers:	72" long x 42" high x 17" wide [1810 x 1080 x 438 mm]	3 to 8+ years	
Chapter 16 - Carousel Style horse:	51" long x 35" high x 11" wide [1295 x 895 x 285 mm]	3 to 5 years	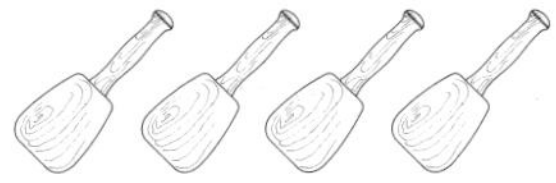

* Sizes are overall dimensions of the completed project, mounted up on its stand or rockers (eg height = floor to top of ears).

** Age ranges are approximate. Children, especially those under 3 years, should be supervised by a responsible adult.

HOW EASY IS IT?

 = Really simple, easy joints, no carving. A weekend project!
(or 2 mallets if you go for the the Toddler or Swinger with carved head)

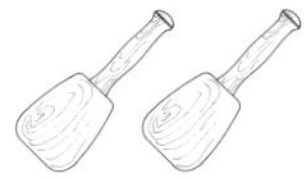 = Easy construction and straightforward method, with simply carved elements.

 = Straightforward construction, projects for reasonably confident woodworkers with some practice at carving.

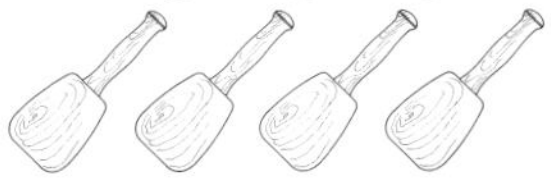 = More ambitious project for experienced carvers.

Not just a childhood plaything! These huge rocking horses were used to teach recruits of the British Cavalry Reserve how to keep proper position & balance during their training for battle in the First World War.

INTRODUCTION

A baby cries and you pick it up and cradle it in your arms, making soothing noises as you gently rock the child. This has the desired effect and the baby's crying subsides, partly because of the warmth and comfort of the cuddle and the soft cooing noises, but undoubtedly the rocking motion has a significant soothing effect. In fact (and research has demonstrated that this is so) rocking is the almost infallible way to pacify a crying baby, unless the child is actually distressed by pain, fear or discomfort. Any parent would surely broadly agree with this, and will have done so from time immemorial.

Rocking is not only soothing for crying babies, it has a similar effect on children of all ages who may rock themselves back and forth if sad or unhappy, or just bored. Mentally disturbed people do it, as do perfectly sane adults in rocking chairs. It is a physical form of the repeated mantra of meditators; a panacea; a way to sooth and ease the mind. On a rocking horse, it is fun too.

Horses (real ones) have been a vital component in the development of almost every human civilization. And since almost every adult concern is imitated in appropriate playthings for children, it is not surprising that toy horses have been made from earliest times. Of course children's toys are frequently roughly used; if a real horse is made to gallop across muddy fields, a toy horse will be made to do the same.

They are often made from perishable materials, so they become broken, worn and are discarded, and few really old toy horses survive to the present day. Nevertheless, a few have done so, made from clay, terra cotta and even wood, that date back several thousands of years. Many of these ancient model horses have been excavated from burial sites, probably made as burial artefacts rather than children's playthings. With a few notable exceptions, ancient toy horses tend to be quite small, certainly too small to be ridden, though sometimes they have wheels like pull-along toys. But if small model horses were made as burial artefacts, I am certain they were also made as children's toys. Could a child who saw one of these little horses resist wanting to play with it? And seeing this, a parent (a craftsman perhaps) would surely want to make one as a toy for his children's amusement and education.

A simple form of toy horse, which dates from at least medieval times, is the hobby horse. At its most basic the hobby horse is a representation of a horse's head, mounted on a stick, sometimes simply fashioned, sometimes beautifully carved and detailed. With a hobby horse it is the rider's legs that do the galloping.

Sometime in the early Seventeenth Century an unknown person had the idea of creating a plaything with the rideability of the hobby horse and the easy movement of the rocking cradle. A brilliant idea: a toy horse big enough for children to actually climb upon and ride. On the earliest rocking horses the rockers were made from two almost semi circular slabs of solid timber, arranged side by side but converging towards the top where a narrow plank formed the seat. On this was fixed a carved horse's head and neck, a seat back and a foot rest strategically placed either side. Made from solid timber, often oak, they were very heavy. But given the right balance and arc of curvature of the rockers, it was quite possible for even a small child to make them rock. The child was in complete control and could vary the rock at will from soothing and gentle to an exciting 'gallop'.

With curved bow rockers, especially if they are made too short, there is a danger that an enthusiastic rider could overturn the horse. This was prevented by cutting "stops" into the rockers

"Ere Jim, I've had this great idea . . ."

at both ends. These restrict the rocking action slightly - the horse can be rocked as far as the stops but no further - and do make it safer. A solid wooden rocking horse is a heavy thing, and overturning on its rider could obviously be injurious. Not that safety seems to have been a very big factor in the early design of these toys.

They were regarded not merely as amusements but as an apparatus for training young (and sometimes not so young) riders for the saddle, and an element of danger was permissible, even welcomed. If the rider was thrown off, she would be instructed to get straight back on and learn to ride properly!

Seventeenth Century rocker - solid timber, very heavy.

Some of these early slab sided rocking horses had the shape of the body and legs of the horse painted or even carved on the rocker sides. But it was not long before it was realised (again by some unknown maker) that a much more attractive and realistic appearance could be achieved by making the rockers out of long and thin bow-shaped arcs of timber and mounting on them a fully carved horse with four separate legs. This gave rise to the characteristic rocking horse of the Eighteenth and Nineteenth Centuries sometimes referred to as mounted on 'Georgian' bows. Apart from being splendid playthings, these can be beautifully carved and finished, and quite a few remain in existence in museums and collections, but only rarely in their original condition.

Bow rockers tend to travel across the floor, crashing into walls and furniture. Also, whilst good design and long bows ensure that the horse cannot be overturned by the rider, other children close by can be at risk from the large moving horse, especially if toes or fingers are caught under the rockers. Adult supervision is needed.

The inventive Victorians produced many patents and designs which attempted to improve upon the bow rocker. Some employing springs or levers enjoyed limited commercial success, but most were too complicated or impractical to be taken up, and probably never left the drawing board. But a patent filed by P. W. Marqua of Cincinnatti USA in 1878 and two years later in Britain, proved to be the one that had all the characteristics of a successful design. It was safer in use than bow rockers, and took up less space, but had a very effective rocking action. It was also simple; easy to make and fit. This is the swing iron safety stand, and it became so successful that it virtually superseded the old bow rocker style. It is much the commonest form of rocking mechanism in use today, except for small toddler size horses where curved rockers remain the favourite.

A more recent version of the slab sided horse, made by the author from plywood and jelutong. Lighter and easy to rock.

There is a tremendous variety of styles, construction methods and finishes used on wooden rocking horses, whether they are made for mounting on bow rockers or swing iron stands. They range from simple constructions with little or no carving or decoration, to beautifully carved horses with fine leather saddlery. As well as the traditional and ever popular dapple greys, there are painted rocking horses in all colours, those with a natural wood finish, and some covered with real skin. There are also stuffed rocking horses covered with skin or fabric, and horses made of papier mache, metal, fibreglass and plastic.

Made by F. H. Ayres c1900; still rocking and with its original dapple grey paintwork, tack and hair (what's left of it!).

When I first became interested in making rocking horses, many years ago now, it was almost a dead craft. This was not surprising since making carved wooden rocking horses is a labour and skill intensive business, not suited to the mass production requirements of modern industry. Some toy manufacturers continued to make rocking horses, but they tended to be of smaller and simpler design, occasionally wooden, more often metal or plastic, or fur fabric covered. Traditional carved wooden rocking horse making came close to extinction.

New horses on traditional swing iron stands - the Swinger and Little Red Rocker

In recent years there has been a great revival of interest in hand craft in general and rocking horse making in particular, and there is now a surprisingly large number of small businesses specialising in traditional rocking horse making (and restoring). Proper rocking horses are no longer as rare as their proverbial manure, and I

find this most gratifying. The surprising response to my earlier books showed that there is a considerable and growing interest in this fascinating craft, and we receive letters from enthusiasts and aspiring makers all over the world. When you have made a horse you may join The Guild of Rocking Horse Makers, which is dedicated to promoting and encouraging the craft (see Appendix).

My rocking horse designs are based on traditional styles, but they are in a continuous state of modification and development. Some designs are quite simple and easy to make, others inevitably more involved. This book contains projects suitable for all abilities, starting with hobby horses, a Toddler's rocker, the Swinger and a Chair horse , designs which involve little or no carving, and which can be successfully accomplished by people with little woodworking experience and few tools. Carved head options are given for those who have not done any carving before, but would like to try. The Little Red Rocker has more interesting carved elements though is still relatively easy to make.

Designs for the 'real' traditional Victorian style of fully carved rocking horse are described in several sizes and styles including mountings on stands and bow rockers, and a design for a carousel style horse is presented as a challenge for more ambitious woodcarvers. The construction method for each project has been kept as straightforward as practicable and none of the designs involves complicated joints. A fairly modest tool kit is all that is needed for the projects in this book, and most home woodworkers will already have the basic tools. Although the carving will require some specialized carving gouges etc (see Chapter 1), it is not necessary to spend a lot of money on tools and equipment before starting to make one of these projects. Indeed, to make the Miniature rocking horse for example, you need little more than a fretsaw and a sharp knife.

A rocking horse is a wonderful vehicle for a child's developing imagination and occupies a special place among playthings. His size, 'personality and solidity set him apart from smaller toys. A child will develop a much more intimate relationship with a rocking horse than with the large impersonal playground swings and see-saws.

A rocking horse can be a very real friend to a lonely child and he possesses, for the younger child, many of the qualities of a real horse with none of the drawbacks. He never needs feeding or exercising on frosty winter mornings, he can look after himself and doesn't resent neglect. He never needs to be mucked out. And he is absolutely tireless; always ready to take the child rider on the most exciting, yet secure imaginative gallops.

To make a fully carved rocking horse can be a challenging prospect, and I am often asked, "Do you think I can do it?" A hard question to answer, except to say that many people have used my designs, even those with limited woodworking and no carving experience, and have made a splendid job of it. We are frequently sent enthusiastic letters and photographs of rocking horses which people have made using our plans, and it is fascinating to see the varied results that arise, because each horse is unique and each maker puts something of him or her self into the project.

A wooden rocking horse is much more than just a toy for the moment, and in spite of the high-tech electronic games now so ubiquitous, remains a firm favourite. He will outlast several generations of young riders and become a family heirloom, passed down to new generations who will always greet him with pleasure. When, after many years of use, his mane and tail and saddle become tattered, his paintwork chipped and cracked, his joints loosen and his mechanical parts become rickety, he can be repaired and refurbished and given a whole new lease of life. Would that we had access to such immortality. The last chapter illustrates some examples of old rocking horses, and looks at collecting and restoring.

I hope this book will encourage many more people to discover the fascination of making rocking horses. To make your own rocking horse and to see it being enjoyed by your children and grand-children will give you a very special sense of achievement and satisfaction.

Above - letting the natural beauty of the timber show through.
Opposite page - new hand carved rocking horses made in the traditional way, with dapple grey paintwork.

Plate 1.1 Practice increases confidence.

CHAPTER 1

GETTING STARTED, TIMBER AND TOOLS

There are projects in this book for woodworkers of all abilities. You do not need a high level of skill to have a go at one and there are no complicated joints. Though some of the designs involve no carving at all, the carved projects are most appealing, and it is the prospect of carving which sometimes concerns people, especially those who have not tackled a project of this sort before. However, over the years many people who have never carved before have used my plans to make highly satisfactory rocking horses. Persistence and a desire to succeed will certainly overcome any doubts you may have.

For your first rocking horse you should choose a design which you feel to be well within your capability. If you are new to carving, choose one of the simpler designs to begin with. When that succeeds it will give you the confidence to go on to one of the more ambitious projects.

PATTERNS & CUTTING LISTS

Throughout this book, measurements are given in inches, followed by the metric equivalent in mm. The cutting lists give the actual finished dimensions (ie after planing) of the timber required. A reasonable allowance for fitting the patterns of the odd shaped pieces - eg legs - onto the timber has been made, but according to the availability of timber, you may vary the widths and lengths specified; for example if you obtain wider timber than that specified for the legs then the length required will be less since you will be able to overlap the leg patterns more on the board.

Actual size patterns or templates will be needed for all the shaped parts: head and neck, ear and eye pieces, neck muscle blocks, legs etc. You can make patterns by scaling up from the drawings in this book, which are all based on one inch square grids, or use the actual size drawings which are available for each project (see Appendix) and transfer them onto card or thin board, using tracing or carbon paper, and cut them out, taking care to leave in place any cramping noggins or bevelling allowances shown on the plan.

Position the patterns carefully on the timber so that the direction of grain conforms as nearly as practicable to that shown on the drawings, pencil round them, and then saw them out, keeping your saw cut just outside the pencil line.

If sourcing and preparing suitable timber proves problematic, timber packs are available with all the initial preparation ready done, to the point where you can start on the assembly - see Appendix - and patterns will not be needed.

TIMBER

Nothing is more disheartening than to spend a great deal of time and effort making your rocking horse only to find that when you bring it into a centrally heated room the joints begin to crack and open up. The way to ensure that this does not happen is to start with good quality timber - this normally means using kiln-dried timber since air dried stock from a timber merchant is rarely of a sufficiently low moisture content - and have good tight joints.

Ideally timber should be stored and worked on in conditions of temperature and humidity similar to

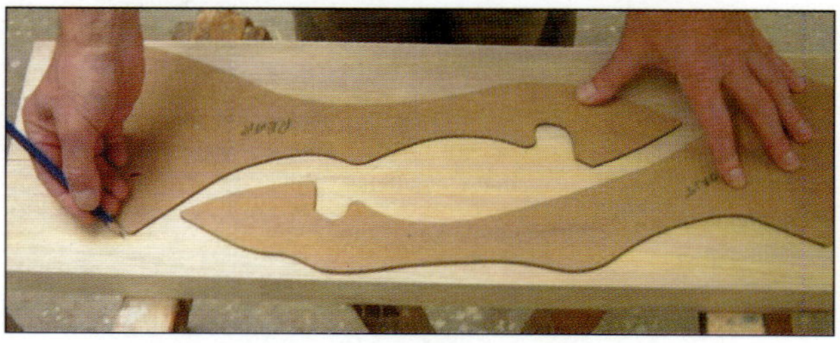

Plate 1.2 The patterns are laid out so that the timber is used in the most economical way; the shaped parts often overlap.

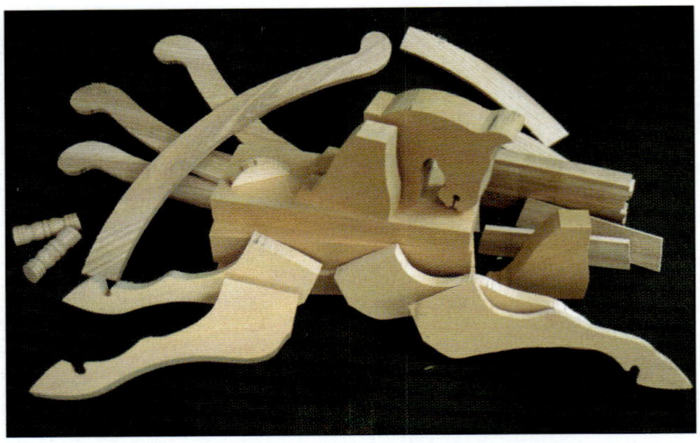

Plate 1.3 All the timber parts for a carved horse, & its bow rockers, prepared to the point at which it is ready for you to start on the assembly & carving.

Plate 1.4 The patterns are pencil marked onto the timber for bandsawing, in this case a Small head. Note the holes drilled to enable the bandsaw blade to be turned. Even so it may be necessary to take several bites at the tighter curves.

Plate 1.5 A Carver's Chop, made of maple with a steel screw & brackets; the ideal holding device for carvers. If you are intending to do a lot of carving it is well worth spending time to make one. They are also available ready made!

those which it will be in when finished. I know this may not be practicable in your particular circumstances. Do recognise though, that if you make your rocking horse in a damp shed outside, and then bring it into a heated room, you may have problems with cracking. Timber will take up moisture from the atmosphere like a sponge, so try to keep it in a dry place (under the bed for example). One man kept and worked on his horse in a corner of the living room while the rest of the family watched TV in the same room, ignoring the dust and woodchips. You may not have such an understanding spouse as that maker, but you have to get your priorities right!

For carving you will need a timber which is relatively easy to carve, stable when assembled, and available in the various thicknesses and widths specified in the cutting lists. In recent years, we have successfully used Tulipwood, often referred to as Poplar (Latin name liriodendron tulipifera) which carves well but is tough enough to take the knocks, is readily available at present, and has an attractive grain pattern which takes stain well, or it can be painted. It is also a plantation grown hardwood from renewable resources (mostly in the US), so avoiding use of tropical hardwoods.

Mahogany, basswood, cherry, sycamore and lime all carve well and have been used in rocking horse making, and many other hardwoods may be both suitable and available. Some may not be obtainable in the dimensions needed for the larger horses, so are more suitable for smaller projects, though of course smaller dimension timber can be laminated up to make larger sizes. Rocking horses have been made entirely from ash, beech or oak, but these are very much harder to carve, and I cannot see a great deal of virtue in making life much harder for yourself than it need be.

Jelutong is an excellent close grained carving timber which is very easy to work and therefore good for beginners. It is ideal for practice heads or for smaller projects such as the Half Size horses which do not have to carry weight, but in my opinion is rather too fragile for larger horses where, if used for head and body, a tougher timber like beech or maple should be used for the legs which have to take a lot of strain. Many of the old

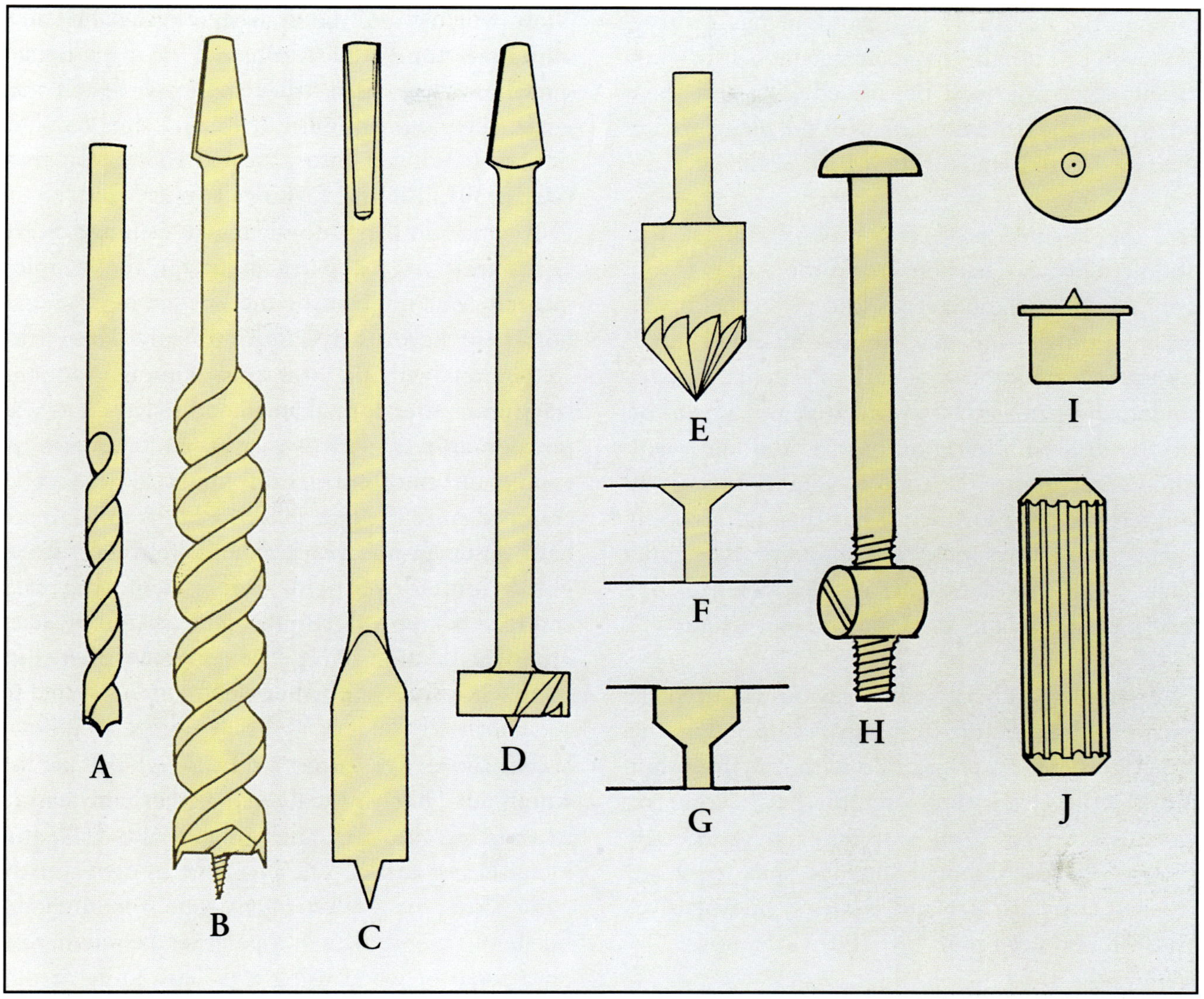

Fig 1. 1 A SELECTION OF DRILL BITS AND JOINTING DOWELS USED IN ROCKING HORSE MAKING. A - *Twist drill for screw and dowel holes.* B - *Auger bit for tail holes.* C - *Flat bit, cheaper than* B, *but not such a clean hole.* D - *Forstner bit, drills clean shallow flat bottomed holes, ideal for eyes.* E - *Countersink bit.* F - *screwhole opened out with countersink bit.* G - *screwhole counterbored, can be filled with a wooden plug to neatly conceal screw head.* H - *screw dowel, for a cheap strong joint.* I - *Centring marker, marks wood at the precise centre of hole to facilitate use of fluted dowelled pegs.* J - *Fluted dowel peg.*

time rocking horse makers used yellow pine or other softwood to make the head and body, with the legs in beech for its greater strength. For a painted dapple grey finish it does not matter if you mix the timbers. But if you intend going for a natural wood finish then you will probably want to use the same type of timber throughout.

On the whole you should avoid using pine or deal such as that supplied for the building industry since it tends to be of coarser grain and poorer quality. Some makers successfully use second hand timber, and I have seen a beautiful horse made from old pitch pine obtained from a demolition contractor, but you have to watch that rusty old nails do not ruin the cutting edges of your tools.

TOOLS and CRAMPS

A fretsaw (hand or power) is needed to cut out the parts for the miniature horse. A hand held jig-saw (saber-saw) can be used for the horses where no part is thicker than 1¾in (45). One maker, who is evidently not afraid of hard work, cut out all the parts for his Medium Size horse by hand with a coping saw, but we use a bandsaw. A small bench-top bandsaw should be quite capable of cutting up to 3in (75) thick timber, the thickest dimension on Medium and Large horses.

We normally keep a ⅜in (9) wide blade in our bandsaw and this will cope with most of the curves, but you will need to drill holes where the bends are tight to allow the blade to turn, and through the mouth. If your bandsaw has a tilting table you can use this to advantage by bandsawing bevels, eg at the tops of splayed legs, and then tidying up the bandsaw cuts with the plane, rather than having to plane off the whole of the bevel.

For the smaller projects - hobby horses, the Toddler's horse, Chair horse and the Swinger, you can make do with no cramps (except for the carved head options) and few tools. You will need compasses, smoothing or jack plane, try square, coping and panel saws, screwdriver, and a hand or electric drill with selection of bits. You may want some other tools - the time to acquire tools is as you feel the need for them - but then do invest in quality. It is always more satisfactory to use a good quality tool that does what it is supposed to do. And you can't blame the tool if it goes wrong.

To assemble a fully carved horse you will need six F-type sliding cramps (or sash cramps). For the Small horse you can make do with only four, but more will speed the assembly, as a rule of woodwork goes, "You can never have enough cramps". I like sliding F cramps since they are efficient, easy to use, and relatively inexpensive. You will also need four 4in (100) G cramps.

Also abrasive paper in various grades - 80, 120 and 180 grit, and 240 and 360 grit if you are going for a super-smooth natural wood finish.

JOINTS & JOINTING
I have tried to use dimensions which are standard timber sizes, but it has not always been possible. In the cutting lists therefore, where non-standard sizes are specified, or where the specified widths or thicknesses prove to be unavailable from your timber merchant, you may have to either cut down a piece to suit, or to joint together two or more pieces to achieve the required dimensions. Some of the designs (eg the Swinger head) require pieces of timber wider than you may be able to obtain. In these cases you will need to glue together two or more pieces edge to edge to make the width needed. Use sash or sliding F cramps.

Nearly all the joints used in these projects are simple butt joints, sometimes employing woodscrews (which hold the joint in position while the glues sets; the strength is in the glue) and sometimes fluted dowel pegs. In the chair horse, screw dowels are used - they are simple to use and make a very strong joint.

GLUE, FILLER and CHOPS
PVA woodworkers adhesive may be used with satisfactory results, particularly for the simpler projects. But for many years on our big rocking horses we have used Cascamite (now known as Extramite), with no problems. This is a strong, waterproof urea-formaldehyde adhesive - a white powder mixed with water - and we use it throughout the construction. Joints do need to be cramped since the glue takes six hours or so to set hard (faster in hot weather), and we usually leave glued joints overnight before removing the cramps. Scrape off surplus glue before it sets, otherwise it could blunt your gouges or even chip them - it is rock hard when set.

Some carvers get rather sniffy about the use of woodfillers, but you will need a filler with which to set in the glass eyes, and probably also to fill any blemishes or cracks. The best type to use is a two part, paste plus catalyst filler of the sort intended for use on wood. Mix in a polythene container or on a scrap of wood using a pallette knife or old dinner knife. Thoroughly mix a small amount of catalyst with the paste according to the instructions (the proportions are usually 1:30), and apply it quickly, since it begins to harden within ten minutes or so (quicker in warm weather). Avoid using motor car body type fillers, which are too hard and inflexible, or decorator's plaster fillers, which are too brittle or too grainy.

A carved rocking horse is an awkward shape to hold securely while you are working on it. The best holding device is a carver's chop mounted on a carving bench. The chop is a wooden vice with high and relatively narrow jaws, usually faced with leather or cork, and a steel screw that allows the jaws to open to about 12in (305). The carver's bench is relatively tall and thin; the carving is thus at a convenient working height and you can work all round it without having to constantly change its position. The bench has a platform base upon which you stand, so your own weight helps to keep the bench immoveable. If you are intending

Plate 1.6 With these six gouges & the round carver's mallet you can carve any rocking horse.

to do a fair bit of woodcarving it is time well spent to make yourself a carver's chop and bench such as this. Plans are available - see Appendix.

However, if you do not wish to go to the trouble of making a chops and bench for what may be only a one-off carving project, you can make do with an ordinary woodwork bench and vice, provided the jaws will open far enough to hold the body. Some makers use a DIY type work bench or 'Workmate' quite satisfactorily, or a large saw-horse onto which the work is clamped, or the horse can be laid on sandbags while you carve it.

CARVING TOOLS and SHARPENING

With the following six gouges you will be able to carve any rocking horse. They have been selected from the gouges in regular use in our own busy workshop, and are the ones I use most:

Straight London Pattern gouges - No. 4 -1in (25) (my favourite, extremely useful shallow sweep tool), No. 5 - 1/2in (13) (useful around the head), No. 9 - 3/8in (16) and No. 8 - 1 1/4in (32) alongee

Plate 1.7 Honing a gouge using a cotton mop. The machine has been turned round so the wheel turns away from you.

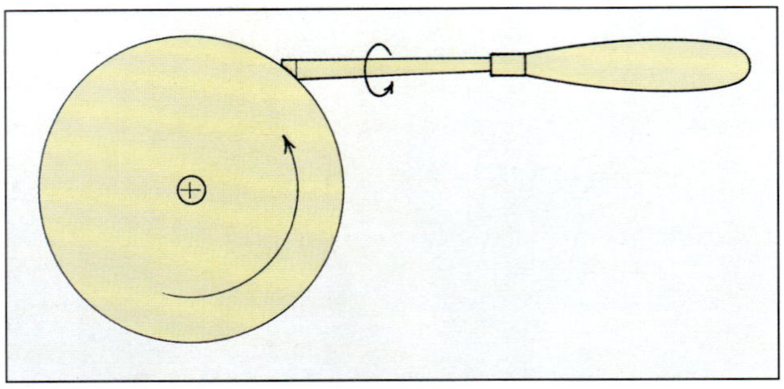

Fig. 1.2 Honing a gouge, showing how the bevel of the gouge rubs against the cotton mop as it turns away from you.

Plate 1.8 (l to r) Carroll drum sander for use in an electric drill. Half round & round Surforms. Microplanes with long lasting stainless steel blades: three different sized round ones & a half round one which is fitted into a hacksaw frame.

Plate 1.9 Drawknife, pull towards you with a slicing action.

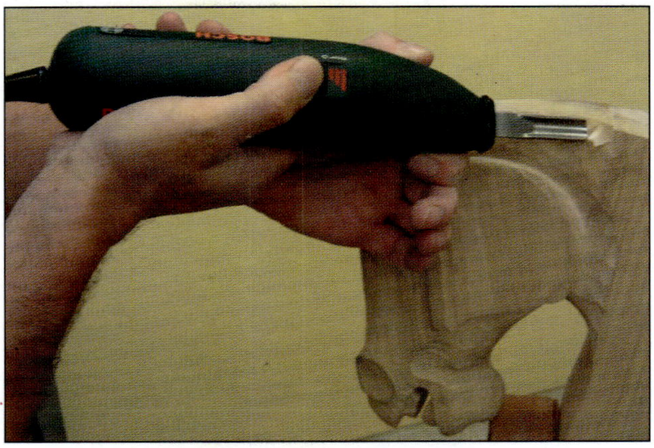

Plate 1.10 Bosch electric carver, makes small clean cuts easy.

(deep sweep gouges for roughing out carving); No. 30 - 3/8in (10) spoon gouge (for hollowing ears and nostrils and other head details) and No. 2 - 5/16in (8) straight corner chisel (for teeth and tongue). For the simpler projects you can make do with fewer or different ones, and a couple of the projects need a few more, smaller gouges.

Some woodcarvers, by no means only novices, have difficulty keeping their gouges sharp. Sharp edges are easily and efficiently accomplished using a rubber wheel for grinding and a cotton mop for honing, both mounted in a 6in (152) grinder. The grinder needs to be set up so that the wheels turn away from you (do this by turning the whole machine round and re-setting the guards). The gouge can then be honed by dressing the mop with a steel cutting compound and holding the bevel against the mop for a few seconds, generally all that is needed to bring back a razor sharp edge.

You will need a mallet; a round woodcarvers mallet is best, since it will wear evenly all round as you use it. It should have a comfortable ash handle and beech or maple head, and not be too heavy - around 22 ounces is quite heavy enough. A few other hand tools will aid the carving: round and curved Surforms, Microplanes or rasps will help you to shape the curves around the neck and body and to remove gouge marks; a drawknife (though it takes a bit of getting used to) is useful for slicing off the waste wood around the body and neck; and a spokeshave will help you to smooth the slow curves.

A router, with suitable cutters, will be useful for the rounding of edges in the Swinger and Little Red Rocker designs, and for cutting the chamfers on stands. But if you do not have one, these mouldings can be done by hand with a rasp, plane or spokeshave, finishing with abrasive paper.

POWER TOOLS for CARVING

There are a number of power carving tools on the market which enable you to produce wonderful carvings in no time at all, if you believe the advertisements. These include pneumatic or electrically driven gouges, rotary rasps with flexible drives, power files, and carving or rasping attachments for angle grinders. I have tried several of these and there is no doubt that they can be very useful. Some of the angle grinder attachments in particular are very effective at removing a lot of waste wood very quickly.

However, they tend to be very fierce and require absolute concentration. You need face and arm protection from flying wood chips, one small slip could spell disaster (even if only to your carving). They are no fun at all to use, and of course you still have to guide the tool, it won't do the job for you. So on balance, and in the interests of 'real' woodcarving, I recommend the traditional mallet and gouge approach. It may be a little slower but it is a lot more satisfying and why, after all, be in such a hurry?

Power assistance can be welcomed however, when you are sanding down. Most of the head and under the chin will have to be sanded by hand, in order to get into all the awkward places, but for the rest of the horse foam backed drum sanding attachments for your electric drill, and pad or orbital finishing sanders can greatly ease what is otherwise a laborious process.

CARVING

Before starting on the carving, study the text and photographs in this book to familiarise yourself with the procedure and the shapes to aim for at each stage. Some people find it helps them to understand and feel the contours involved if they make a practice model in clay or play dough.

It may also help you to look at real horses, but do not let this confuse you. What we are making here is a rocking horse and not a carving of a real horse. The rocking horse tends to be stylised, with simplified forms, and although it must be unambiguously recognisable as a horse, and will probably have many of the features and contours of a real horse, it need not imitate a real horse in every respect. What is absolutely right for a rocking horse can be quite unlike a real one. Conversely, carvers who try to make a realistic horse may find that it is visually unsatisfactory as a rocking horse. A knowledgeable horse lady once asked me, "Why is it that your rocking horses do not look like real horses?". I replied simply that it is because they are not real horses.

Plate 1.11 An Arbortech attachment used in an angle grinder. For the fast removal of waste wood, but it is very fierce!

More information on carving is given with each project. All the drawings, photographs and instructions in this book are aimed at ensuring that you achieve a successful result; a rocking horse that will be both fascinating for you to make and a delight for its riders. I can give you the information that I have found, by experience, to be helpful in achieving this, but I cannot, nor would I want to, take the tools from your hands.

In the end the rocking horse you make will be yours, and it will be unique. Even starting from the same basic design, each person produces a different result. Let this fact give you pleasure in your own achievement, rather than be a source of irritation that you are not getting it 'correct'. If you do become frustrated with it however, and feel that it is just not coming right for you, leave it completely alone for a while before taking up your tools again for another go. You will then see it with fresher, calmer eyes, and it will certainly come good in the end.

Plate 1.12 Mallet and gouge - the real thing!

Plate 2.1 Finished hobby horses 1, 2 & 3, varnished & decorated with coloured tape.

CHAPTER 2

Hobby Horses

Children don't need much to get their imaginations going and I have seen a child having great fun riding an ordinary broom as if it were a horse. These four designs have heads that are rather more horse-like than a broom, but they should be well within the capability of even a beginner at woodworking, and few tools are needed. Basically a hobby horse is a stick with a representation of a horse's head at the top and (usually) a wheel at the bottom. This is what I call a "hobby horse" although the term is, confusingly, sometimes used to describe rocking horses mounted on stands.

You will need a fretsaw or coping saw, a drill with $\frac{1}{2}$in (13) and $\frac{3}{4}$in (19) bits, abrasive paper, PVA adhesive, and a pair of compasses.

HOW TO MAKE IT

HOBBY HORSE Number 1

The first design is very simple: the head, wheel and connecting pieces are all made from $\frac{3}{8}$in (9) thick plywood. Birch ply tends to be the best quality, and a piece 10 by 12in (254 x 305) will be big enough for all the parts. The stick and handle are $\frac{3}{4}$in (19) diameter ramin dowel, the handle being 7in (178) long with both ends sanded to round them over, and the stick approx 30in (760) long (though you can vary the length of stick to suit the height of the potential rider). You will also need a short piece of $\frac{1}{2}$in (13) ramin dowel approximately $1\frac{1}{2}$in (38) long for the axle. Make sure, by testing on a piece of scrap wood, that the drill bits make holes in which the dowel will be a close fit; dowel does tend to vary in diameter.

Make a pattern of the head shape out of thin card, pencil round it onto the plywood and saw out. Note that you should leave on the piece at the bottom of the neck marked A on the plan. Sand the edges smooth and mark the position of the eyes on both sides. The eyes can be very simply done by drilling very shallow $\frac{1}{2}$in (13) holes, just through the first lamination of the plywood. Also mark and saw out a 5in (127) diameter disc for the wheel. Sand the edge to round it over a little, and drill a $\frac{1}{2}$in (13) hole through the centre. Enlarge this hole slightly to enable the wheel to spin freely on the axle. Do this by wrapping a piece of abrasive paper round a pencil and rubbing it vigorously through the hole. The connecting pieces are a sandwich of three pieces of plywood glued together. Cut some strips of the plywood to finish $1\frac{1}{8}$in (29) wide. For the head end

Plate 2.2 Cutting out a plywood hobby horse wheel with a coping saw.

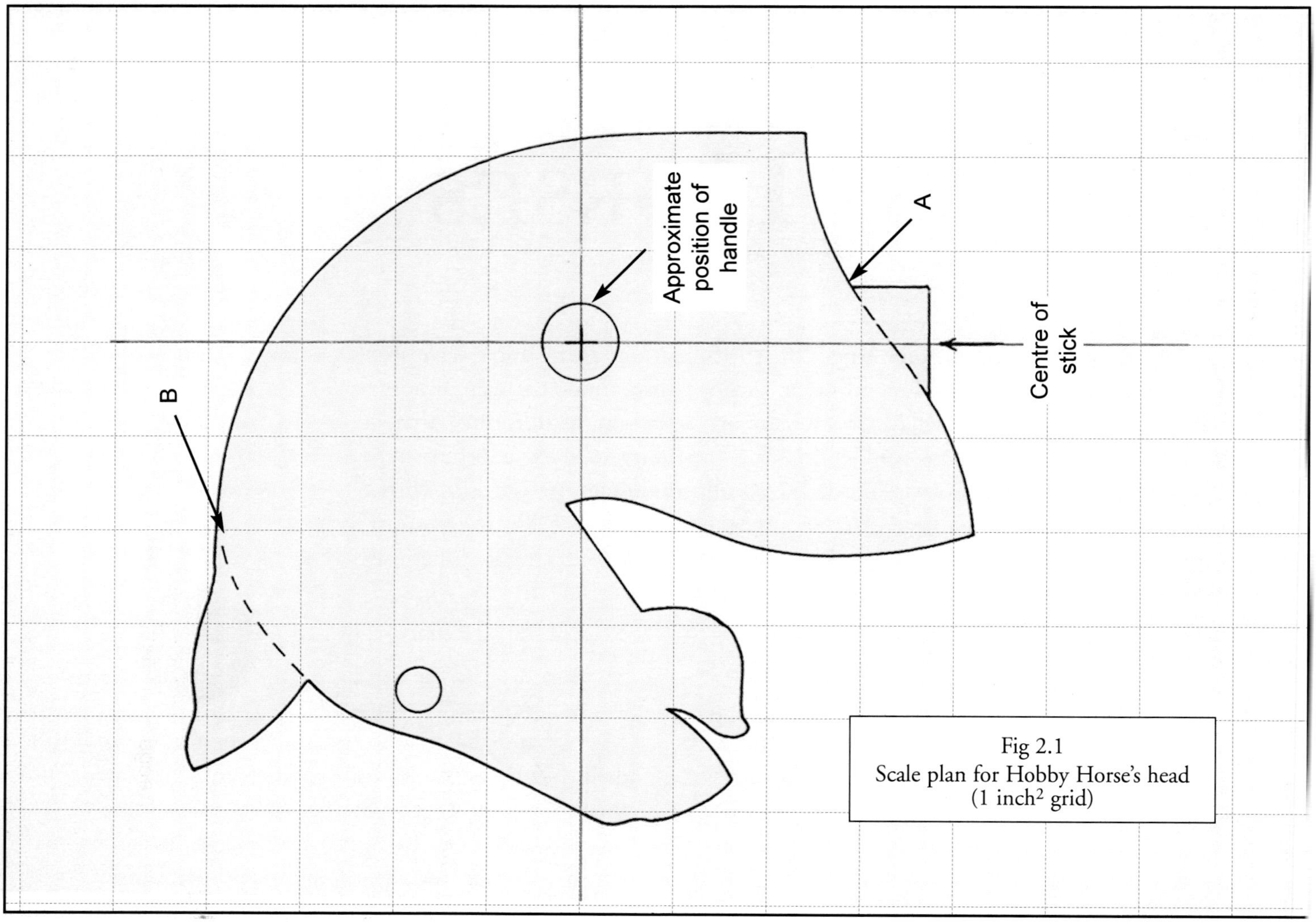

Fig 2.1
Scale plan for Hobby Horse's head
(1 inch^2 grid)

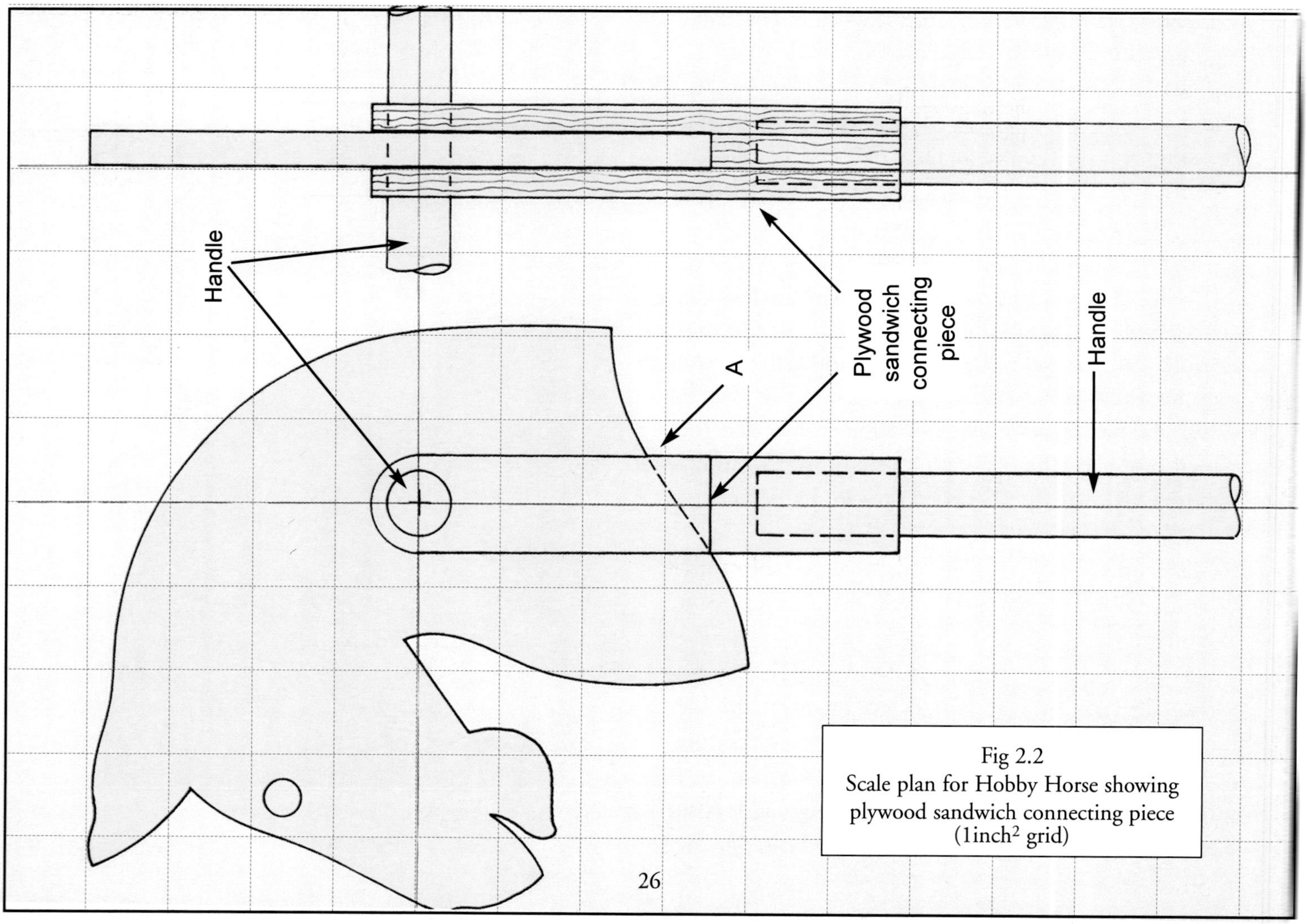

Fig 2.2
Scale plan for Hobby Horse showing plywood sandwich connecting piece
(1inch^2 grid)

Fig 2.3
Scale plan showing plywood sandwich connecting piece for wheel end
(1inch² grid)

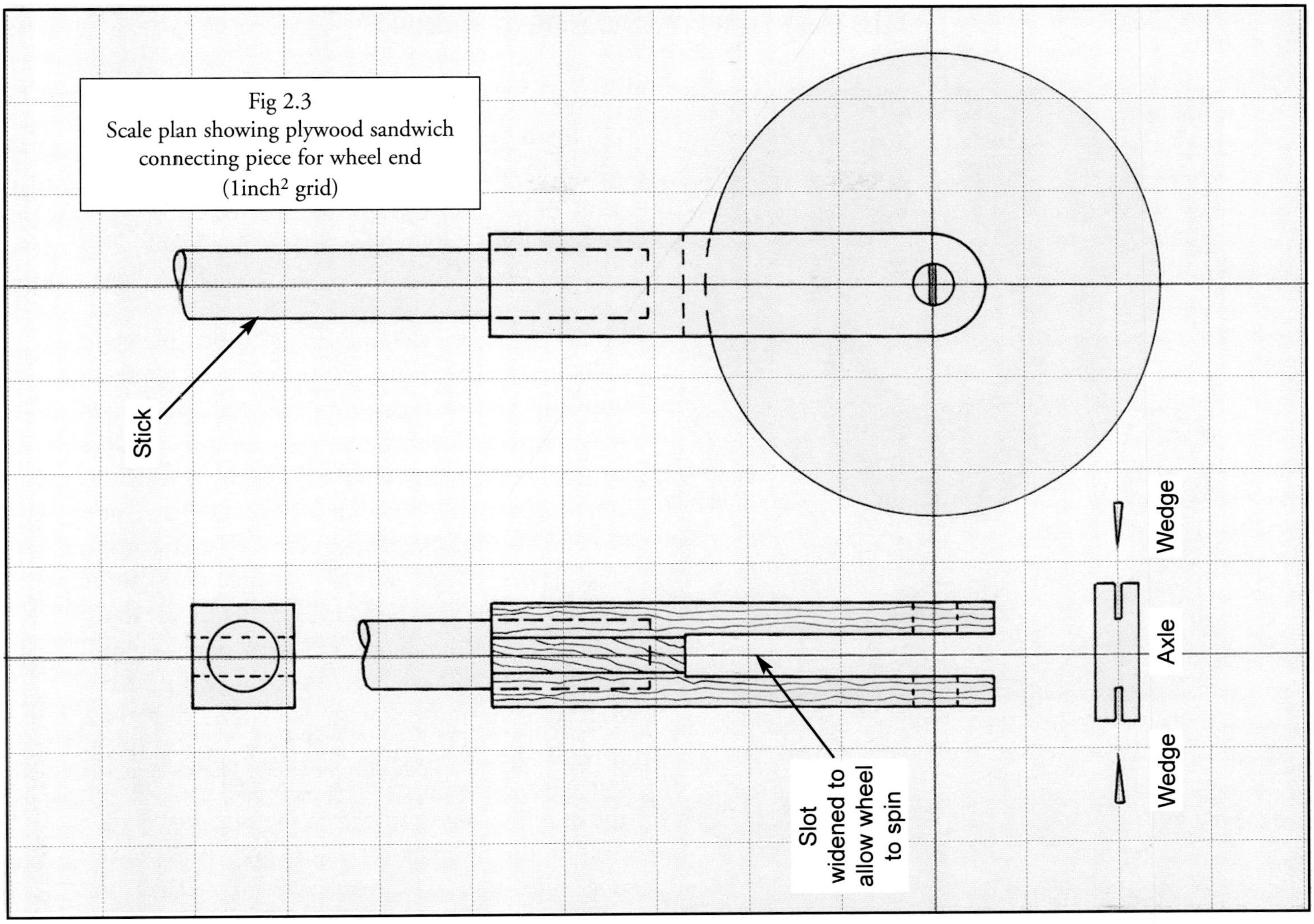

Fig 2.4
Scale plan showing solid wood connecting piece for wheel end
(1inch² grid)

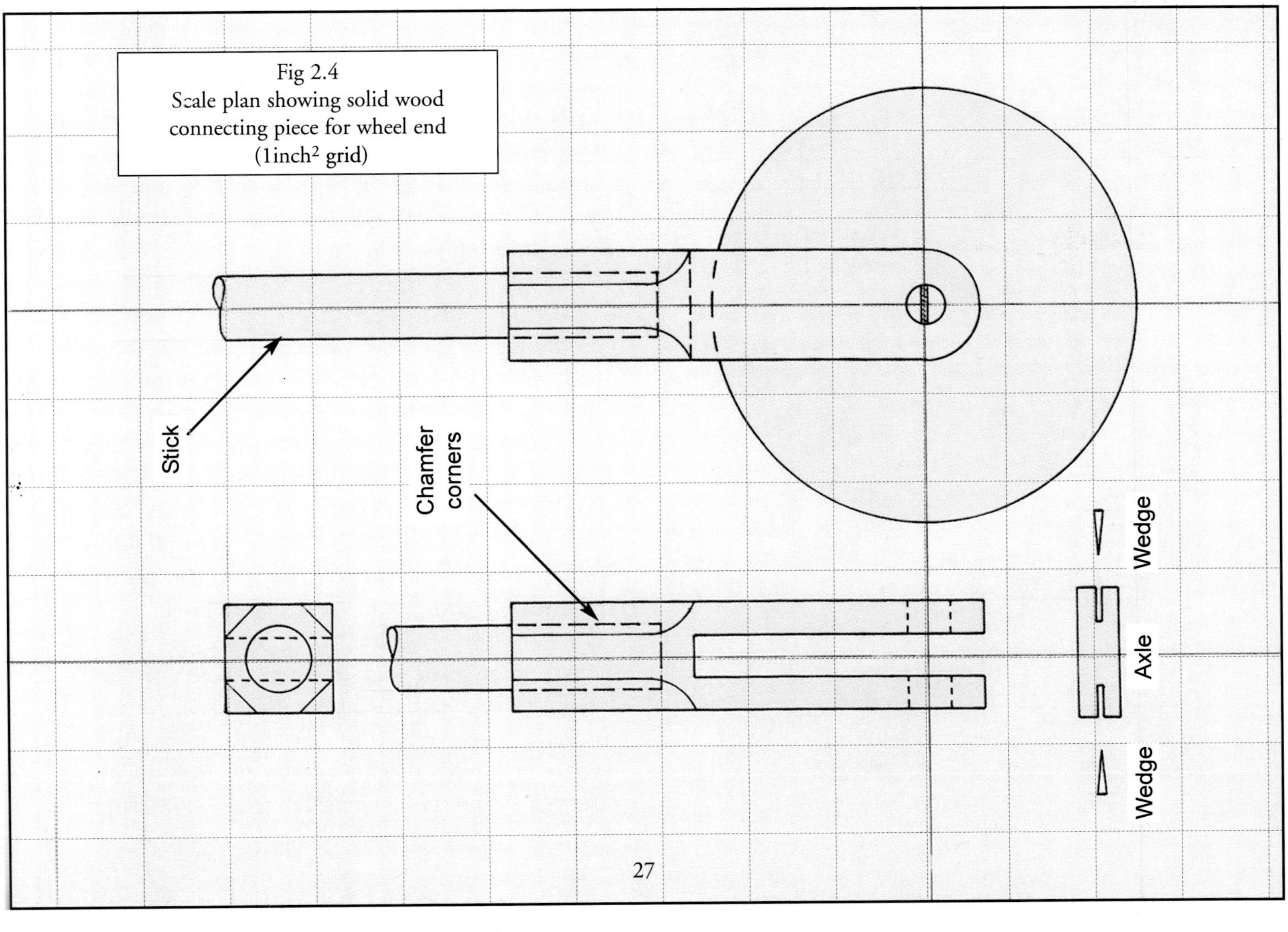

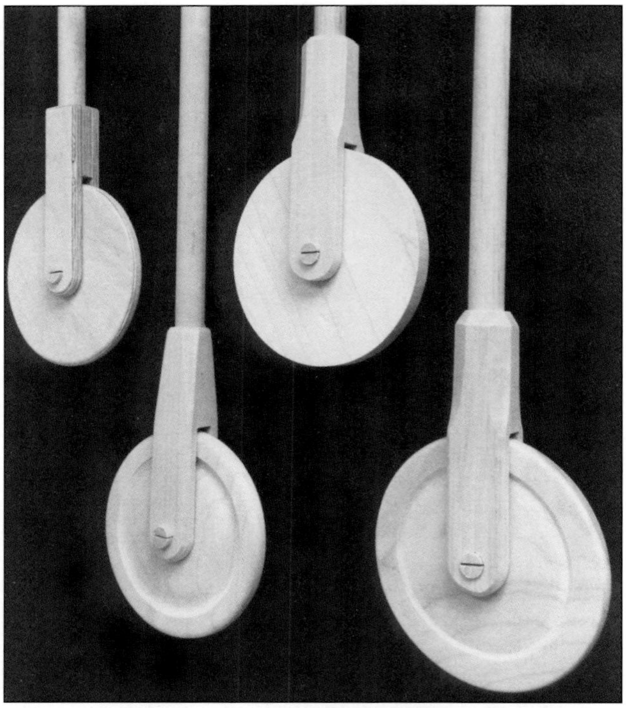

Plate 2.3 Hobby horse wheels. On the left is a plywood wheel and connecting piece; the other three have solid wood connecting pieces and wheels.

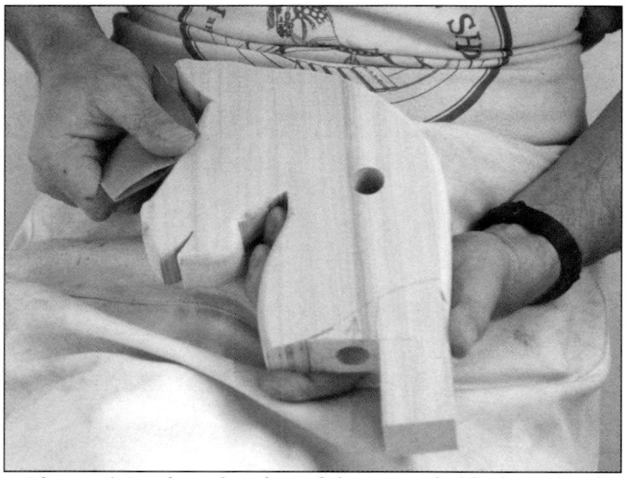

Plate 2.4 Sanding the edges of the 'No 2' hobby horse head. Note the hole for the stick, and the piece that has been left below the base of the neck to make it easier to hold.

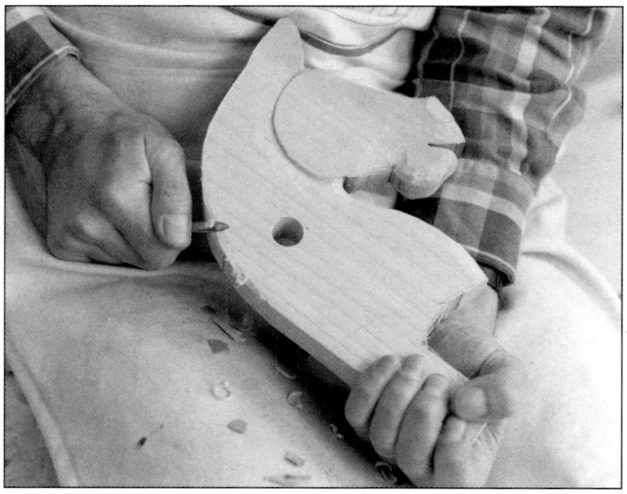

Plate 2.5 Carving the No 3 hobby horse head with a penknife.

connecting piece you will need two strips $6^3/_8$in (162) long and one piece $2^1/_4$in (57) long. For the wheel end you will need two pieces $5^1/_2$in (140) long and one piece $2^1/_8$in (54) long. Mark, saw and sand off a rounded end on each of the four longer strips.

Glue together the parts for the plywood connecting piece, making sure that you align them correctly. Cramp them until the glue dries if you have cramps. If not, place them on a flat surface with a heavy weight on top. Sand smooth all round. The next job is to drill a $^3/_4$in (19) hole into the end of each connecting piece for the stick to fit into. This is the tricky bit - the hole needs to be straight down the middle to a depth of about $1^3/_4$in (45). A holding vice under a power drill press is best, but we have done this with a hand drill, judging by eye, with the connecting piece held firmly in a vice, and it is not difficult especially if you get someone to help you line up the drill by looking at it from the side. But if your drill bit does wander off course and breaks out at one side, you will just have to remake the connecting piece.

Glue the head end connecting piece onto the neck, so that it is tight up against the piece marked A on the bottom of the neck. Mark and drill the $^3/_4$in (19) hole for the handle, which passes right through the connecting piece and neck, and glue in the handle. Then glue the stick into its hole in the connecting piece.

Tuck a piece of spare $^3/_8$in (9) plywood between the two legs of the wheel end connecting piece and mark and drill the $^1/_2$in (13) hole for the axle. There is a $^3/_8$in (9) gap between the legs of the connecting piece - the same as the thickness of the wheel - so clearly if you insert the wheel it will be too tight to spin. You need to ease the situation by paring away one lamination of the plywood at the inside of each leg. You will find you can do this quite readily with a knife or a sharp chisel.

Prepare two small wedges from a piece of scrap wood. Make a saw cut into each end of the axle. Tuck the wheel in position and push through the axle, applying a little glue at each end, but making sure you do not get glue on the wheel, then apply a little glue to the wedges and tap them into the saw cuts at either end of the axle. Saw off the excess ends of the axle, and glue the lower connecting piece onto the stick, lining up head and wheel. Sand smooth all round and your hobby horse is finished, ready to varnish and/or paint.

HOBBY HORSES Numbers 2 and 3

These designs employ the same head pattern as Number 1, but instead of plywood the head is cut from solid wood 1¼in (32) thick. Solid wood gives you the opportunity to do a bit more shaping on the head, and no connecting piece is necessary since the stick hole is drilled right into the neck. Number 2 merely has rounded over edges and drill hole eyes, but Number 3 is carved or whittled to give rather more of a three dimensional horse's head shape, and real glass eyes are fitted. When marking out the pattern on the timber make the direction of the grain run more or less along the direction of the ears; if the grain runs across the ears they will more readily snap off. Also, as well as leaving on the piece marked A on the drawing (until after the stick hole has been drilled) it is a good idea to leave a bigger piece of waste wood on the bottom of the neck to give you something to hold on to while carving it.

The carving can be done with a sharp penknife, plus a couple of small carving gouges if you have any, say a No. 5 - ½in (13) and a No. 4 - 1 in (25) straight London pattern. Pencil in a few guide lines before you start to carve - the shape of the ears, the curve of the cheek and the approximate positions of eyes and nostrils. The ears are separated with a coping saw, down to the dashed line marked B on the drawing. Aim to give the head a slight taper from the full width at the eyebrow down to the mouth, with just the nostrils sticking out. The glass eyes are set into shallow recesses with wood filler.

The wheel end connecting piece can be laminated from plywood as described above, or made of solid wood 1¼ x 1¼ x 5½in (32 x 32 x 140) cut as shown in the drawings, and enhanced with some chamfering at the corners. The wheel can also be made of plywood as above, or from solid wood, and if you have a lathe, can be turned to ensure it is exactly round and to give 'tyres'. When you cut the slot for the wheel in the connecting piece make sure the wheel has enough clearance to spin.

Plate 2.6 The parts prepared ready to start on the carving. Note the pencilled guidelines.

Plate 2.7 Ears are separated and the rough carving done.

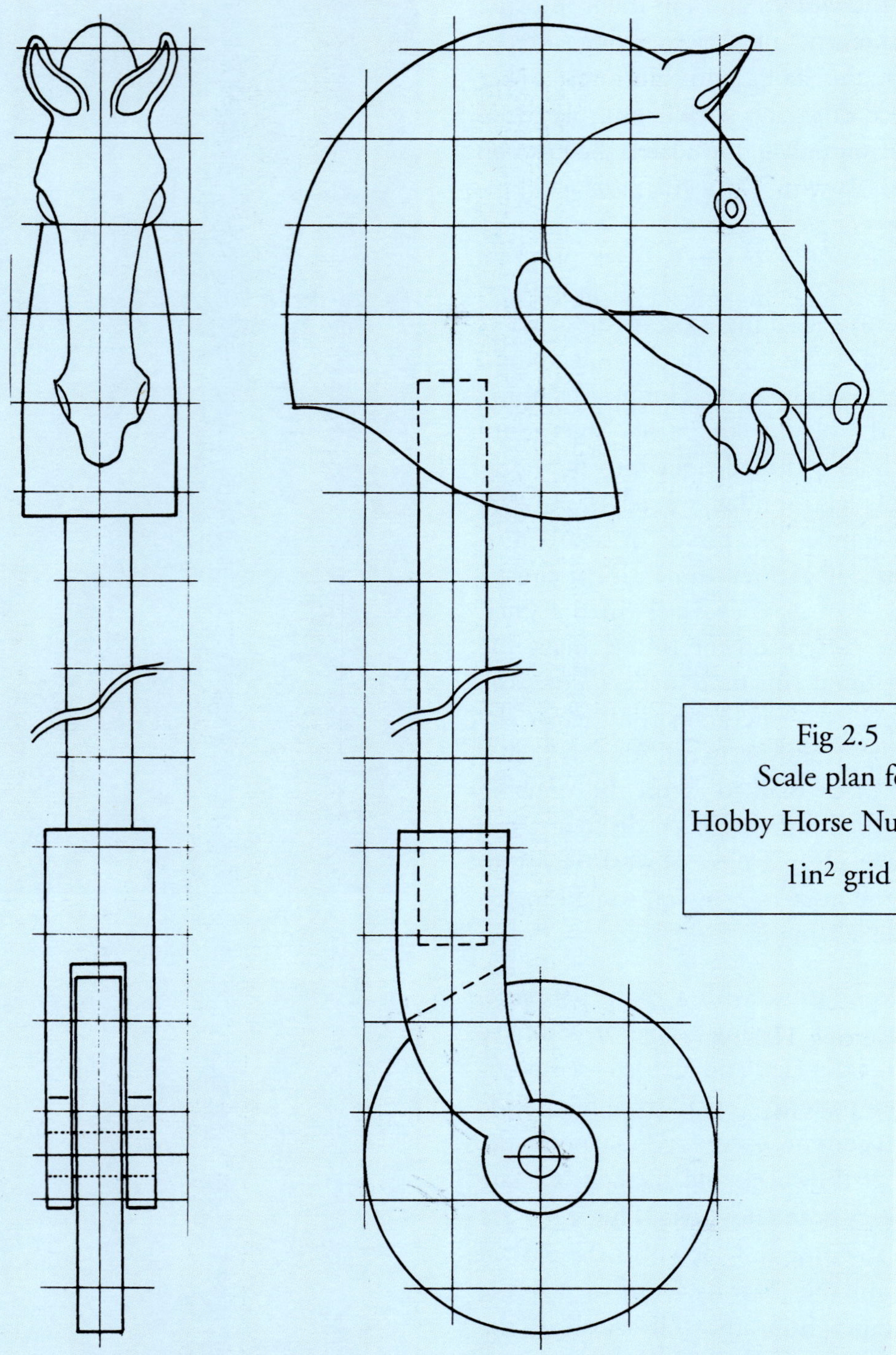

Fig 2.5
Scale plan for
Hobby Horse Number 4
1in^2 grid

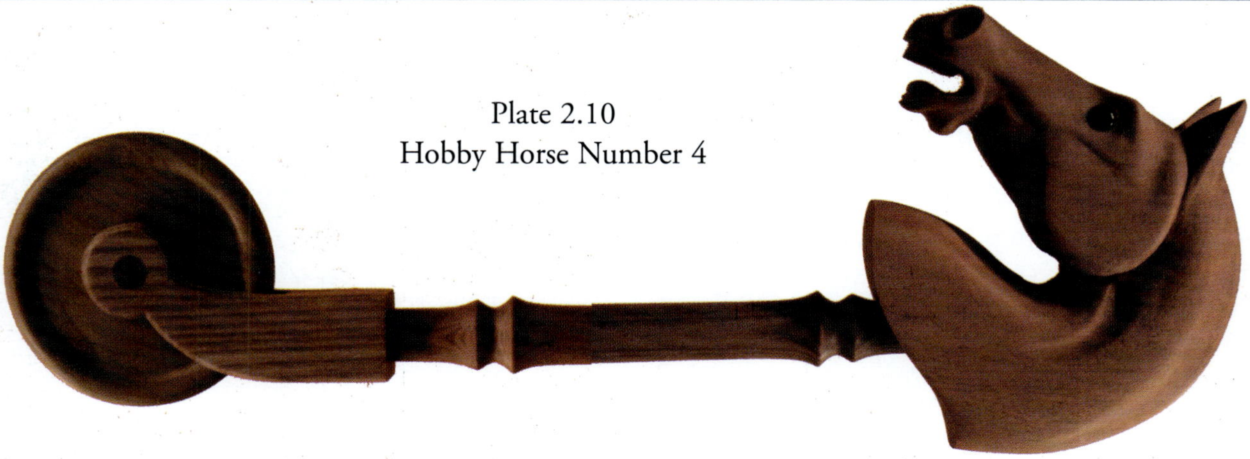

Plate 2.10
Hobby Horse Number 4

HOBBY HORSE Number 4

This is an opportunity to practice carving a horse's head with as much detail as you can manage, but because the head is small you will be able to do most of the carving sitting down with the head on your knee, working with just a knife and a couple of small carving gouges.

The wheel end connecting piece is cut from a piece of wood $1^1/_4$in thick x $2^1/_2$in wide x $4^1/_2$in long (32 x 64 x 114). Drill the $^3/_4$in (19) hole for the stick, and the $^1/_2$in (12) hole for the axle before cutting out the rest of the shape. The mount is notched just over $^1/_2$in (13) wide to allow the wheel to spin. The wheel is $^1/_2$in (13) thick and 4in (102) diameter and a flat disc will serve, but if you have a lathe you can turn a better shape for the wheel, as in the pictures. A length of $^3/_4$in (19) diameter ramin dowel can be used for the stick, or again if you have a lathe you can turn up an 'improved' stick with a few fancy beads as shown. A short length of $^1/_2$in (13) diameter dowel is used for the axle, as above, which has a sawn slot at each end and is glued and wedged firmly in place, ensuring that the glue does not impede the spinning of the wheel.

The head and neck are cut from a piece of tulipwood or jelutong $1^3/_4$in thick x $6^3/_4$in wide x $5^3/_4$in long (45 x 171 x 146). Some $^1/_2$in (13) holes are drilled to ease the sawing out round the tighter curves, and it is easier to drill the $^3/_4$in (19) hole for the stick before cutting out the head and neck. The ears are separated with a coping saw and the first gouge cuts determine the positions of nostrils and eyes. Carve the head so that it tapers from eyebrow to mouth with just the nostrils sticking out, and round over all the 'square' corners.

Take it carefully and cut a little from each side in turn to maintain the symmetry. Examine your head to see if any more shaping can be done, and when you are satisfied it is as good as you are going to get it, stop carving and give it a final sand all round. The glass eyes are $^3/_8$in (10) diameter and are set into shallow sockets with wood filler.

There are dozens of variations on the basic hobby horse. I hope these ideas give you an interesting starting point.

Plate 2.8 The carving complete, the head is ready to sand.

Plate 2.9
The completed Number 4 hobby horse head.

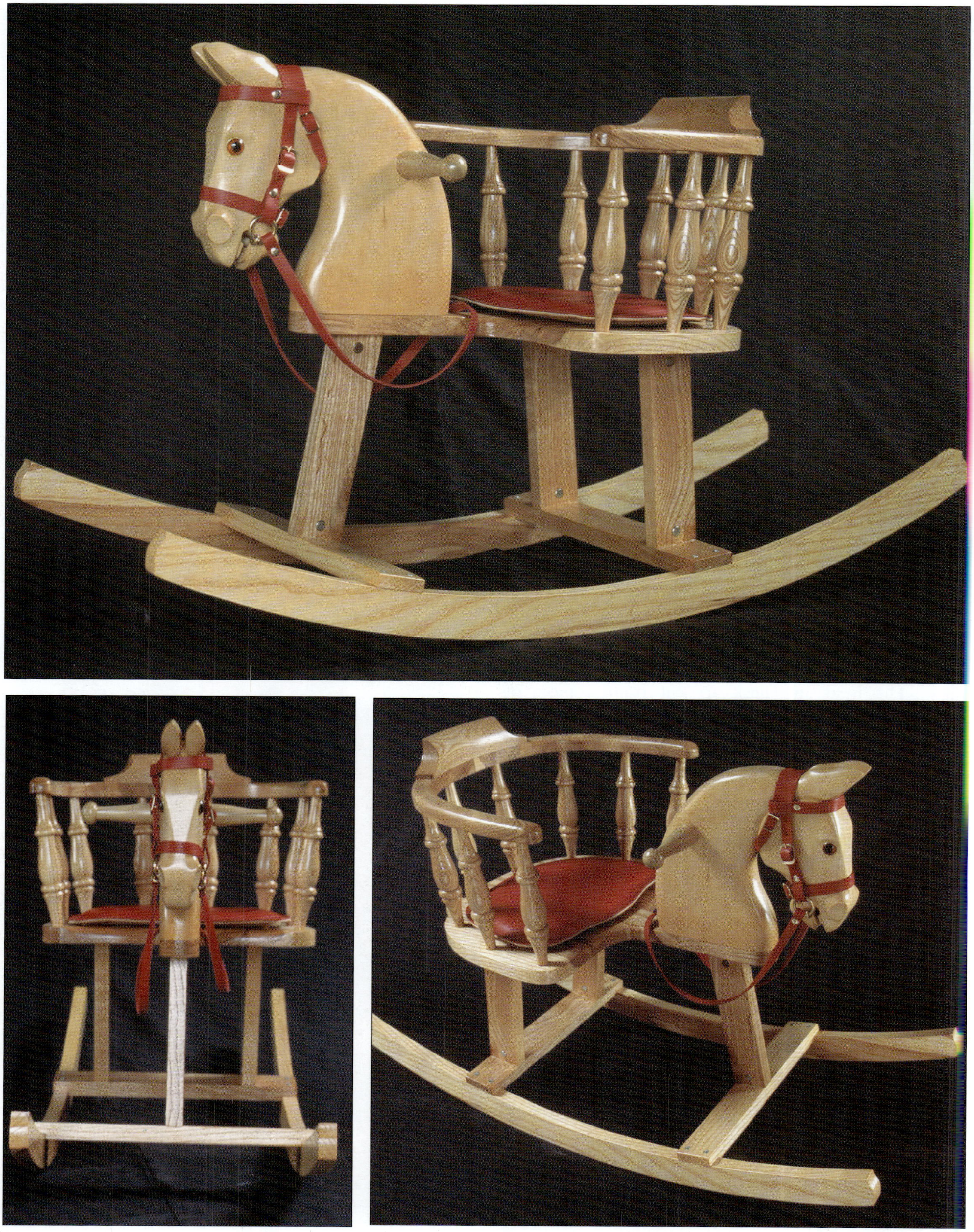

Plates 3.1, 3.2, 3.3 The completed Chair Horse

CHAPTER 3

Chair Horse

This design is based on a style of rocking horse dating from the 1920s. It is an excellent plaything for the younger child, the chair providing a very secure seat. The solid wood rockers and chair with turned spindles is sturdy and attractive, enhanced by a leather bridle and padded seat. The Chair horse is a perfectly straightforward project to make, and the head offers the opportunity to try your hand at carving a simple horse's head.

PREPARATION

Make actual size card patterns of all the parts, position them on the timber and cut out. The Chair Horse described here has turned spindles and handles, the making of which requires use of a lathe. If you don't have one, ready turned spindles, and all the other parts, are available, and it would be perfectly feasible to simplify the design and make the spindles and handle out of ordinary round $^{1}/_{2}$in (13) ramin dowel, and the seat out of plywood or MDF instead of solid timber.

In the accompanying photographs, the chair, rockers, legs and seat are made in ash, the head is jelutong. After turning, the chair spindles finish at $7^{1}/_{2}$in (190) long overall and $^{1}/_{2}$in (13) diameter at each end. The handles are turned to finish $4^{1}/_{4}$in (108) long overall with a $^{3}/_{4}$in (19) long peg or spigot, $^{1}/_{2}$in (13) in diameter to set into the hole either side of the neck. The seat is made from a solid piece of timber but, if you are unable to obtain the required width, it will have to be made up from two or three pieces edge jointed together (see Chapter 1).

The hardware you will need is: 8 off 1 in (25) x 6g countersunk woodscrews (to fix cross pieces to rockers), 2 off $1^{1}/_{2}$in (38) x 8g countersunk woodscrews (to fix head to seat) and 6 off $1^{1}/_{4}$in (32) x M6 screwed cross dowels (to fix legs to seat and cross pieces).

MAKING THE HEAD

This is a simple head cut from $1^{3}/_{4}$in (45) thick timber. No additional pieces are glued on the sides. Pencil in the approximate positions of the eyes and nostrils, and the curve of the cheek. On the underside of the neck mark with compasses where the neck is rounded front and back. Also pencil mark a centreline all round the head and neck, and the shapes of the ears looking from the front. All the carving can be accomplished with a 1in (25) No. 4 London Pattern gouge and a $^{1}/_{4}$in (6) straight chisel, with a coping saw to cut out the

CUTTING LIST	*Thickness x width x length*	*Thickness x width x length*
	Inches	**Millimetres**
Head and Neck	$1^{3}/_{4}$ x $8^{3}/_{4}$ x 14	45 x 222 x 356
Seat	$^{3}/_{4}$ x 14 x $18^{3}/_{4}$	19 x 356 x 476
Seat back - sides (both)	$^{3}/_{4}$ x $4^{3}/_{4}$ x 27	19 x 121 x 686
Seat back - curved centre piece	$1^{3}/_{4}$ x 2 x $8^{1}/_{2}$	45 x 51 x 216
Legs x 3	$^{3}/_{4}$ x $1^{3}/_{4}$ x 8	19 x 45 x 203
Cross Pieces x 2	$^{3}/_{4}$ x $1^{3}/_{4}$ x 13	19 x 45 x 330
Rockers (both)	$^{3}/_{4}$ x $7^{1}/_{2}$ x 37	19 x 190 x 940
Chair Spindles x 8	$1^{1}/_{4}$ x $1^{1}/_{4}$ x $8^{1}/_{2}$	32 x 32 x 216
Handles (both)	$1^{1}/_{4}$ x $1^{1}/_{4}$ x 10	32 x 32 x 254

Plate 3.4 The nostril is defined, carving up towrads the eyes.

Plate 3.5 Cutting into the cheek.

Plate 3.6 Thinning and rounding the lower jaw.

ears, and 120 and 180 grit abrasive paper.

Carve back the areas where the nostrils will be, so that they angle back at either side. Pencil in the oval shape of the nostrils and carve back all round to allow them to project.

With the coping saw, cut away the waste between and on the outside of the ears. With the gouge round over the "corners" above the eyes, up to the base of the ears, and below the eyes, down to the top of the nostrils.

Make a chisel cut straight in along the line of the cheek, and carve in towards this cut with the gouge from the waste (ie neck) side. Below the cheek, down towards the mouth and lower jaw, the timber is pared away until it finishes approximately 1³⁄₈in (35) wide. The bottom of the lower jaw is rounded.

With the head upside down and using the gouge and mallet, chop away the waste at the rounded ends front and rear. Continue to round over the neck up towards the ears, and at the front. Shape the ears but avoid making them too sharp. Once you have reached a stage where you feel happy with the overall shape you have achieved you can take up the abrasive paper and smooth away the wrinkles. Then drill the ⁵⁄₈in (16) diameter holes, ¹⁄₈in (3) deep, for the glass eyes, which are set into their recesses with woodfiller. Glue the two handles in place.

The head will be secured to the seat with glue and screws (though it occurs to me that if you think you might want to remove the head, to work on it some more or replace it with a different one, it could easily be fixed on with screwed cross dowels and not glued).

MAKING THE SEAT AND ROCKERS

The curved seat back is made from two pieces joined at the middle, and these two pieces are initially cut out as shown by the dashed line on the plan: they have flats so that the two pieces can be glued and cramped together. You may like to reinforce this join with a single dowel peg, but in any case the joint is strengthened and the two halves fixed securely together with the short

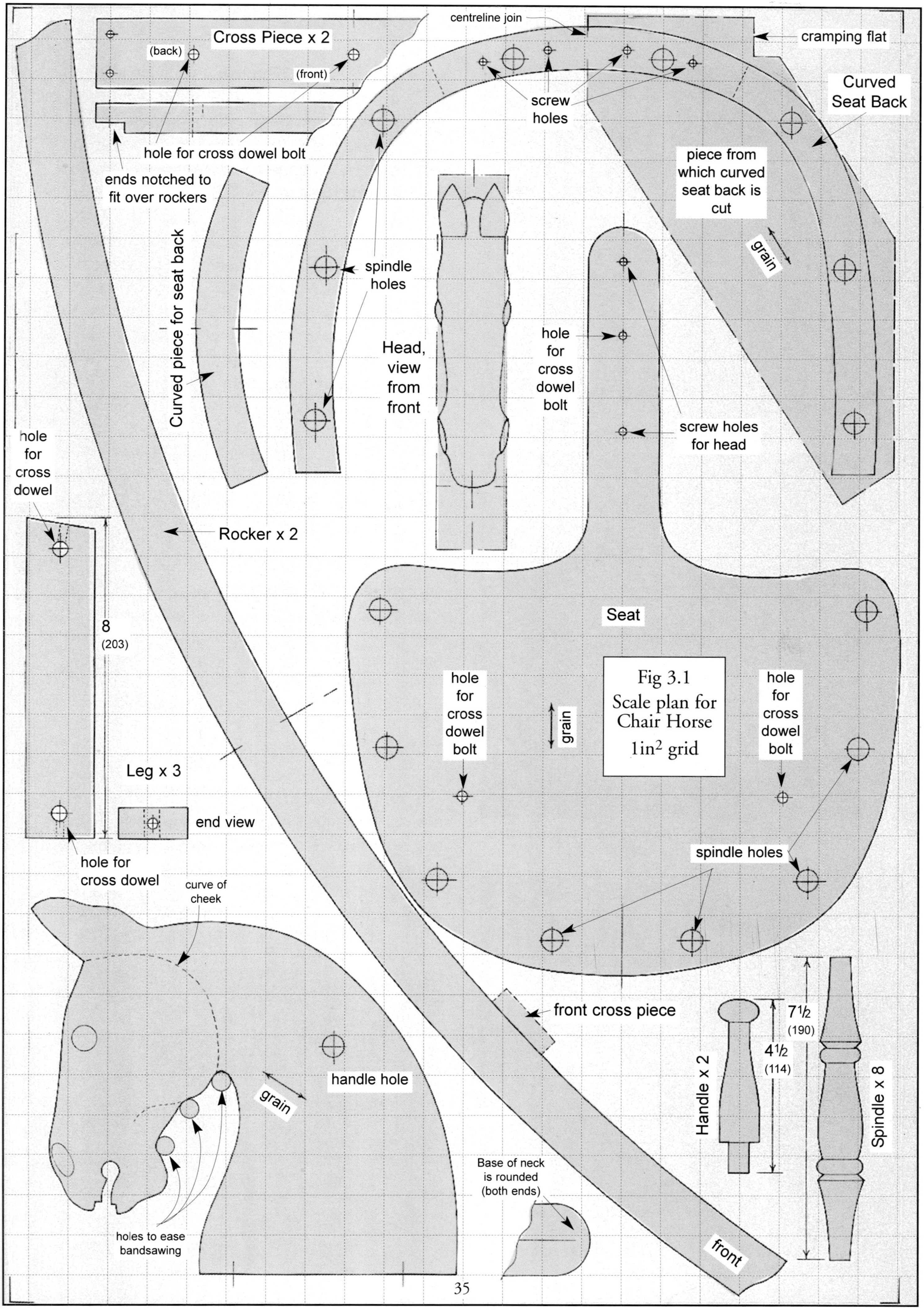

Fig 3.1
Scale plan for Chair Horse
1in² grid

Plate 3.7 Rounding the neck

Plate 3.8 Go with the grain - here the gouge is bevel side up to round the neck.

Plate 3.9 Gluing up the two halves of the seat.

curved piece which fits on top and is glued and secured with screws from underneath. Before you fix this piece mark the full curve of the seat back and cut out. (If you have the facilities and inclination, it would be perfectly possible to steam bend the seat back.)

The seat has eight spindles and the holes to receive them are drilled no more than 3/8in (10) deep into the seat and curved seat back. Note that the seat back has a rather bigger radius than the seat, so allow for the splay of the spindles by angling the drill as you make the 1/2in (13) diameter holes using, ideally, a Forstner bit.

This angling is not great - only about 5°. Ensure that you tilt the drill by eye (get someone to help sight the drill) the correct way. This seems to be a difficult part of the operation, but it is not as hard as it seems, because if your holes are not quite angled correctly, the wood is pliable enough to ensure that the assembly will be strong and secure once the parts are glued and tapped together. The ends of the spindles can be trimmed, if necessary, to get them to enter the holes, and when you have the tops and bottoms of all the spindles just resting in their holes, and glue has been applied, use a wooden mallet to tap them firmly home.

The three legs are each bevelled at 9° at the top and are secured through the three holes in the seat, and to the cross pieces with the screwed cross dowels. The single front leg is secured through a bolt hole in the centre of the front cross piece and in the projection at the front of the seat. The two rear legs are secured to the rear cross piece and seat through bolt holes 8in (203) apart, 4in (102) either side of the centre point. The ends of the

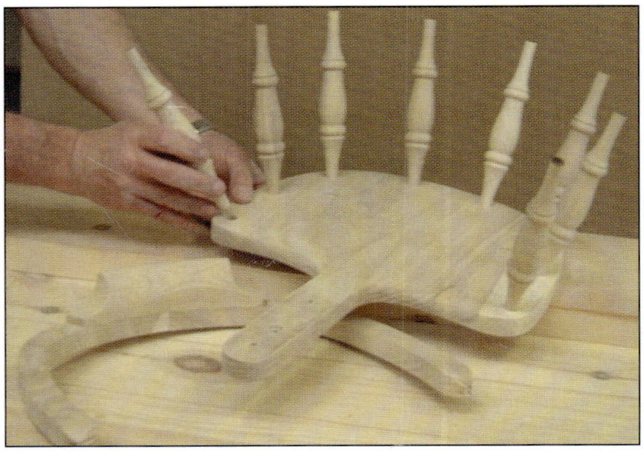

Plate 3.10 Fitting spindles. Note the seat back, ready to fit.

cross pieces are notched to sit over the rockers to which they are secured with glue and wood screws. The front of the front cross piece is 8in (203) from the front end of the rockers. This gives the horse decent balance when it has the added weight of the rider in the seat. Fit the whole thing together dry before gluing up, to ensure that it all goes together neatly; it may be necessary to adjust the angle of the bevel at the top of the front leg in order to get the cross pieces to sit neatly on the rockers.

Plate 3.12 Fixing front leg with a cross dowel.

FINISHING

Give the horse and rockers a final sand all round, making sure you take off any sharp corners, and it is ready to varnish. Three coats of varnish will be sufficient, gently rubbing down between each coat. The head is enhanced by a small bridle and reins in red leather which simply buckles on. We also made a padded cushion out of soft red leather to soften the seat.

This is an interesting project and a splendid and attractive little horse which will give its young riders lots of fun.

Plate 3.11 The seat.

Plate 3.13 Cross pieces are glued and screwed to rockers.

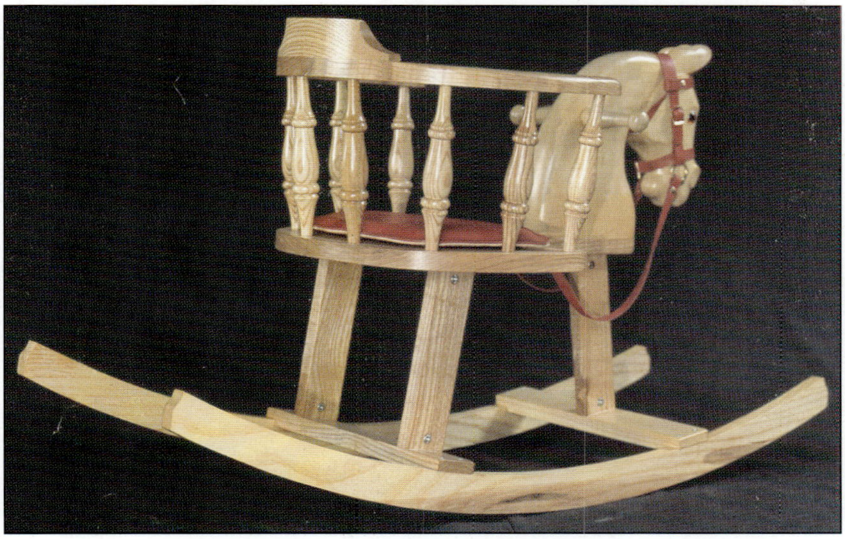

Plate 3.14 The Chair horse complete, with buckle-on bridle, glass eyes & a padded cushion on the seat.

Plate 4.1 (left) Completed Toddler's horse with simple cut out head.

Plate 4.2 (below) Carved head version with screwed on bridle.

Plate 4.3 (inset below) With buckle-on bridle.

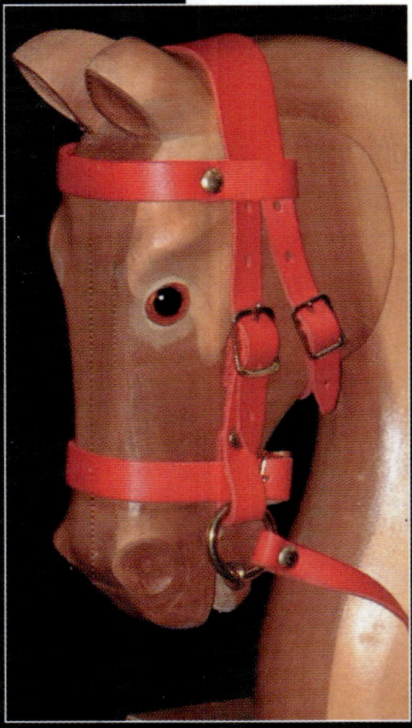

CHAPTER 4

A TODDLER'S ROCKING HORSE

Based on the historic seventeenth century slab-sided style, this rocking horse is ideal for younger riders and is the simplest of my designs to make. Although it may not be your idea of a 'proper' rocking horse - not having legs or a mane and tail and so on, it does have a lot to commend it. Of course small children need to be supervised, but is a relief for parents to have a rocking horse that little ones can really enjoy without the need for constant help to get on and off. And because it is low to the ground, if the rider should fall off it's not far to fall (but do let it rock on a soft carpet).

Riders have complete control, and may wish just to rock very gently. But if they are bolder, it will reward them with a very exciting ride. I have seen mothers jump with anxiety as their youngsters vigorously rock this horse to the extremity of its rockers. But they have little need for concern since it is virtually impossible to overturn.

PREPARATION

The basic head and neck are 'silhouette' shapes without carving, but an alternative carved version is also given, an opportunity for novice carvers. The head, rump footrests and seat battens are solid timber, but the seat, rocker panels and seat back are cut from 3/8in (9) thick plywood - birch faced ply tends to be the best quality.

The cross pieces are 3/4in (19) thick, so for these either use a thicker plywood or board, or laminate up to the thickness required by gluing together two pieces 3/8in (9) thick. The handle is a length of ramin dowel with the ends rounded over with abrasive paper. Place the patterns carefully on the wood and pencil round them. The seat back is cut from the same piece as the rocker panels, and the straight top edges of the rocker panels are to be bevelled, so leave an allowance of 1/8in (3) for this. If you mark the positions of all the screw holes on the patterns you can prick mark them through onto the wood. Woodworkers' PVA glue is used throughout the assembly, together with 30 x 1in (25) countersunk head wood screws.

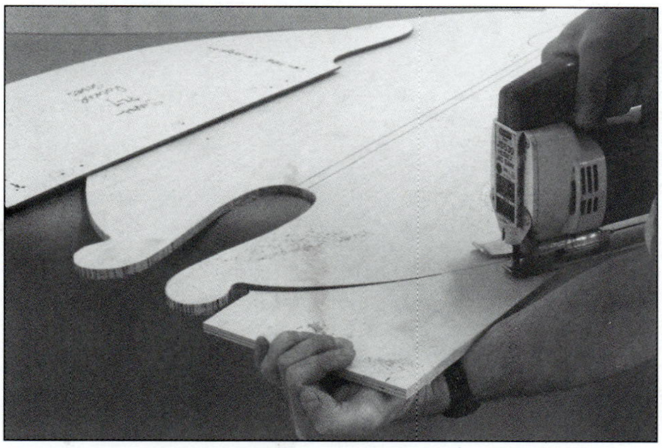

Plate 4.4 Cutting out plywood rocker panels with a jigsaw.

CUTTING LIST	*Thickness x width x length*	*Thickness x width x length*
	Inches	**Millimetres**
Head and neck	1 1/4 x 8 x 12	32 x 203 x 305
Rump	1 1/4 x 3 3/4 x 6	32 x 95 x 152
Footrests	3/4 x 2 3/4 x 14	19 x 70 x 356
Seat Battens (x 2)	3/4 x 1 3/4 x 15 3/8	19 x 45 x 391
Seat	3/8 x 6 7/8 x 18 7/8	9 x 175 x 480
2 Rocker Panels and Seat Back	3/8 x 24 x 36	9 x 610 x 914
Cross Pieces (x 2)	3/4 x 9 1/2 x 9 1/2	19 x 241 x 241
Handle	3/4 diam x 7	19 diam x 178

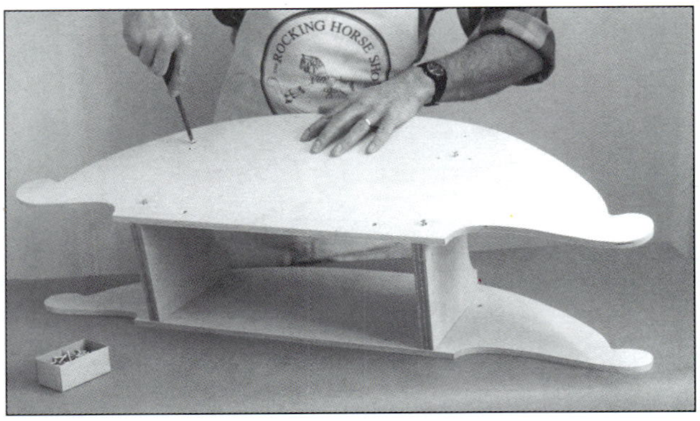

Plate 4.5 Gluing and screwing rocker panels to cross-pieces.

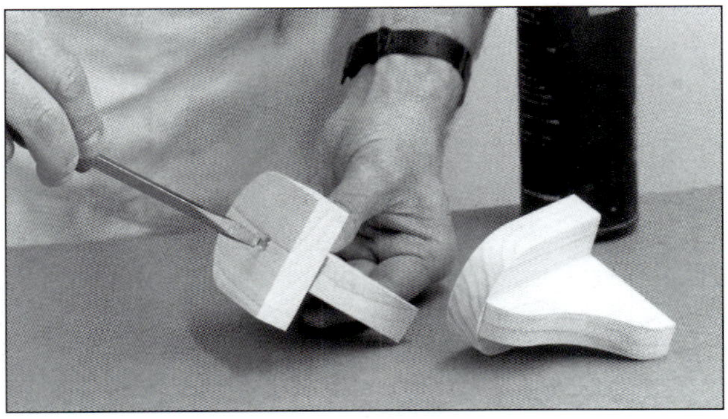

Plate 4.6 Assembling footrests.

Plate 4.7 The silhouette head and the rump have been glued and screwed to the seat from underneath and the seat back is being fixed in position.

Plate 4.8 Gluing on the ear and eye pieces and neck muscle blocks for the carved head.

HOW TO MAKE IT

Saw out all the shapes and drill the screwholes, and the $\frac{3}{4}$in (19) hole through the neck for the handle. Hold the two rocker panels together and pencil mark them 'left' and 'right'. Countersink the screw holes on the outside of each panel so that the screw heads will sit just below the surface of the ply - except for the three holes for the footrest which are countersunk from the inside.

Glue and screw on the seat battens so that they project about $^1/_8$in (3) above the rocker panel and plane off the bevel to an angle of 10°. Now glue and screw on the cross pieces with the tops of the cross pieces flush with the tops of the rocker panels. With the plane, adjust the bevelling along the top so that the seat will sit flat down neatly.

Take the seat and countersink from the top for the four screws that will secure it to the seat battens, and from underneath for the neck and rump. Screw the seat temporarily in position (without glue) so you can plane off the edges either side until they are flush with the rocker sides.

Unscrew the seat and glue and screw on the rump, centrally, at the back. The bottom of the ply seat back is bevelled (the angle is 15°) with the plane to fit neatly down onto the seat when it rests back against the rump. Glue and screw in position.

On the head, the eyes can be simply indicated by drilling a shallow hole, or they can be painted on later, or glass eyes may be fitted. Glue and screw on the head and neck centrally at the front, and

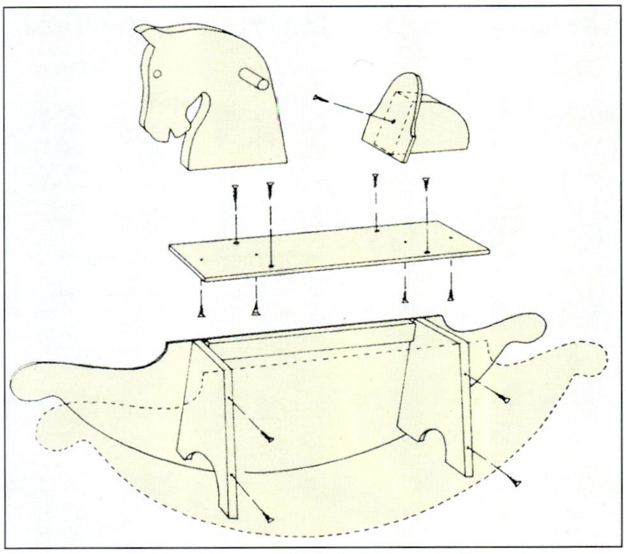

Fig 4.1 Exploded drawing of Toddler rocking horse assembly

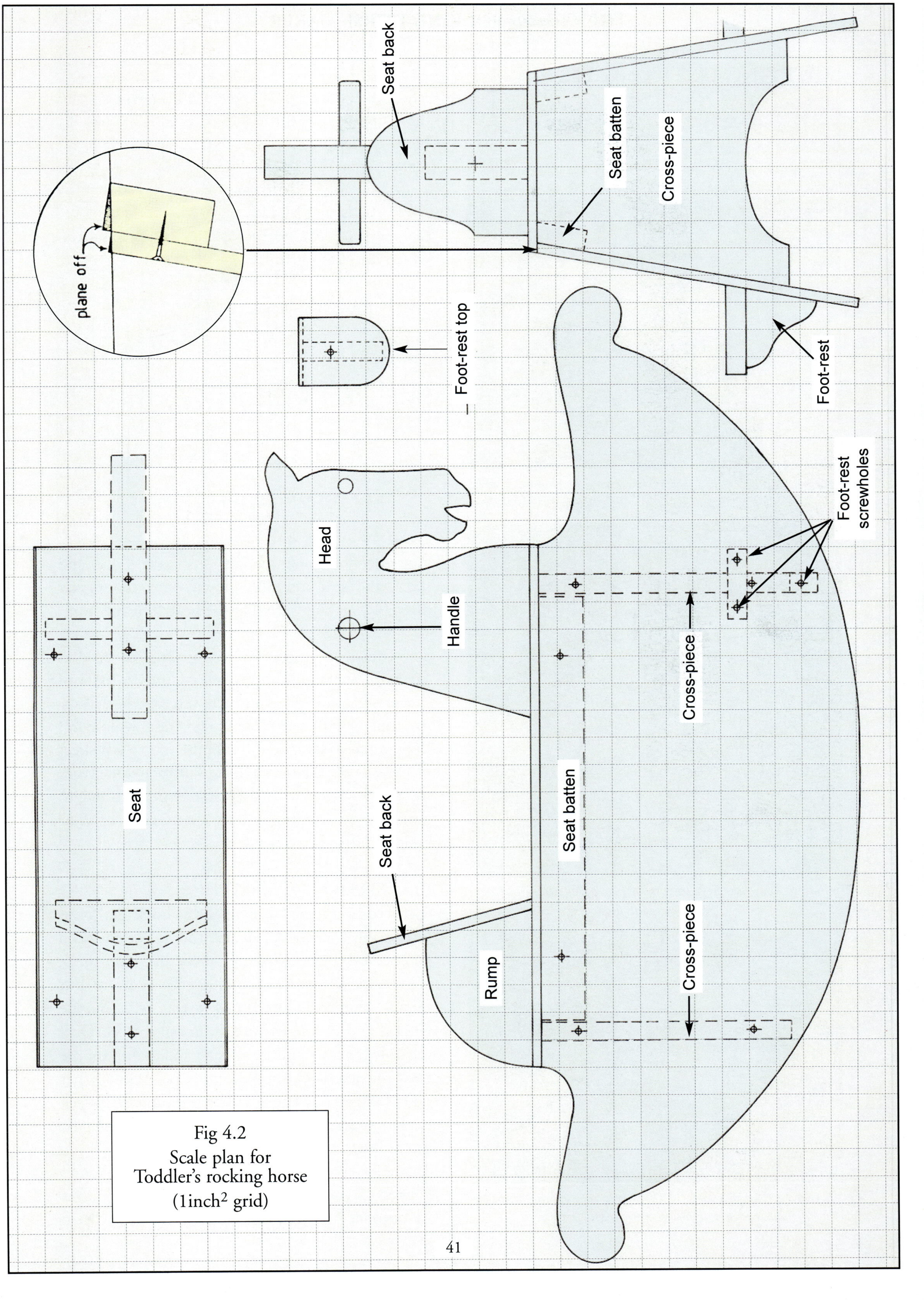

Fig 4.2
Scale plan for
Toddler's rocking horse
(1inch^2 grid)

CUTTING LIST - Carved Head	*Thickness x width x length* Inches	*Thickness x width x length* Millimetres
Head and Neck	1 3/4 x 8 x 12	45 x 203 x 305
Neck Muscle Blocks	3/4 x 5 3/4 x 15	19 x 146 x 381
Ear and Eye Pieces	3/8 x 2 3/4 x 8	10 x 70 x 203

Plate 4.9 Carving the taper of the neck. A block screwed onto the base of the neck will be used to hold the work in the vice.

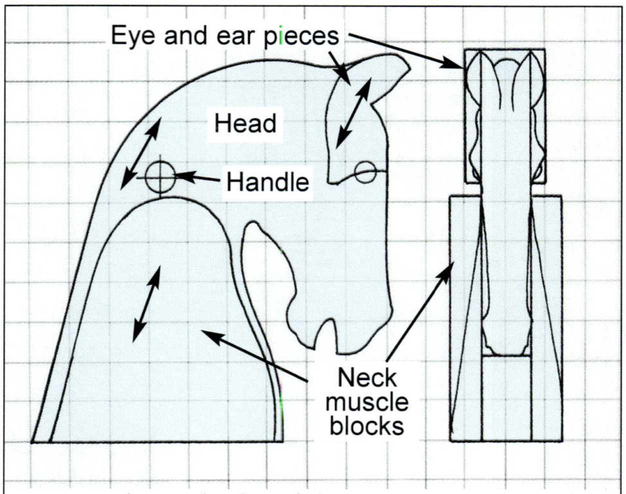

Fig 4.3 Scale plan of alternative carved head (1inch² grid)

Plate 4.10 Separating the ears with a coping saw. Note the pencilled guide lines.

Plate 4.11 Cutting along the cheek line with a straight chisel. Note the carving of the nostrils and eye pieces.

glue the dowel handle into its hole. Glue and screw the seat assembly down onto the rocker assembly, making sure that the head is at the front.

The end of the top of each footrest is bevelled at 10° with the smoothing plane. The two parts of each footrest are glued and screwed together. Make sure that the inner face of the footrests will lie flat to the rocker sides, by rubbing them on a flat sheet of abrasive and glue and screw in position, from the inside. After a final sand down all-round to remove any roughness and sharp corners your rocking horse is ready for finishing.

ALTERNATIVE CARVED HEAD

A carved head really enhances this horse and is an interesting challenge, but not too ambitious, as a practice carving. The shape of the head and neck is the same as for the silhouette version above, but thicker timber is used and extra neck muscle blocks, and eye & ear pieces, are glued on. Drill the hole for the handle and glue and cramp on the neck muscle blocks and ear and eye pieces either side as shown in Plate 4.8. The bottom of the neck is planed and sanded flat so that it can later be fitted down neatly onto the seat.

For the carving you can make do with two gouges - a number 4 - 1inch (25) and a number 9 - 5/8in

Plate 4.12 The rough carved head.

Plate 4.13 The finished head, ready to fix onto the seat.

(16) straight London pattern. Start by clamping the head upside down in your vice and on the underside pencil in a centreline and the shape of the base of the neck which is an egg shape, 'thick end' towards the front. With the larger gouge and mallet chop down at the waste side of this line. Watch that the wood does not split away too much (don't be too greedy!) and guide the cutting edge of the gouge so that the front and rear of the neck begin to take on a rounded shape and the muscle blocks at the sides taper in towards the neck. Screw a small block of scrap wood onto the base of the neck to hold onto (in the vice) when you turn the head the right way up.

Pencil a centre line all round the head (to help you keep the symmetry), the shapes of the ears (a coping saw will be used to cut away the waste between the ears), the curve of the cheek, and the approximate positions of the nostrils. With the 1in (25) gouge cut back the corners at an angle for the nostrils, pencil in the oval shapes of the nostrils and pare the wood back all round.

As you carve, study the accompanying photographs, which should give you a good idea of the shapes and contours to aim at. Work steadily, cutting a little from each side in turn, aiming to create pleasing rounded contours. The ears are pointed, but should not be left sharp. Once you have carved the head to a shape with which you can feel satisfied, sand it smooth.

Glass eyes really set off the head. They are 5/8in (16) diameter and are set into recesses 1/8in (3) deep with wood filler. Glue the handle in its hole, glue and screw the head onto the seat, centrally, at the front, and sand down thoroughly all round.

FINISHING

The horse can be either clear varnished or painted. It may be fitted with a simple bridle and reins, using leather strapping secured to the head with 1/2in (13) brass round head screws, or a small buckle-on bridle may be fitted. Some makers have further decorated the rocker panels with painting or pictorial transfers, and added a padded seat. This is a sturdy and attractive little rocking horse, and will give great pleasure to its young riders.

Plate 4.14 At nine months, Lynn can almost reach the footrests. This painted version also has painted eyes.

Plate 5.1 (below)
The completed Swinger rocking horse, made of tulipwood with simple cut-out head.

Plate 5.2 (right)
The carved head version, with buckle-on bridle, mounted on a stained ash stand.

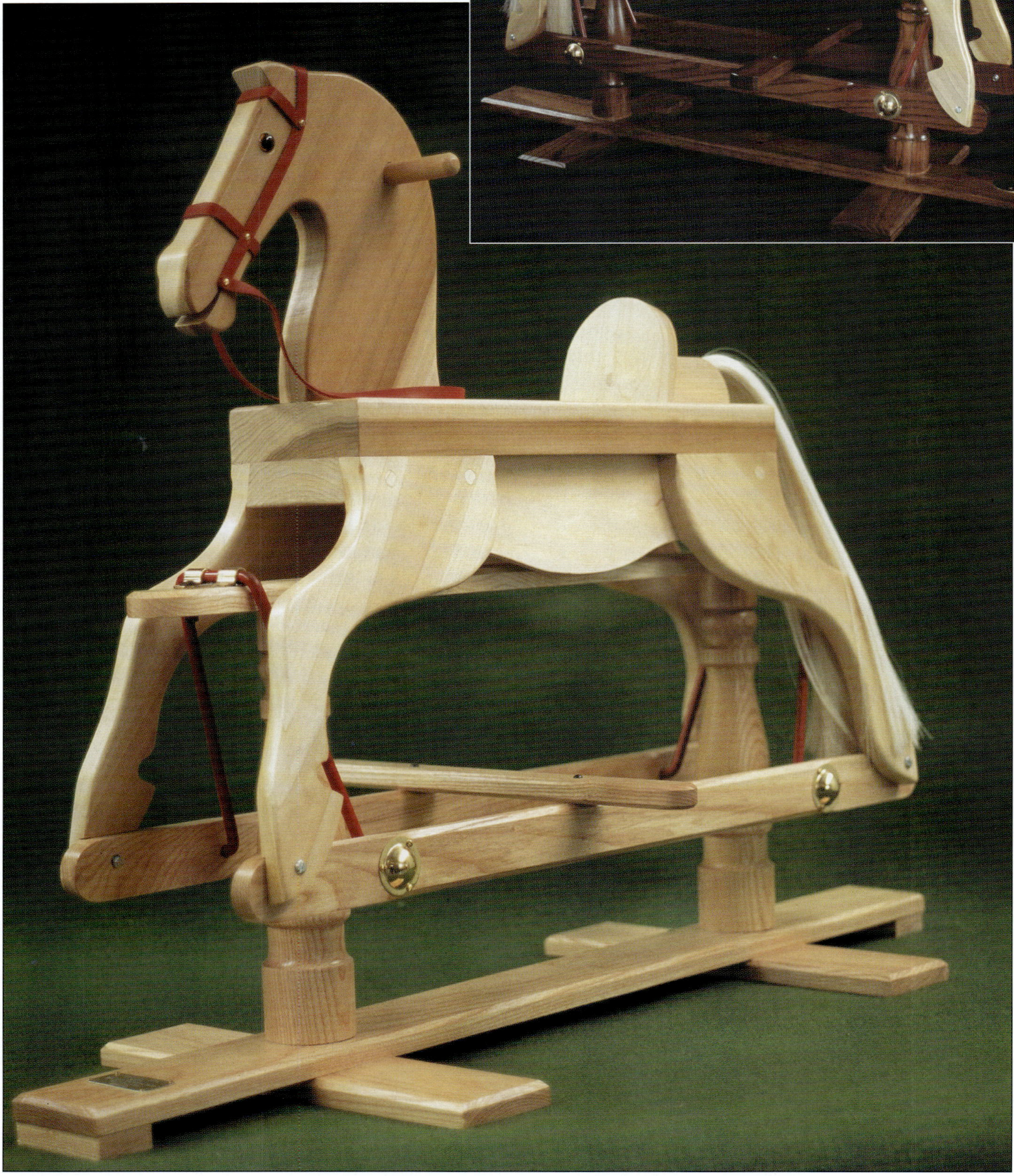

CHAPTER 5

THE SWINGER

The idea behind this design is for an attractive and easy-to-make rocking horse for children up to the age of six or so. Mounted on a 'proper' swing iron safety stand so that it has a good rocking action, it is simple to make because the construction is very straightforward and involves no carving, though an alternative head is given for those who would like to have a go at carving.

PREPARATION

First, prepare the timber. The horse can be made entirely of tulipwood except for the handle, which is ramin dowel, and the body sides, which are birch faced plywood. Note that the two pieces for the head and neck are glued together edge to edge to make a piece approx. 11 1/2 x 12in (292 x 305).

HOW TO MAKE IT

Make actual size patterns for the head, rump, back rest, legs and body sides, and transfer the shapes onto the timber. Note that the tops of the legs are to be bevelled at 10° so an allowance of approximately 3/16in (5) should be left on the straight top edges. When you have cut out all the parts, mark on them the positions of the screw holes. The screwholes on the seat and leg fixing blocks are counterbored as shown in the drawing. Drill a 3/4in (19) hole through the neck for the handle, and into the rump for the tail.

The sides of the leg fixing blocks are bevelled to 10°, as are the straight tops of the legs, and the bottom of the seat back is bevelled to 15°. Mark the bevels onto the wood and carefully plane off, making sure the bevels run the right way, to give you two left legs and two right ones.

If you have a router with a rounding over cutter, you can do the rounding over of the top edges of the seat and round the head before assembly. Note the places where the edges are *not* rounded over:

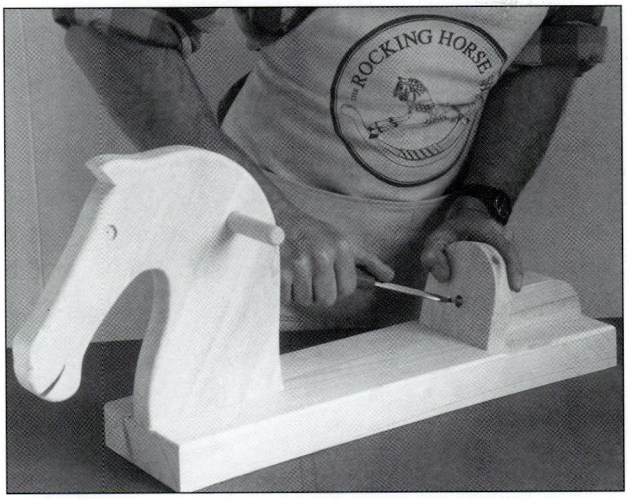

Plate 5.3 Screwing on the seat back. The rump and the neck were glued and screwed in position from underneath the seat.

CUTTING LIST

	Inches (*Thickness x width x length*)	Millimetres (*Thickness x width x length*)
Head and Neck (x 2)	1 3/8 x 5 3/4 x 12	35 x 146 x 305
Handle (round dowel)	3/4 diam x 7	19 diam x 180
Back Rest	7/8 x 4 1/2 x 4 1/4	22 x 114 x 108
Rump	1 3/4 x 1 3/4 x 5	45 x 45 x 127
Seat	1 3/4 x 5 3/4 x 21	45 x 146 x 533
Legs (all four)	7/8 x 6 x 72	22 x 152 x 1830
Leg Fixing Blocks (x 2)	1 3/8 x 4 1/2 x 5	35 x 114 x 127
Body sides (plywood) (x 2)	1/4 x 4 x 11	6 x 100 x 279
Foot Rest	3/4 x 1 3/4 x 17	19 x 45 x 432

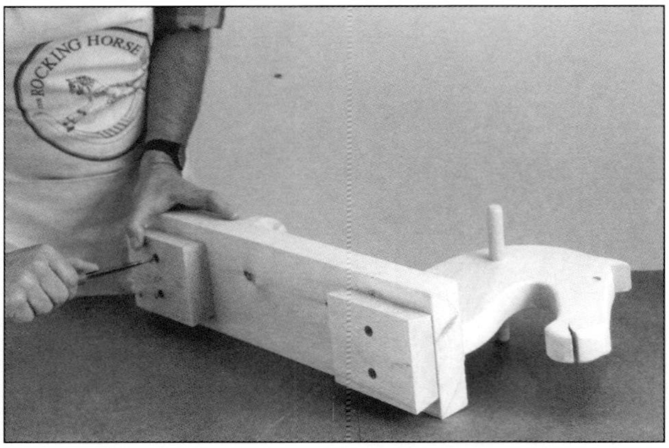

Plate 5.4 Screwing the leg fixing blocks to the underside of the seat.

Plate 5.5 Screwing on the legs.

the front of the ears, the nostrils, and on the seat where the head and rump are to be fixed down. In the absence of a router the rounding over can be readily accomplished after assembly with a rasp or Surform, and smoothed off with abrasive paper. Timber packs are available in which all this initial preparation has already been done, see Appendix.

Glass eyes are set into shallow recesses $^5/_8$in (16) diameter and $^1/_8$in (3) deep with soft wood filler.

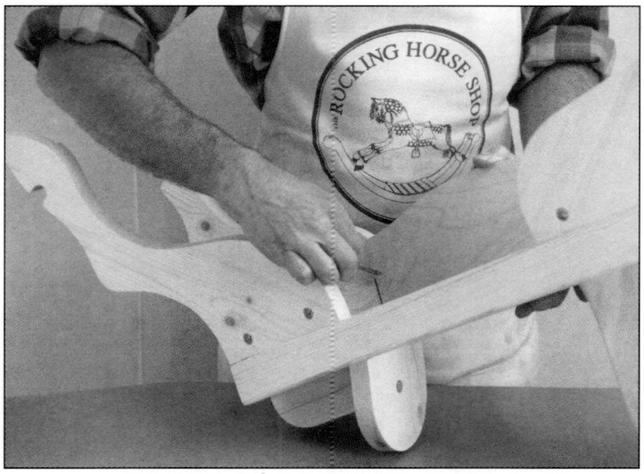

Plate 5.6 Glue and screw the plywood body sides to the inside of the legs.

For the assembly, use PVA glue and countersunk steel woodscrews: 2 x 2$^1/_2$in (64) 10g for fixing neck to seat, 14 x 1$^3/_4$in (45) 10g - 1 each for fixing rump to seat and back rest to rump, 4 for screwing leg fixing blocks to seat and 8 for securing legs to leg fixing blocks. You should counterbore for the screws through the seat and leg fixing blocks. The rest can be countersunk so their heads sit just below the surface to be filled with woodfiller, or you may like to set them a little deeper and cover the screwheads with wooden plugs. You will also need 4 x $^1/_2$in (13) 4g screws, 2 to fix on each of the body sides.

When fixing on the head, rump and leg fixing blocks make sure that they are aligned centrally on the seat and that the bevels on the leg fixing blocks will allow the legs to fit in neatly under the seat. Also, an obvious point, but easily overlooked in the excitement of getting it all together, do make sure that the front legs are at the head end (it has been done!). Round the ends of the handle with abrasive paper and glue it into its hole in the neck. When the glue has set and you have filled or plugged all the visible screw holes, give the whole thing a thorough sand down, taking care not to scratch the glass eyes.

CARVED HEAD

This head gives you an opportunity to try your hand at carving; you need only a couple of gouges to do it - a number 4 - 1in (25) and a number 9 - $^5/_8$in (16) straight London pattern gouge.

Mark the shapes onto the timber, noting the direction of grain, cut out and glue up, then plane and sand the bottom so that it will fit down flat onto the seat. With the head upside down draw an 'egg' shape (see photo) onto the base of the neck, thick end towards the front. With the large gouge cut away the waste all round, until the neck tapers gently up to the top where it is rounded over.

A small block of timber screwed onto the base of the neck will give you something to hold onto when you turn the head right way up. Pencil in the centre line all round the head and neck, the shapes of the ears, the curve of the cheek and the approximate positions of the nostrils. With the 1in (25) gouge cut back the corner at an angle for the

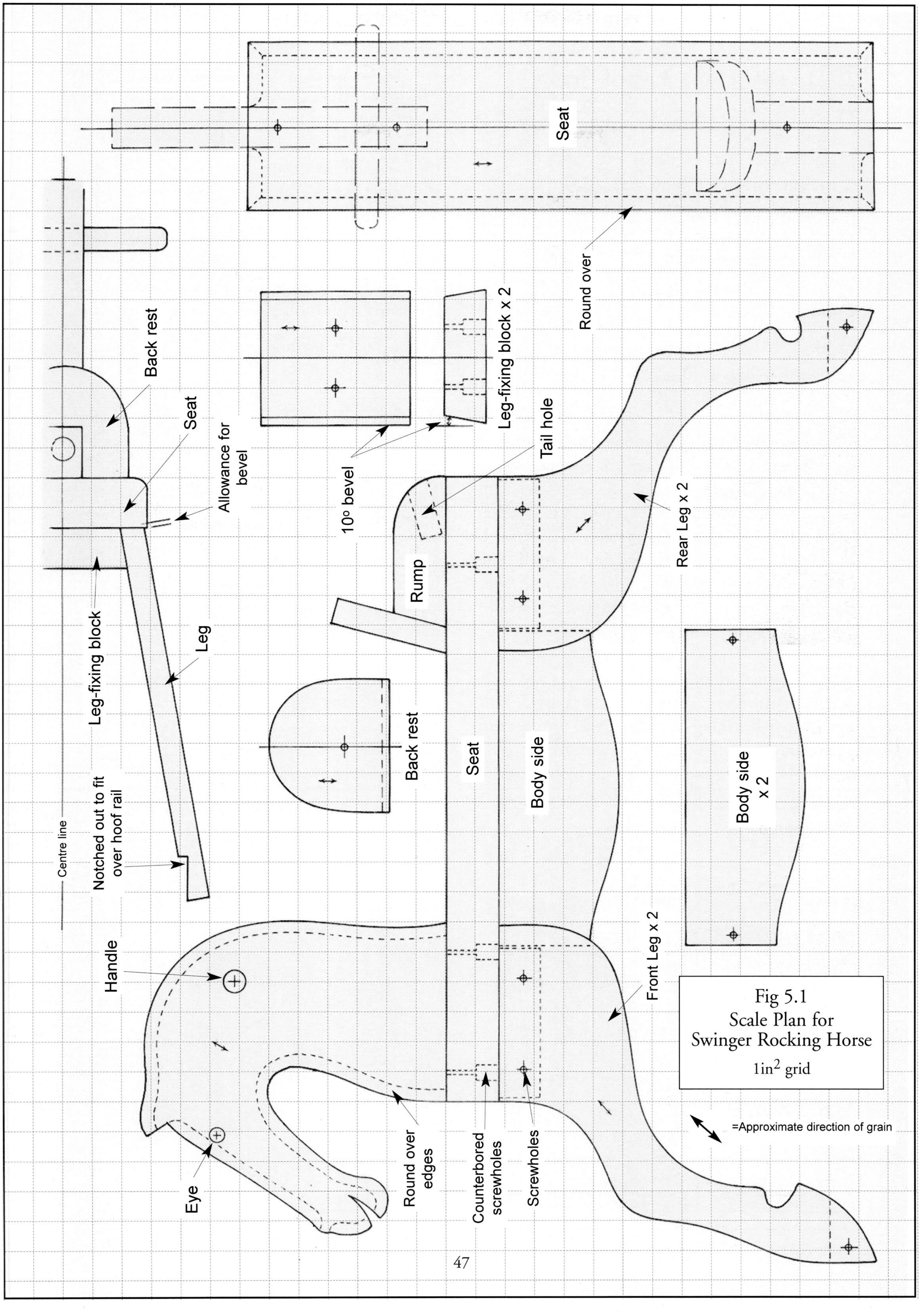

Fig 5.1
Scale Plan for
Swinger Rocking Horse
1in^2 grid

CUTTING LIST - Carved Head	*Thickness x width x length* Inches	*Thickness x width x length* Millimetres
Head and Neck	$1^3/_4$ x $8^3/_4$ x 14	45 x 222 x 356
Neck muscle blocks (both)	$1^1/_4$ x 8 x 14	32 x 205 x 356
Ear and eye pieces (both)	$^1/_2$ x $3^3/_4$ x 9	13 x 95 x 230
Handle (round dowel)	$^3/_4$ diam x 9	19 diam x 230

nostrils, mark the shapes of the nostrils and carve back all round.

Carve steadily, a little from each side in turn, following the photographs opposite, and try to take clean, slicing, paring cuts with your gouge.

FINISHING

When the hooves have been notched, for details of which please refer to Chapter 13, you can drill a screw hole through each hoof and screw on temporary hoof rails with $1^1/_4$in (32) 8g screws. These temporary hoof rails enable you to varnish the hooves and prevent them getting chipped. The horse can now be varnished. Give it two or three thin coats of clear satin polyurethane varnish, lightly sanding down between coats.

I usually varnish right over the glass eyes and then scrape the varnish off them when it has dried. This is easier than brushing carefully round the eyes and the varnish does not stick very well to the glass anyway. The bridle and reins for the basic head are made up using $^3/_8$in (9) wide red leather strap, a total length of about 56in (1425) will be enough for both, and they are fixed to the head with $^1/_2$in (13) 4g round head brass screws. For the carved head a buckle on bridle may be fitted, which is similar in size to the bridle for the Small carved horse. The tail, usually synthetic, but real horsehair may be used, is glued into its hole and secured by tapping in a wooden wedge underneath.

That completes the horse which can now be mounted up on its stand. For details of how to make the stand, please refer to Chapter 11. This horse does not normally have stirrup irons. Instead, the wooden footrest is screwed onto the top of the hoof rails so that it projects evenly either side, something solid for children to rest their feet on. It is positioned so that when the horse is rocked right forward the footrest does not quite touch the stand post.

Altogether, this is a super little rocking horse which will give a great deal of pleasure to children.

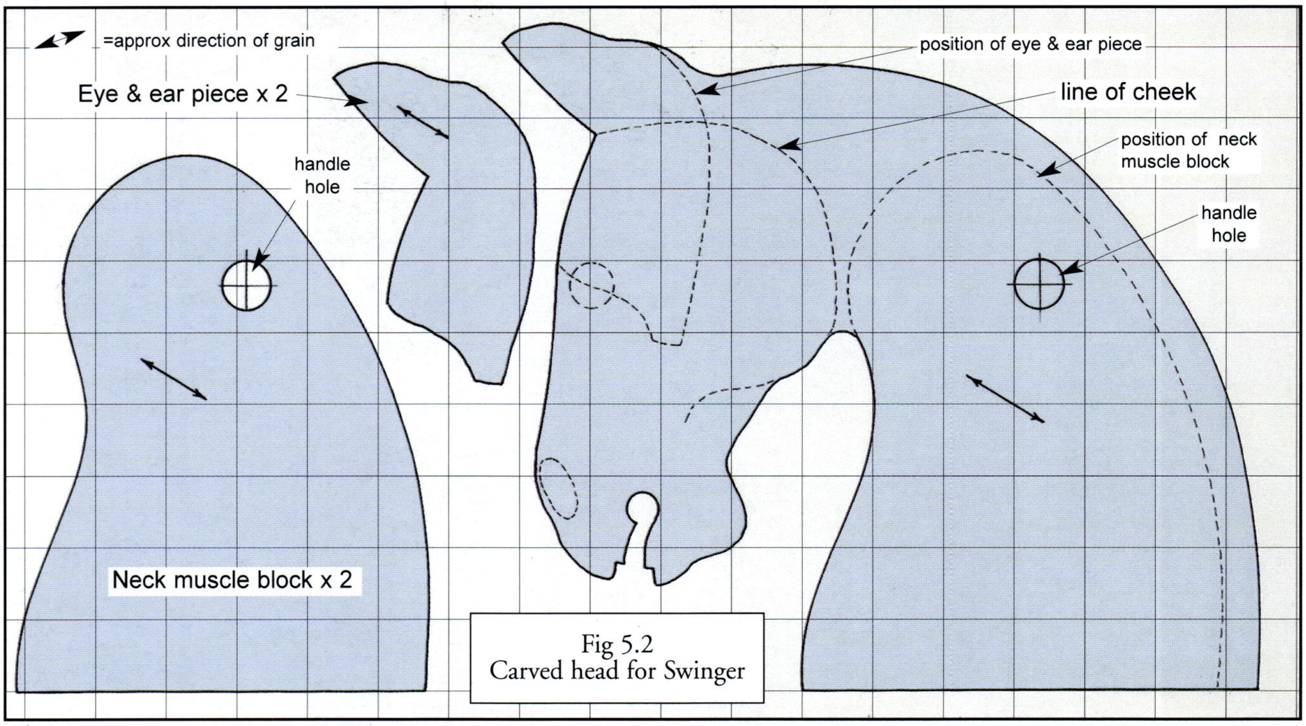

Fig 5.2
Carved head for Swinger

Opposite page - Plates 5.7 to 5.18 Making the carved head. Note the 'egg' shape at the base of the neck in the top middle picture.

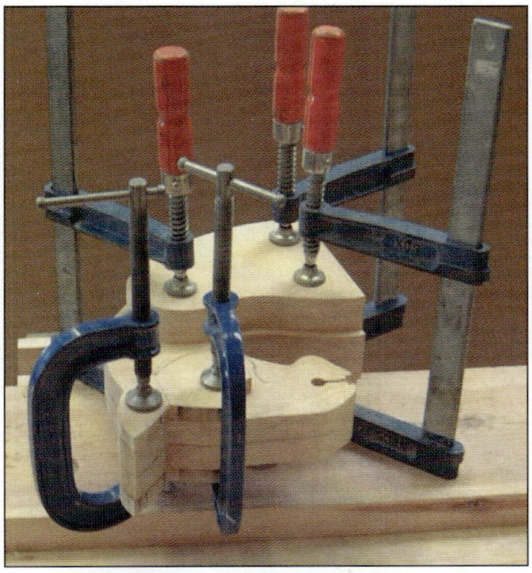

Plate 6.1 The finished horse with buckle on bridle, reins and brass bit.

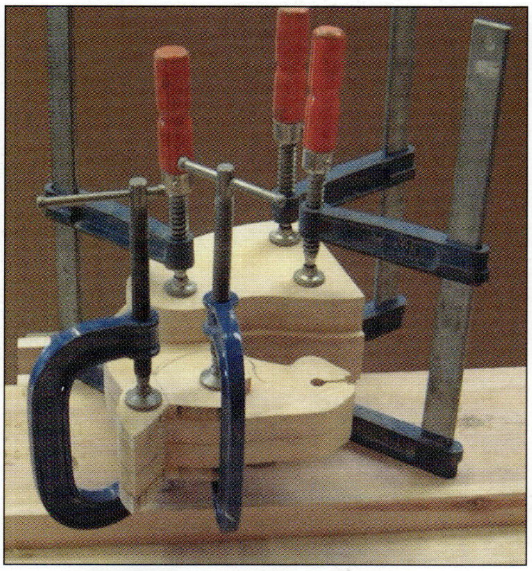

Plate 6.1 The finished horse with buckle on bridle, reins and brass bit.

CHAPTER 6

Little Red Rocker

This design combines the straightforward construction of the Swinger enhanced by a carved head, neck and upper body. It is an excellent rocking horse for children up to the age of six or so, and the carved elements are nicely complemented by the red leather bridle and saddle. Choose a timber which carves readily - the horse in the accompanying photographs is made out of tulipwood - and prepare your timber according to the cutting list below:

PREPARATION

Make full size patterns of all the parts and mark them out carefully on the timber, then bandsaw out. Note that the two ears and two eye pieces shown on the plan are cut from offcuts of the same piece from which the head and neck and the two neck muscle blocks are cut. The grain should run in the direction of the arrows on the plan. The ears are bandsawn to 1in (25) thick and the eye pieces to 3/8in (9) thick. Leave an allowance of 3/16in (5) on the top straight edges of the legs for the 10° bevel.

The plan shows counterbored screwholes in the seat for fixing it to the head and rump, but you may prefer to use fluted dowel pegs, with centring markers to locate the holes, in which case the cramping noggin on the neck will aid the cramping down. Cramping noggins are also left on the tops of the neck muscle blocks, and the ears.

HOW TO MAKE IT

First glue and cramp the eye pieces to the head, making sure that the top edges are flush with the top of the head. When set, remove the cramps and sand the top flat with coarse (80 grit) abrasive

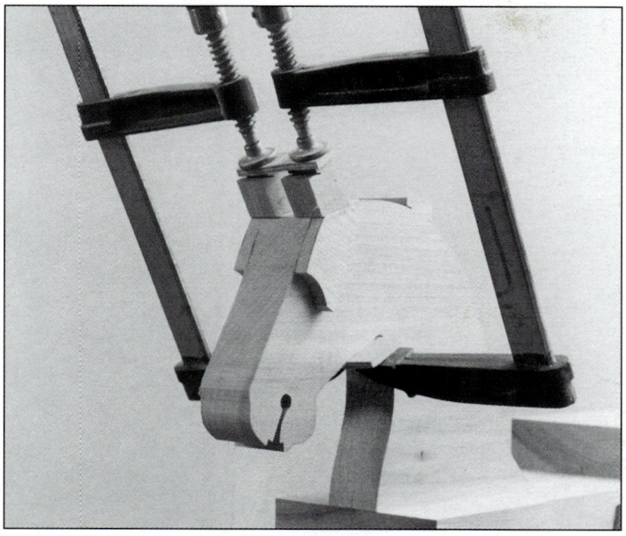

Plate 6.2 Gluing and cramping ear and eye pieces to head.

CUTTING LIST	*Thickness x width x length* Inches	*Thickness x width x length* Millimetres
Head & Neck, & both Neck muscle blocks	1 3/4 x 8 3/4 x 23	45 x 222 x 603
[NB The Ears & Eye pieces are also cut from the above piece]		
Seat	1 3/4 x 5 3/4 x 21	45 x 146 x 533
Rump	1 3/4 x 5 3/4 x 8	45 x 146 x 203
Leg fixing blocks (x 2)	1 3/8 x 4 1/2 x 5	35 x 114 x 127
Legs (all 4)	7/8 x 6 x 72	22 x 152 x 1830
Body Sides (x 2)	1/2 x 4 1/2 x 10 7/8	13 x 114 x 276
Battens (x 2)	3/4 x 3/4 x 10 7/8	19 x 19 x 276

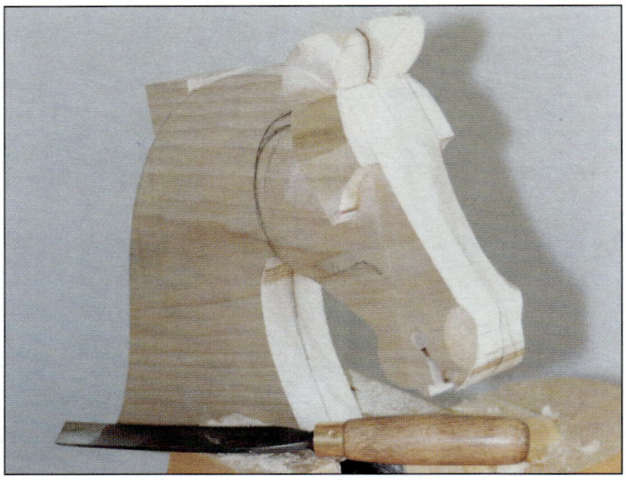

Plate 6.3 Carving ears & nostrils using large shallow gouge.

Plate 6.4 Carving along cheek line. Note eye piece has been carved back, and nostrils further defined.

Plate 6.5 Head rough carving complete, ready to sand off – note teeth and shape of lower jaw.

paper wrapped round a flat block of wood, and similarly sand the bottoms of the ears flat, so that they will fit down neatly onto the top of the head. The outside edges of the ears are flush with the outside edges of the eye pieces. Since sticking-out ears are always vulnerable to knocks, you may like to strengthen each ear joint with a ¼in (6) fluted dowel peg 1in (25) long. Glue on the ears. Now you are ready to tackle the head carving.

CARVING THE HEAD

Pencil in some guidelines: a centreline to help you keep the symmetry, the shapes of the ears, approx. positions of eyes and nostrils, and the curve of the cheek. The waste around the ears is removed with a coping saw.

With the 1in (25) gouge carve an angle where the nostrils will be. Pencil in the oval shapes of the nostrils and cut back all around until they stand proud. Then carve off the corners above the eye, up towards the base of the ears. The eye piece remains at its full thickness just above the eye (the eyebrow), but below the eye it is carved to run smoothly into the surrounding wood. With a straight chisel cut the line of the cheek then pare back the wood on the waste (neck) side of this line. Under the throat the front of the neck will eventually be rounded.

Below the cheek the head is gradually tapered down to the mouth, which finishes about 1⅜in (35) wide. Carefully cut away the mouth to reveal the teeth, and round over the corners at the back of the lower jaw. Carve steadily, taking a little from each side in turn and stand back from time to time to examine your progress.

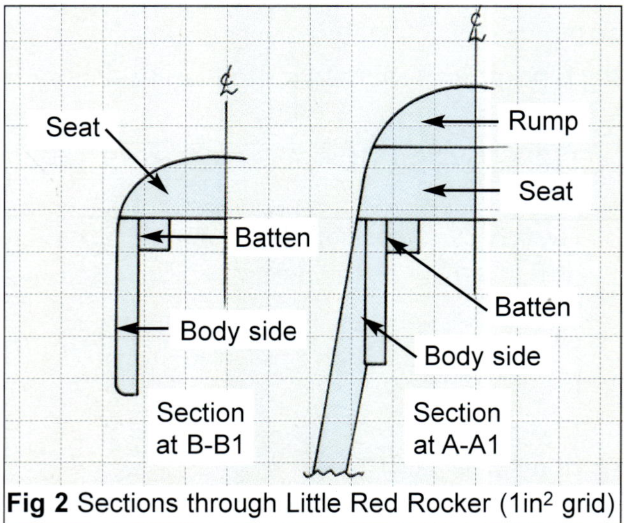

Fig 2 Sections through Little Red Rocker (1in² grid)

CHAPTER 6

LITTLE RED ROCKER

This design combines the straightforward construction of the Swinger enhanced by a carved head, neck and upper body. It is an excellent rocking horse for children up to the age of six or so, and the carved elements are nicely complemented by the red leather bridle and saddle. Choose a timber which carves readily - the horse in the accompanying photographs is made out of tulipwood - and prepare your timber according to the cutting list below:

PREPARATION

Make full size patterns of all the parts and mark them out carefully on the timber, then bandsaw out. Note that the two ears and two eye pieces shown on the plan are cut from offcuts of the same piece from which the head and neck and the two neck muscle blocks are cut. The grain should run in the direction of the arrows on the plan. The ears are bandsawn to 1in (25) thick and the eye pieces to 3/8in (9) thick. Leave an allowance of 3/16in (5) on the top straight edges of the legs for the 10° bevel.

The plan shows counterbored screwholes in the seat for fixing it to the head and rump, but you may prefer to use fluted dowel pegs, with centring markers to locate the holes, in which case the cramping noggin on the neck will aid the cramping down. Cramping noggins are also left on the tops of the neck muscle blocks, and the ears.

HOW TO MAKE IT

First glue and cramp the eye pieces to the head, making sure that the top edges are flush with the top of the head. When set, remove the cramps and sand the top flat with coarse (80 grit) abrasive

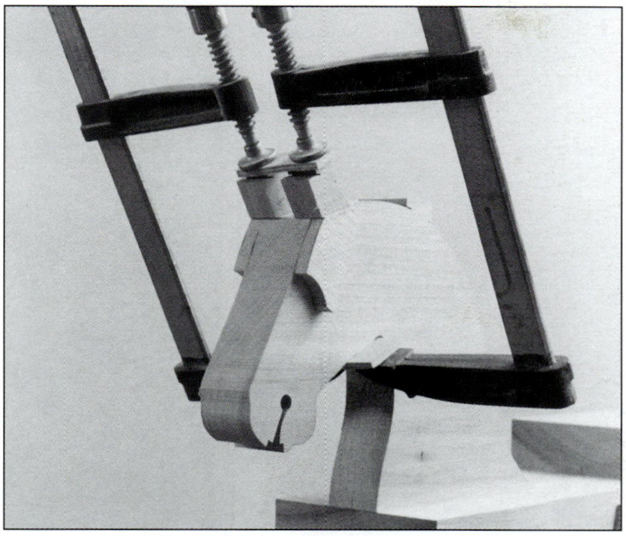

Plate 6.2 Gluing and cramping ear and eye pieces to head.

CUTTING LIST	*Thickness x width x length* Inches	*Thickness x width x length* Millimetres
Head & Neck, & both Neck muscle blocks	1 3/4 x 8 3/4 x 23	45 x 222 x 603
[NB The Ears & Eye pieces are also cut from the above piece]		
Seat	1 3/4 x 5 3/4 x 21	45 x 146 x 533
Rump	1 3/4 x 5 3/4 x 8	45 x 146 x 203
Leg fixing blocks (x 2)	1 3/8 x 4 1/2 x 5	35 x 114 x 127
Legs (all 4)	7/8 x 6 x 72	22 x 152 x 1830
Body Sides (x 2)	1/2 x 4 1/2 x 10 7/8	13 x 114 x 276
Battens (x 2)	3/4 x 3/4 x 10 7/8	19 x 19 x 276

Plate 6.3 Carving ears & nostrils using large shallow gouge.

Plate 6.4 Carving along cheek line. Note eye piece has been carved back, and nostrils further defined.

Plate 6.5 Head rough carving complete, ready to sand off – note teeth and shape of lower jaw.

paper wrapped round a flat block of wood, and similarly sand the bottoms of the ears flat, so that they will fit down neatly onto the top of the head. The outside edges of the ears are flush with the outside edges of the eye pieces. Since sticking-out ears are always vulnerable to knocks, you may like to strengthen each ear joint with a 1/4in (6) fluted dowel peg 1in (25) long. Glue on the ears. Now you are ready to tackle the head carving.

CARVING THE HEAD

Pencil in some guidelines: a centreline to help you keep the symmetry, the shapes of the ears, approx. positions of eyes and nostrils, and the curve of the cheek. The waste around the ears is removed with a coping saw.

With the 1in (25) gouge carve an angle where the nostrils will be. Pencil in the oval shapes of the nostrils and cut back all around until they stand proud. Then carve off the corners above the eye, up towards the base of the ears. The eye piece remains at its full thickness just above the eye (the eyebrow), but below the eye it is carved to run smoothly into the surrounding wood. With a straight chisel cut the line of the cheek then pare back the wood on the waste (neck) side of this line. Under the throat the front of the neck will eventually be rounded.

Below the cheek the head is gradually tapered down to the mouth, which finishes about 1 3/8in (35) wide. Carefully cut away the mouth to reveal the teeth, and round over the corners at the back of the lower jaw. Carve steadily, taking a little from each side in turn and stand back from time to time to examine your progress.

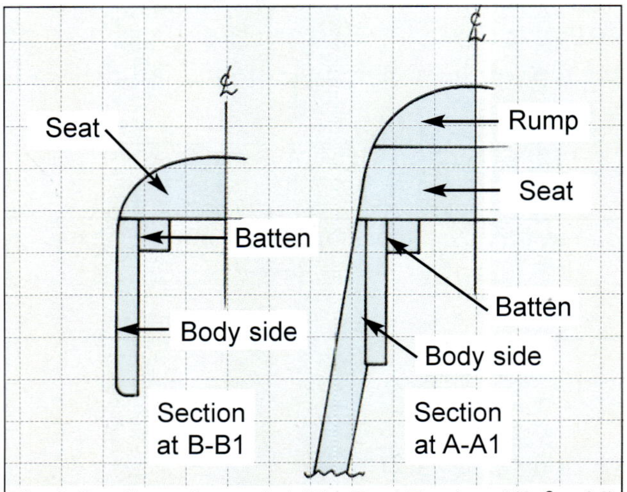

Fig 2 Sections through Little Red Rocker (1in^2 grid)

Plate 6.6 Both neck muscle blocks and the rump can be glued on in one go if you have enough cramps.

Plate 6.7 Head and neck muscle blocks have been glued and pegged down to seat – and some of waste wood sawn away.

FITTING IT TOGETHER

When you fix down the neck ensure that it is positioned centrally on the seat. Plane the bottoms of the neck muscle blocks so that they fit neatly onto the seat and neck each side, then glue and cramp them in position. The fronts of the neck and neck muscle blocks should all be flush with the front edge of the seat. Glue on the rump, which is not shaped at all prior to assembly.

Pencil in the curved shape of the seat and rump. If you have a bandsaw that will cut to a depth of six inches you can turn the horse on its side and bandsaw off the waste from rump and seat. If your bandsaw table will tilt, set it to 10° and bandsaw down each side, keeping the seat full width - 5¾ in (146) - at the bottom. This angled saw cut is rather deep through the neck and your bandsaw may not be big enough to cope, in which case you can saw it by hand, or carve away the waste with your biggest gouge and a mallet.

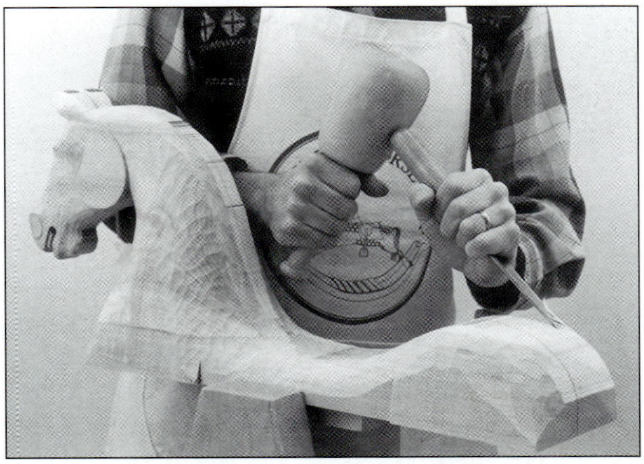

Plate 6.8 Carving the rump with a mallet and gouge.

CARVING THE BODY

The neck muscle blocks should be carved to run smoothly into the neck, which is rounded over at the top. You can use a bigger gouge and mallet here, and also to round over the rump and seat. At this stage do not carve right down to the lower corners of the seat block. When you are getting close to the final roughed out shape, leave the carving while you fix on the legs and body sides. Check that the outer face of the legs will be flush with the lower edge of the seat, and glue and screw

Plate 6.9 Use a Surform (or Microplane or rasp) to further shape neck and rump. Carving stops short of the bottom edges of the seat.

Plate 6.10 Dry-fit legs and leg fixing blocks so legs can be marked and notches sawn out to accommodate the body sides (fitted at right angles to the underside of the seat and flush with the outside edges of the seat).

Plate 6.11 Fitting body sides with their battens.

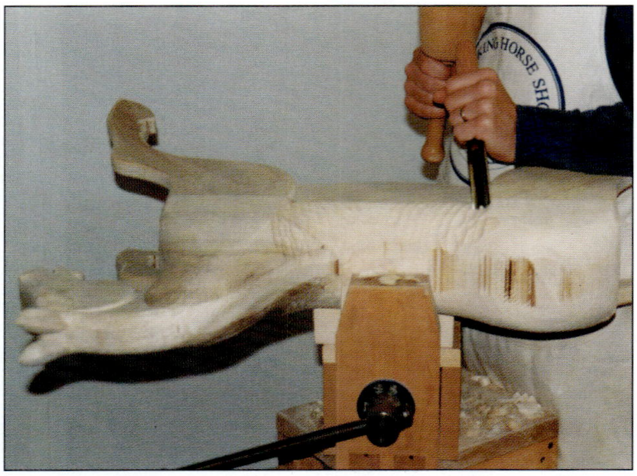

Plate 6.12 Further carving of body – aim for gentle curves.

on the leg fixing blocks centrally to the underside of the seat. The ends of the leg fixing blocks should be flush with the ends of the seat. Then screw on the legs temporarily (without glue) while you mark for the notches which are sawn from the inside of each leg. These notches enable the body sides to be fitted at right angles to the underside of the seat and flush with the edge of the seat in the middle (where the seat is narrower).

The corners of the legs and the lower edges of the body sides are rounded over. This can be most easily accomplished before assembly with a rounding over cutter in a router, if you have one. Take care not to round over that part of the leg which will be against the leg fixing block. If you do not have a router, use a Surform or rasp and abrasive paper after assembly. Glue and screw the legs and body sides in position. To prevent the body sides from being crushed in when you put the horse in your vice, tuck pieces of scrap wood tightly between them.

A half round Surform is very useful for removing gouge marks and further rounding the rump, seat and neck which should run smoothly down to the legs and body sides. The rounding of the corners of the legs is carried on up the corners of the seat to run smoothly into the curve of the neck and rump. When you have achieved a satisfactory shape, sand smooth all over, starting with a fairly course abrasive, then progressively finer ones - 120, 180, and 240 grit - until you lose all blemishes and scratch marks. Fill or plug the screw holes and drill a ¾inch (19) hole for the tail. Please refer to Chaper 13 for details of hoof notching, and to Chapter 11 for how to make the stand.

FINISHING

Fit a pair of 5/8in (16) diameter glass eyes by cutting recesses 1/8in (3) deep and set the eyes in with woodfiller. The horse can then be varnished - two or three thin coats of a satin finish varnish will look good, sanding down lightly between coats.

Plate 6.13 The carving complete – sanded smooth, glass eyes fitted, and given a coat of clear satin varnish.

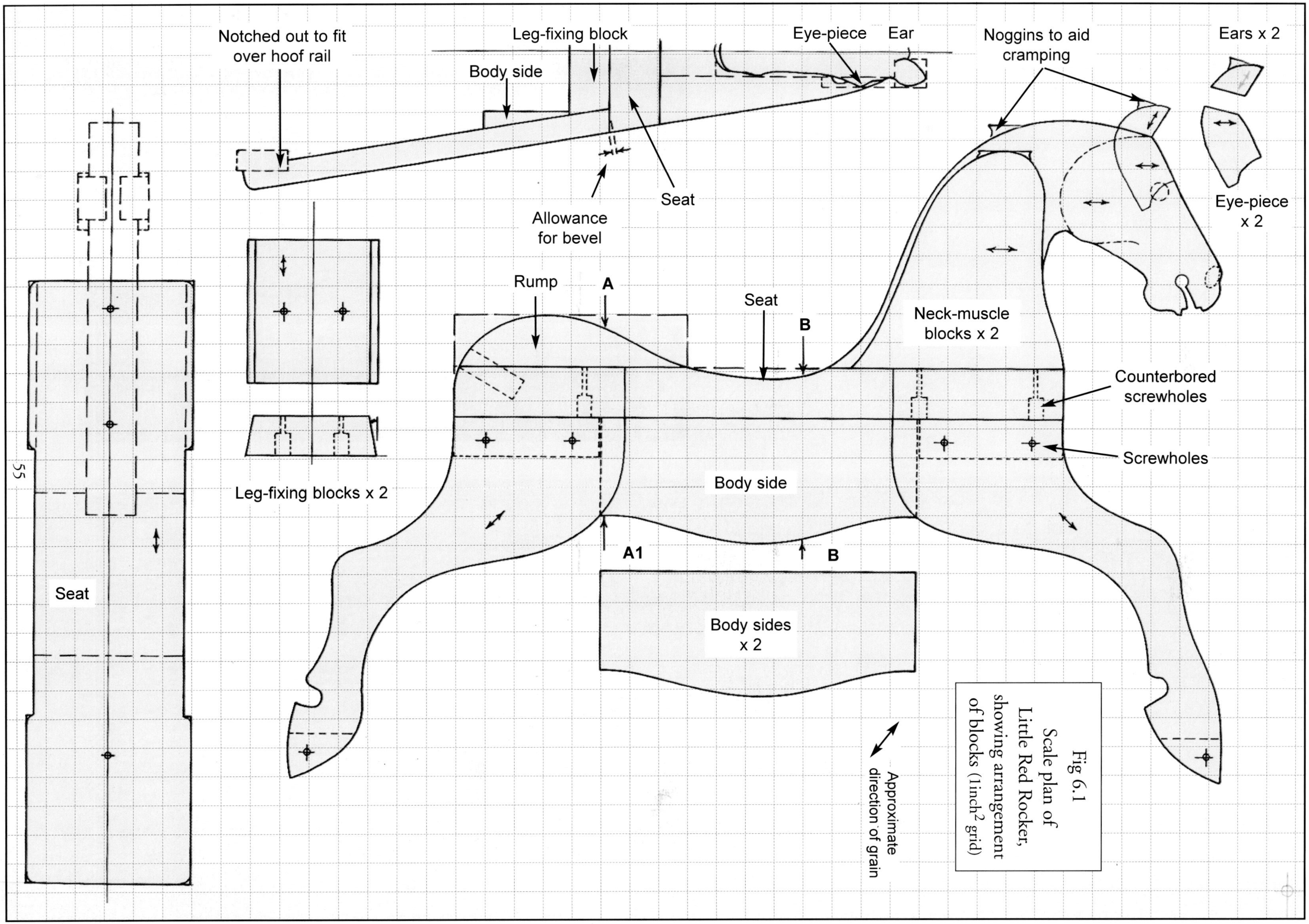

Fig 6.1
Scale plan of Little Red Rocker, showing arrangement of blocks (1inch^2 grid)

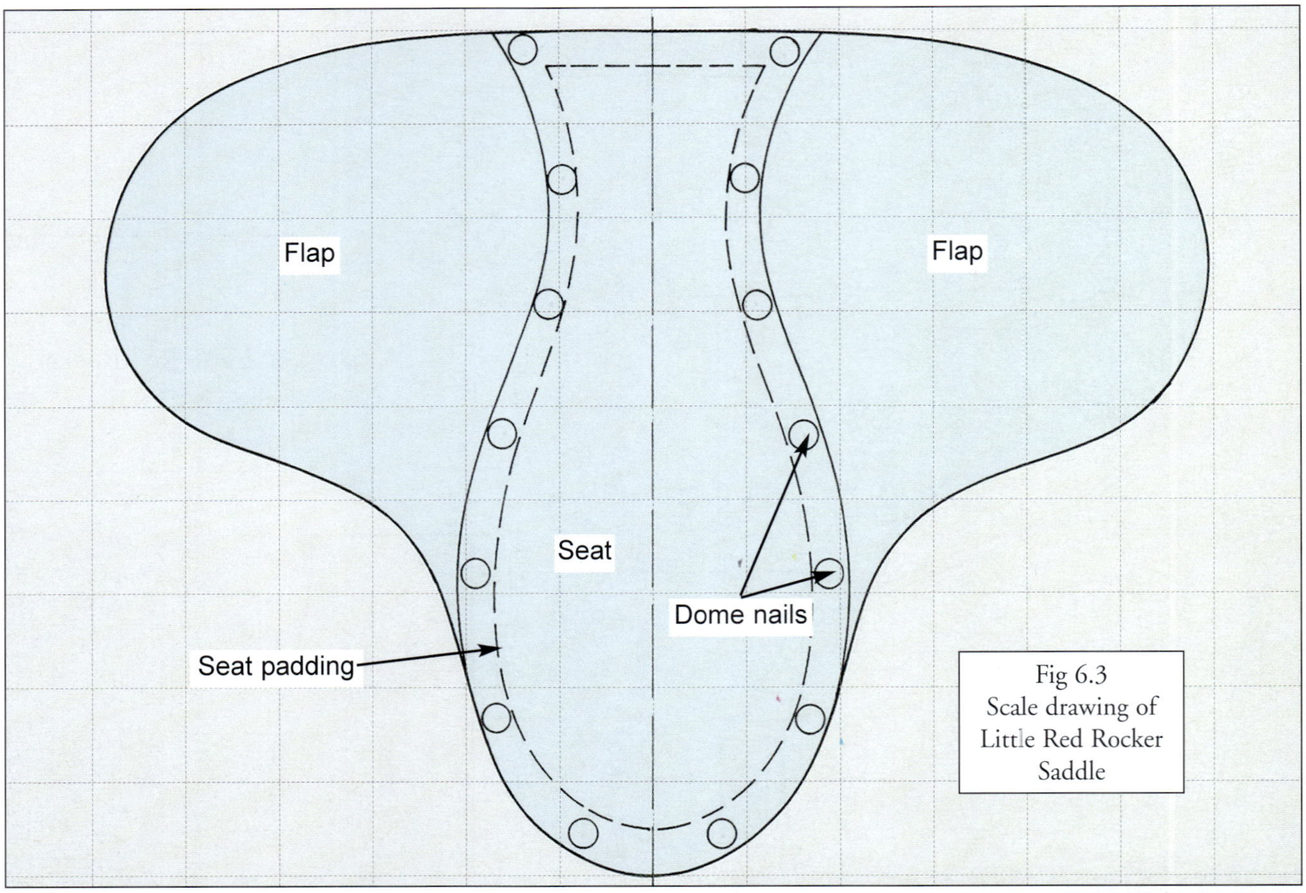

Fig 6.3
Scale drawing of
Little Red Rocker
Saddle

A pair of small stirrup irons riveted to a length of ¾in (19) leather strap 21in (552) long is placed over the horse's back towards the front of the saddle and nailed on in the middle. The simple red leather saddle is padded with ½in (13) thick foam rubber. Damp the leather a little with water to make it flexible, and press it over the contours of the horse. Nail in place with ½in (13) brass dome head nails spaced evenly along the crease lines and round the back.

A 'deluxe' version of the Little red Rocker saddle has stiffer leather flaps and adjustable stirrups.

The tail, synthetic or real horsehair, is glued into its hole and secured with a small wooden wedge tapped in underneath so it is out of sight. The bridle and reins are made up from red leather strapping. The bridle has little brass buckles and a brass bit, so is simply buckled onto the head. For details of bridles refer to Chapter 14. The Little Red Rocker is now almost ready to be lifted onto the stand where it is secured to the hoof rails with either 1¼in (32) no. 8 screws or 3/16in (5) bolts and nuts. It is finished, a delightful and impressive little horse. All it needs now is a rider.

Plate 6.14 Rear view of the completed horse mounted on its swing iron safety stand.

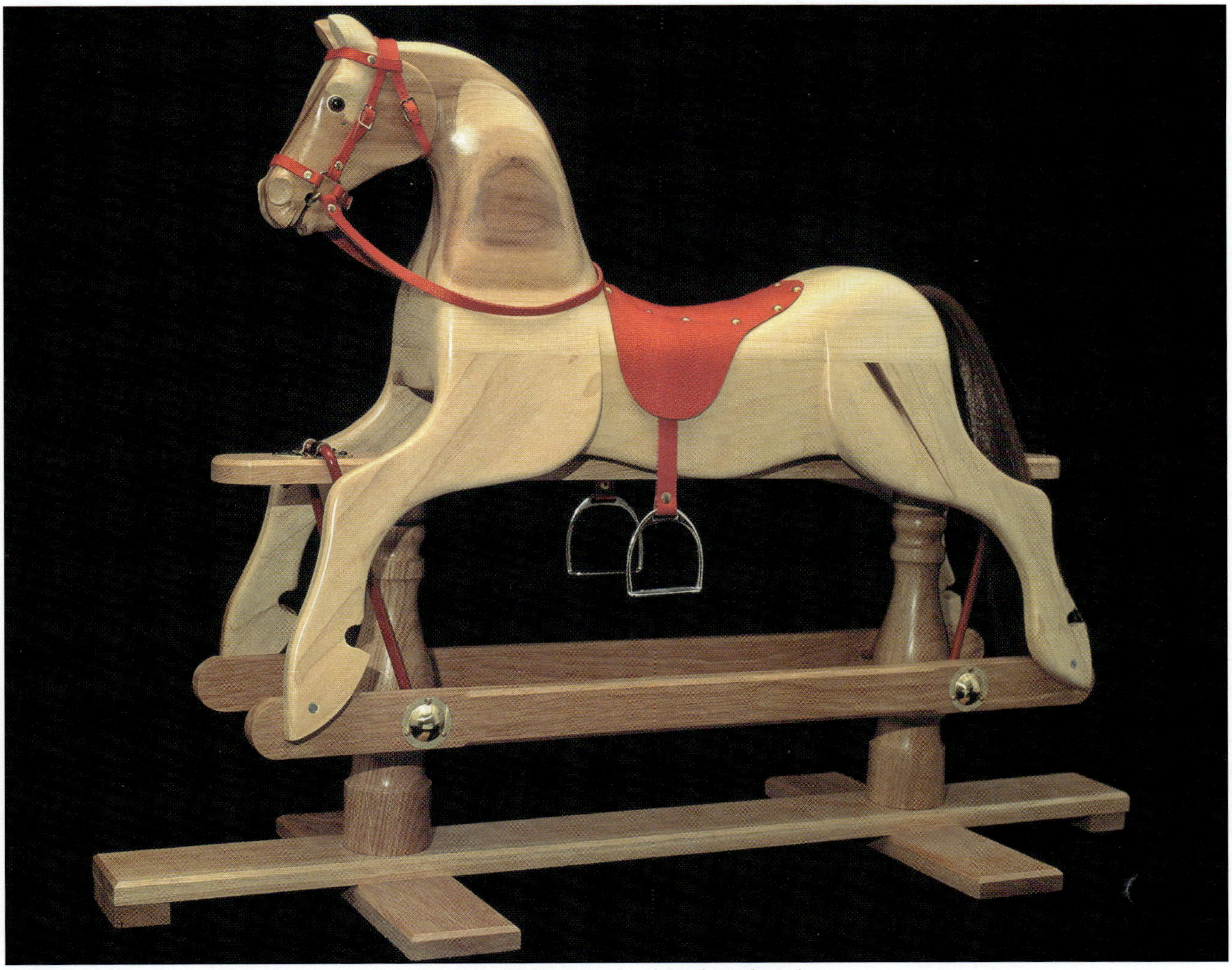

Plate 6.15 The Completed Little Red Rocker.

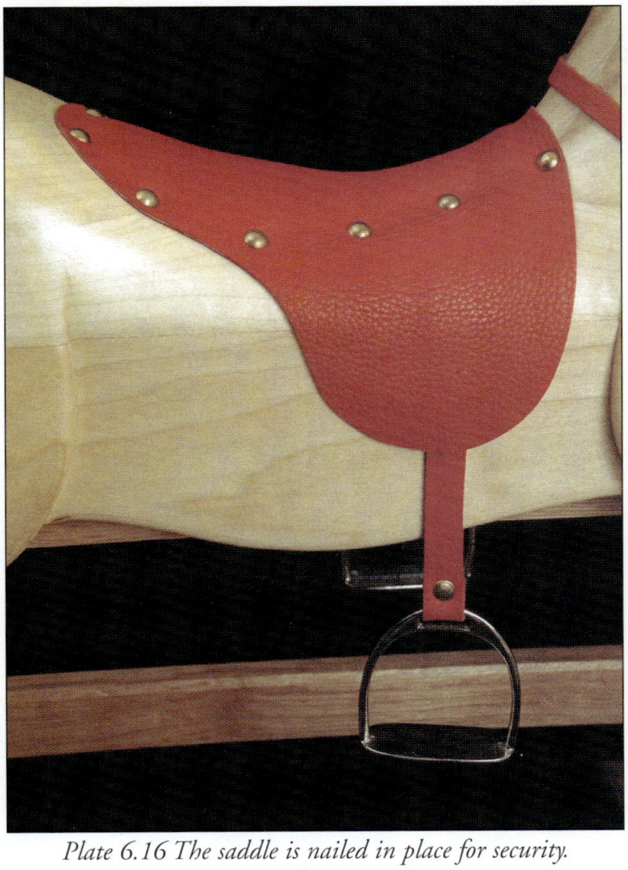

Plate 6.16 The saddle is nailed in place for security.

Plate 6.17 The tail in place.

Plate 7.2 Miniature rocking horse in dolls house nursery.

Plate 7.1 Twelfth scale rocking horse for a dolls house.

CHAPTER 7

A DOLL'S HOUSE MINIATURE ROCKING HORSE

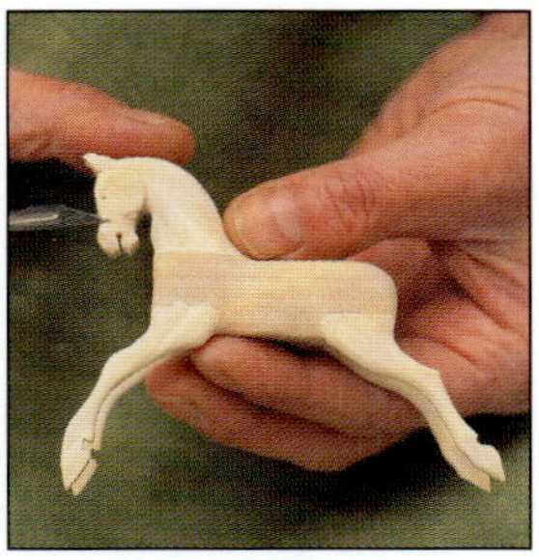

This is a twelfth scale doll's house size version of the Large rocking horse described in Chapter 10. I found that making a rocking horse on such a small scale after being accustomed to the full-size versions presented peculiar problems; you certainly need a good eye and steady hand and everything has to be handled so much more delicately. On the other hand few tools are needed, the materials are relatively inexpensive, and the whole project, including tools, can be kept in a small box.

PREPARATION

The horse is made from lime, basswood or similar close grained, easy to carve timber. Model craft suppliers often stock prepared timber in suitable dimensions, but avoid balsa, which is too fragile.

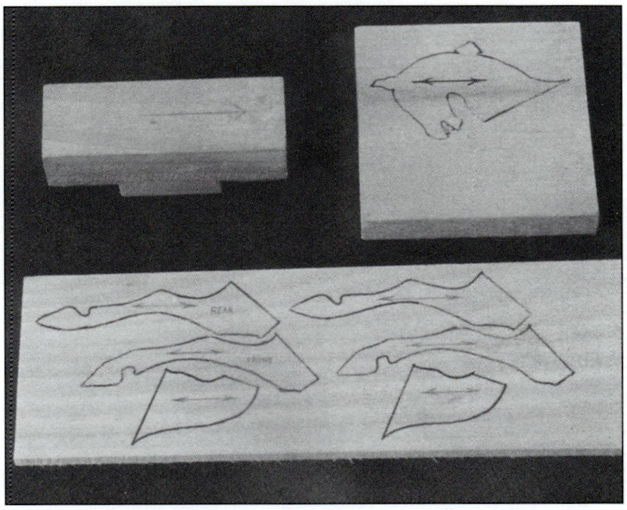

Plate 7.3 Mark shape onto the wood, noting direction of grain.

HOW TO MAKE THE HORSE

Trace the patterns for the head and neck, legs and neck muscle blocks onto the wood and cut out carefully with a fret saw. Avoid having short grain running across those parts vulnerable to breakage (ie legs and ears) by keeping the direction of grain running in approximately the same direction as the arrows on the plan.

The body is a solid block and should be marked for the notch at each corner to receive the legs. These notches can be cut out with a sharp chisel or knife and note that they are angled so that the legs splay out, leaving 9/16in (14) between the legs at the body end, and 13/16in (20) between the hooves (approximately!). Mark the body block with an arrow pointing to the front, and glue on the neck, making sure it is central. Then glue on the neck muscle blocks at either side. Use aliphatic resin glue and small cramps, or 'Superglue', in which case you need no cramps, for the assembly. Then

Plate 7.4 Cutting out the parts with a fret saw.

CUTTING LIST for Horse	*Thickness x width x length*	*Thickness x width x length*
	Inches	**Millimetres**
Head and neck	3/8 x 1 1/2 x 2 3/8	10 x 38 x 60
Body	13/16 x 13/16 x 2 3/8	20 x 20 x 60
Legs (all 4) and 2 neck muscle blocks	3/16 x 2 x 5 1/2	4 x 50 x 140
Saddle block	1/8 x 1/4 x 5/8	3 x 6 x 16

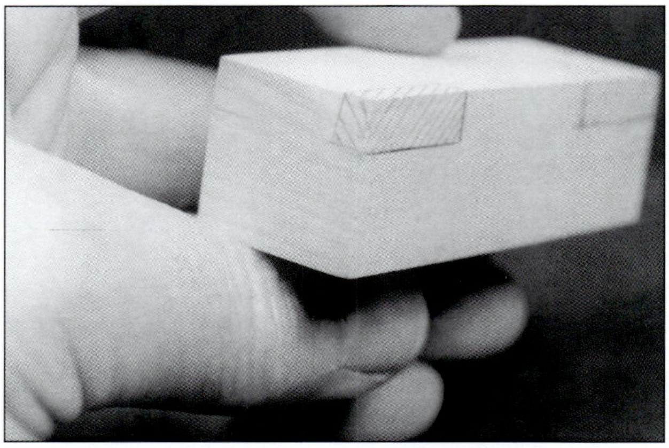

Plate 7.5 Mark the body for the leg notches.

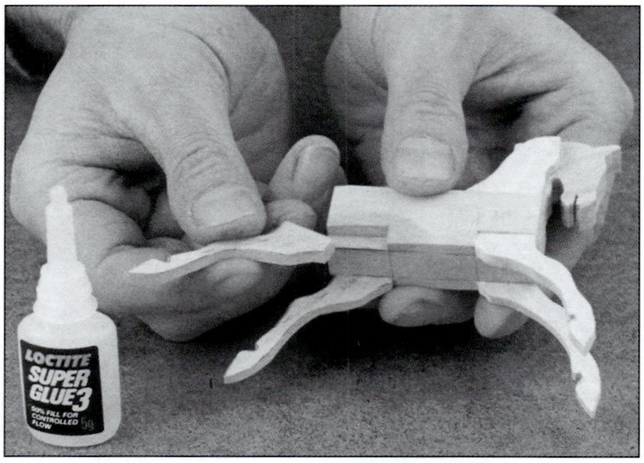

Plate 7.6 Gluing the horse together with 'super glue'

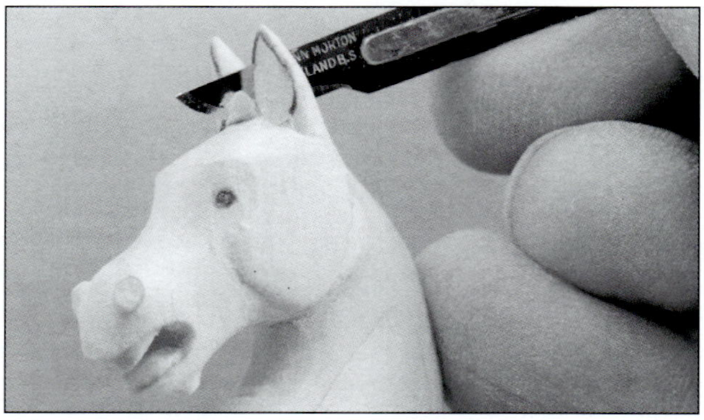

Plate 7.7 Carefully carving ears.

Plate 7.8 Carving the miniature horse.

glue on the legs. It is a good idea to give extra security to the leg fixings by dowelling them to the body. Wooden cocktail sticks make good dowels. Drill two holes to fit your cocktail sticks through the top of each leg and into the body. Put a little glue onto the dowel, push in firmly and cut off.

When the glue has set the carving can commence. You will need a really sharp small pointed knife for this. A scalpel is ideal, and of course you will have to take care not to cut yourself (too many times). Remove all the square corners, taking a little from each side in turn to keep the symmetry, and carving gradually towards the desired shape. You will probably find it helpful to refer to the photographs in Chapters 8, 9 and 10. Of course each person's carving is unique - this is what gives each horse its own character.

When you start to carve the head, mark the cheeks and the eye positions. The head tapers to approximately 3/16in (5) wide at the mouth. Carve the teeth with care since the grain is short here and it is all too easy to end up with a toothless horse. If you have one, a small round burr tool will be useful for hollowing out the nostrils and ears.

When you are happy with the shape of your horse, sand him all over with 180 grit abrasive paper to remove your carving marks, then with finer grade abrasive papers - 240 and even 360 grit to achieve a nicely rounded smooth finish. Take particular care when sanding the head, ears and hooves, to leave your carving sharp. Mark the position for the saddle block, cut a 1/8in (3) wide groove, glue the saddle block in place and then sand lightly so the

Plate 7.9 Sealed, sanded and painted pale grey.

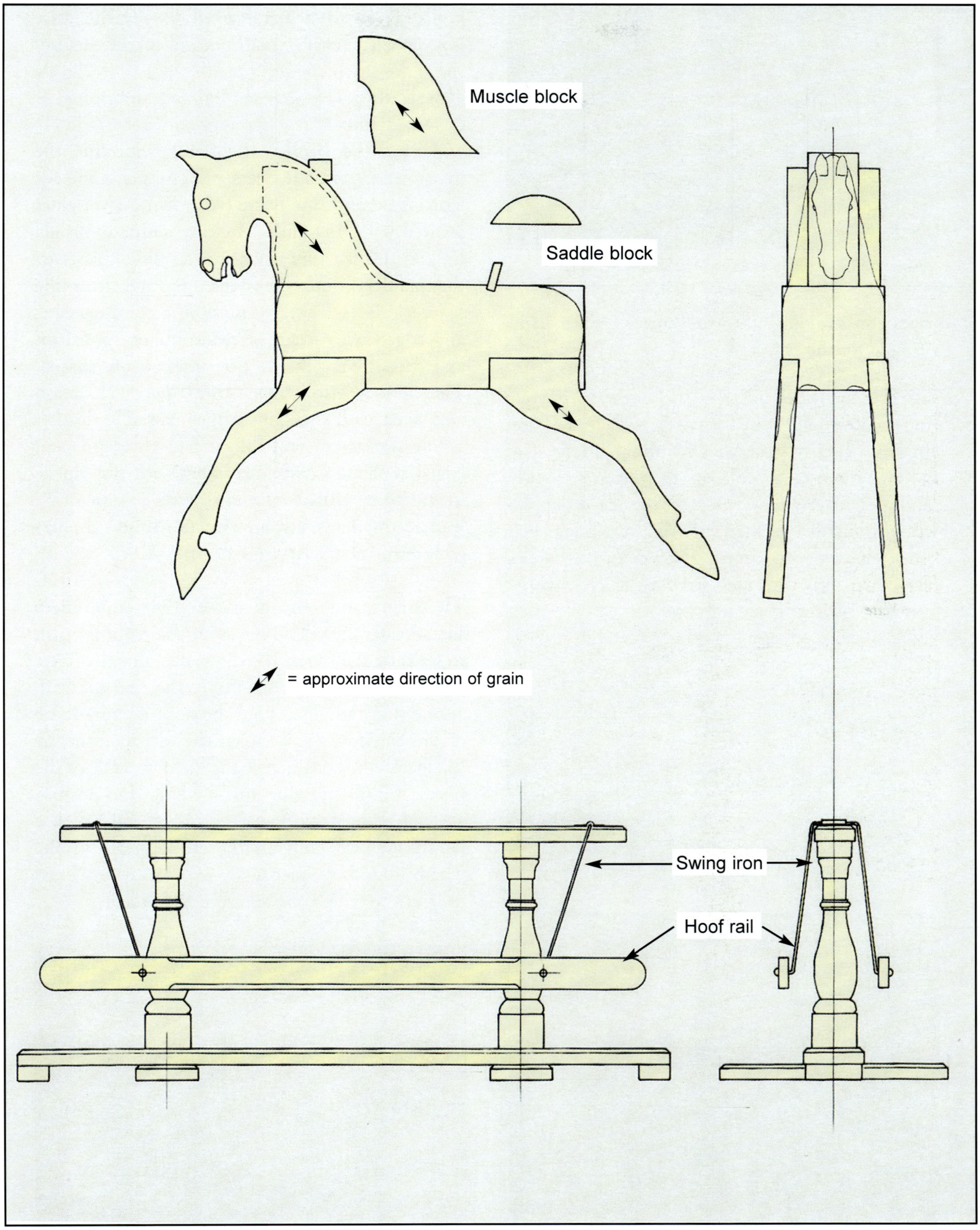

Fig 7.1 Actual Size plan for twelfth scale Miniature Rocking Horse and Stand.

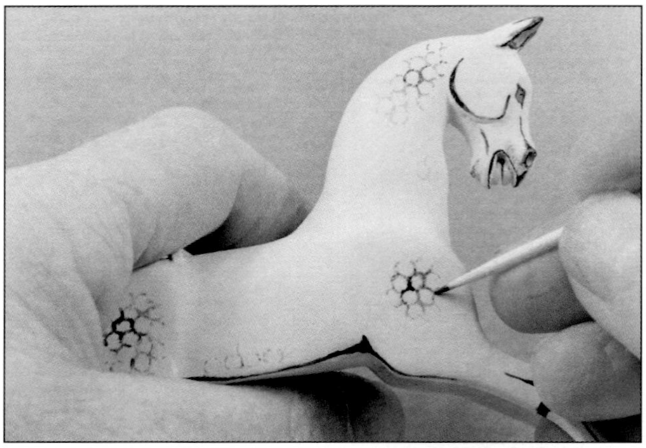

Plate 7.10 Dappling with a cocktail stick. The hooves have been painted black.

edges run smoothly into the horse. Drill a $^{3}/_{32}$in (2) hole for the tail.

Rub a grain filler all over the horse with your finger tips, and sand smooth with very fine abrasive paper. Use acrylics for the painting; give the horse two or three coats of pale grey, lightly sanding between coats. Dab on the black dapples with the end of a cocktail stick or a very fine pencil brush - have a practice first - and paint the hooves black. Two tiny pins are used for the eyes, which are painted brown with a black dot for the iris, and rimmed with red. The mouth, the inside of the ears and nostrils are painted red. Finally, the horse is given a thin coat of matt or satin acrylic varnish.

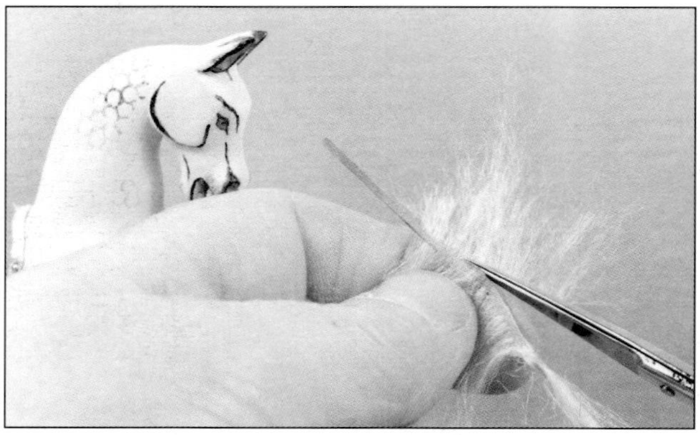

Plate 7.11 Preparing the mane.

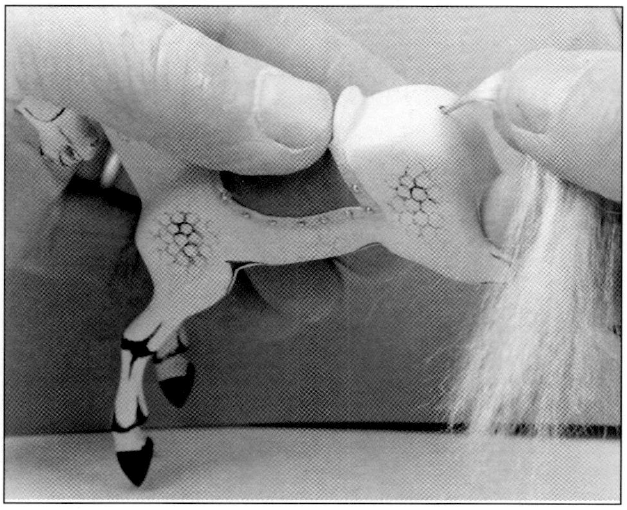

Plate 7.12 Glueing in the tail, note saddlecloth has been fitted.

The leather for the saddle and strapping is extremely thin. Cut strips approximately $^{1}/_{32}$in (1) wide for the bridle, $^{1}/_{16}$in (2) wide for the martingale, stirrup leathers and crupper. Glue the martingale onto the horse (with white PVA glue) secured with tiny nails. The tiny nails are pushed in, and this is easier if you prick guide holes. Put the saddlery onto the horse, starting with the saddlecloths, which are cut from red carpet tape, and edged with $^{1}/_{16}$in (2) wide ribbon, glued on and decorated with the tiny nails evenly spaced. The chest rosette is made from $^{1}/_{16}$in (2) ribbon and fixed with a slightly larger nail. The leather saddle seat is cut and folded and glued on, and edged with tiny nails. Accessories for this horse, including tiny brackets and stirrups in cast silver, leather, tiny nails, etc, are available from suppliers of accessories, see Appendix.

The mane and tail are made from embroidery thread carefully teased out with a stiff toothbrush to separate the fibres. For the mane, glue the fibres onto a $^{1}/_{32}$in (1) wide strip of leather, cut off flush at one side and glued onto the neck, leaving some of the hair to hang between the ears to form the forelock. For the tail, glue together the ends of the fibres, roll up and glue into the hole, and push in a small wooden wedge to hold the tail up at a jaunty angle. Finally fit the crupper and bridle. The bridle 'cheek pieces' are led to two tiny brass bit rings to which the reins are also attached.

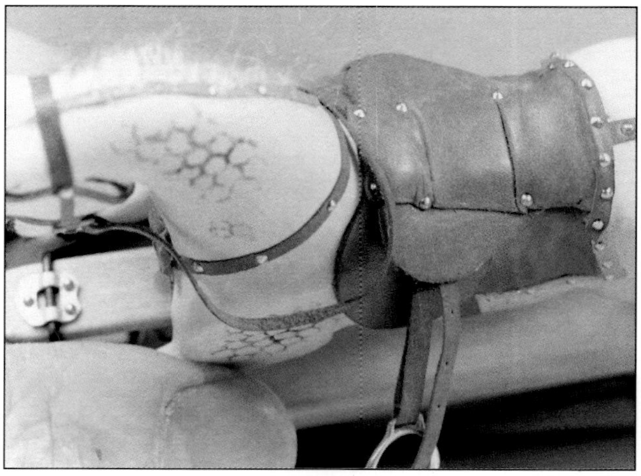

Plate 7.13 Saddle arrangement.

CUTTING LIST for Stand	*Thickness x width x length* Inches	*Thickness x width x length* Millimetres
Top Rail	1/8 x 5/16 x 4 3/8	3 x 8 x 110
Bottom Rail	1/8 x 15/32 x 5	3 x 12 x 127
Cross pieces (x 2)	1/8 x 15/32 x 1 3/4	3 x 12 x 45
End pieces (x 2)	1/8 x 1/4 x 7/16	3 x 6 x 11
Posts (x 2)	3/8 dia x 1 7/8	10 diam x 48
Hoof rails (x 2)	1/16 x 1/4 x 4 5/8	2 x 6 x 118

HOW TO MAKE THE STAND

Chamfer the top edges of the stand rails and cross pieces. The posts can be left round, or tapered, or if you have a lathe, turned to the pattern shown in the drawings. If turned, leave a 1/8in (3) diameter peg 5/32in (4) long, top and bottom, and reduce the diameter of the post at the top to 9/32in (7). The posts are 1 5/8in (40) long between the top and bottom rails.

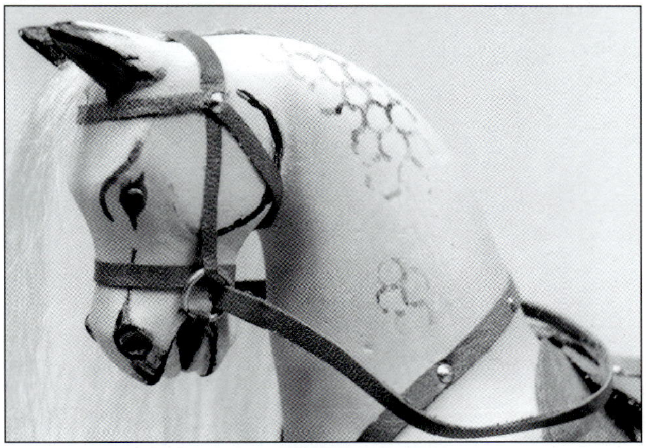

Plate 7.14 Bridle and reins.

Mark the positions of the posts carefully on the top rail. Hold the top rail centrally on the bottom rail and carefully drill a 1/8in (3) hole through both pieces. Also drill a 1/8in (3) diameter hole 1/32in (1) into the exact centre of the cross piece, then glue it all together. If you have left the posts square (or tapered them), you can cut them off to the exact length between the rails, which is 1 5/8in (40), and fix them in place with cocktail stick dowel pegs. Glue on the end pieces and, when dry, trim off the pegs or dowels at the tops and bottoms of the posts and lightly sand smooth. Make the hoof rails and drill 5/64in (2) holes for the swing irons. Lightly sand, stain and varnish the stand and hoof rails.

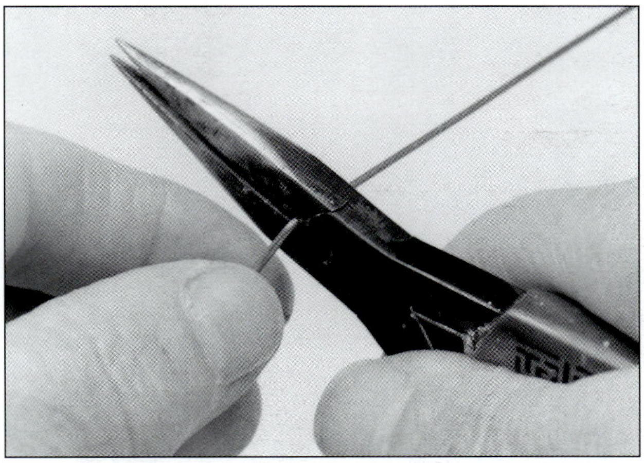

Plate 7.15 Bending the swing irons.

Make the swing irons by bending 1/32in (1) brass wire to the shape of the pattern. Ensure both are the same. Tiny cast silver brackets secure swing irons to the top rail of the stand and are fixed on with tiny nails. Cut notches in the hooves so they will fit over the hoof rails and glue them on. Drill through hooves and hoof rails and glue in tiny nails to hold the hooves securely. Fit the ends of the swing irons through the holes in the hoof rails. The ends can be secured with a nut which is just glued on.

Make sure that the swing irons move freely and that the horse rocks properly - then stand back, relaxed and satisfied, and wait for the admiring comments.

Plate 7.16 The completed miniature rocking horse.

Plate 8.1 The completed Half Size horses, on stand and bows, with porcelain riders.

Plates 8.2 and 8.3 (below) The Half Size horse under construction.

CHAPTER 8

THE HALF SIZE
TRADITIONAL CARVED ROCKING HORSE

This fully carved Victorian style horse is a great project, particularly for those new to the craft. The construction and carving are similar to the larger versions, but because of its size making this horse requires few tools. Indeed the carving can be accomplished almost entirely with a penknife and sandpaper, though some specialist carving tools will certainly make the project easier, as detailed below.

PREPARATION

This horse is 'Half Size' in that it is half the dimensions of the popular Medium Size horse in Chapter 10: the body is 12in (305) long against the Medium Size horse's 24in (610) long body. The Half Size horse is for dolls to ride, and since it does not have to take the strain of children riding it, a soft timber which is easy to carve, such as jelutong or basswood, is recommended. The horse is mounted on a traditional swing iron stand. Modifications for bow rocker mounting are described in Chapter 12.

Apart from a small bandsaw or jigsaw (sabersaw) for cutting out the parts, other tools required are: electric hand drill with various bits up to 5/8in (16); a small drum sanding attachment is also useful; handsaw, coping saw, smoothing plane and a pair of compasses.

For the carving we recommend these gouges:
No. 9 - 5/8in (16) and No. 4 - 1in straight London Pattern gouges; No. 30 - 3/8in (10) spoon gouge, 1/4in (6) chisel (preferably skew end). A No. 9 - 1/8in (3) will also be useful for the finer detail round the head. A round Surform, abrasive paper (and penknife).

HOW TO MAKE IT

Start with the head, which is easier to carve before it is fitted onto the rest of the horse. Pencil a centreline all round the head and down the neck, and the shapes of the ears looking from the front. On each side pencil in the line which indicates the base of the ears and curves round to mark the edge of the cheek. Use the coping saw to cut away the waste from around the ears and to separate them.

With a large shallow gouge carve the fronts of the ears so they angle back slightly and curve in to meet the glue line at either side. The head timber remains thickest, 1 3/4in (45), where the ears flare out and the eyebrows. In the area of the cheeks it is pared back to approx 1 1/2in (38) thick. Round off the corners above the eyes to meet the base of the ears. With the large gouge cut away for the nostrils which angle back at each side. Pencil in the oval shape of the nostrils and cut back all round. Above the nostrils the corner is pared away right up to the eye, and below is curved to the mouth. The front of the head tapers from eyebrow to mouth with just the nostrils sticking out.

Carve around the 'cheekbone' until it stands up

CUTTING LIST - Half Size Horse	*Thickness x width x length* Inches	*Thickness x width x length* Millimetres
Head and neck	1 3/4 x 5 3/4 x 11	45 x 146 x 280
Neck Muscle blocks (both)	1 1/4 x 4 1/4 x 13	32 x 108 x 330
Upper & lower body blocks x 2	1 1/4 x 4 1/4 x 12	32 x 108 x 305
Middle body blocks: - Sides x 2	1 1/4 x 1 3/4 x 12	32 x 44 x 305
- Ends x 2	1 1/4 x 1 3/4 x 1 3/4	32 x 45 x 45
Legs	7/8 x 4 x 36	22 x 100 x 914
Saddle Block	3/8 x 1 x 3	10 x 25 x 76

only about 1/16in (1.5), and use a small gouge to narrow and round it so it flows neatly into the surrounding areas. Below the cheek the wood is carved away to taper towards the mouth and lower jaw. The mouth should finish about 1 1/4in (32) wide. Round off the 'corners' below the cheek and the lower jaw. With a small chisel cut away around the mouth to reveal the teeth. Just below the eyebrow cut in circular recesses about 3/8in (10) diameter, 1/8in (3) deep for the glass eyes to fit into, but do not fit them yet. Hollow out the nostrils and ears slightly. The head is finished off with abrasive paper.

THE BODY

The body is essentially a hollow rectangular box with upper, lower and four middle body blocks. No shaping is done on the body (apart from sawing out the corners of the lower body block to receive the legs - see below) prior to assembly.

Glue the neck down centrally to the upper body block, using the neck cramping noggin if need be. When the adhesive has set the neck muscle blocks are glued in place, one at each side of the neck. Ensure a good fit to neck and upper body block. Glue the middle body blocks - sides and ends - together and to the upper body block.

Make a card pattern of the upper face of the lower body block, and the ends, as shown on the plan, and pencil the lines at each corner onto the timber. The lower body block is notched out with angled saw cuts at each corner to receive the legs: 5° for the front legs, 8° for the rear ones (as near as you can). Glue onto the middle body blocks.

The lower parts of the legs can be rough shaped before fixing them to the horse, using a Surform or rasp. The shaping consists of rounding the legs and making them a little thinner in the area below the 'knees'. Do not round over the bottoms of the hoofs.

The legs are now fixed onto the lower body block. These are important joints so true up the sawn surface of the notches carefully for the legs to fit to. The waste pieces sawn from the lower body block can be used to help to position cramps. Now to carve the body and neck.

Pencil in the centre line along the top of the body and down the rear end, and down the chest, to aid you in keeping the horse symmetrical. With the horse on its side pencil in the curve of the rump and saw off the waste. Also, saw off the neck cramping noggin. Take your largest gouge and proceed to cut away the waste at all corners (a horse has no corners!). Rough shape the neck to taper up towards the top, where it is rounded over.

With the horse upside down, round off the inside corners of the tops of the legs so they run smoothly into the body. The lower body block at the front is shaped to leave a bulge in the middle, while at the rear a 'valley' between the legs curves up towards the tail. With the horse on its side again, pencil a cross near the centre of the middle body block at each side to indicate the highest point of the swell of the belly - forward of this point, from the back of the front leg round to the base of the neck, and back of this point, from the front of the rear leg round to just in front of where the saddle block will be placed, the body is thinner.

The main fault with beginners is not removing enough wood, leaving the horse looking too boxlike. There is plenty of timber to cut away and very little danger of cutting through to the hollow in the middle. Aim to achieve gentle curves, not steep depressions. The profiles shown (which relate to letters shown on the plan) give a guide to the contours to aim for.

Round the 'shoulders' but leave them proud of the area above, where the wood is cut in towards the neck, and below where the top corners of the legs are rounded in towards the chest. The chest is concave in the middle but bulges out in the centre at the bottom. At the rear, curve the rump down to run into the rounded corners of the rear legs. Use a Surform to remove the ripples left by the gouges, and finish by sanding down thoroughly all over. Drum sanding attachments in your electric drill are useful here. Fill blemishes with a proprietary woodfiller, preferably the two-part, paste and hardener type.

FINISHING

The following explains those aspects of the finishing process which apply specifically to the

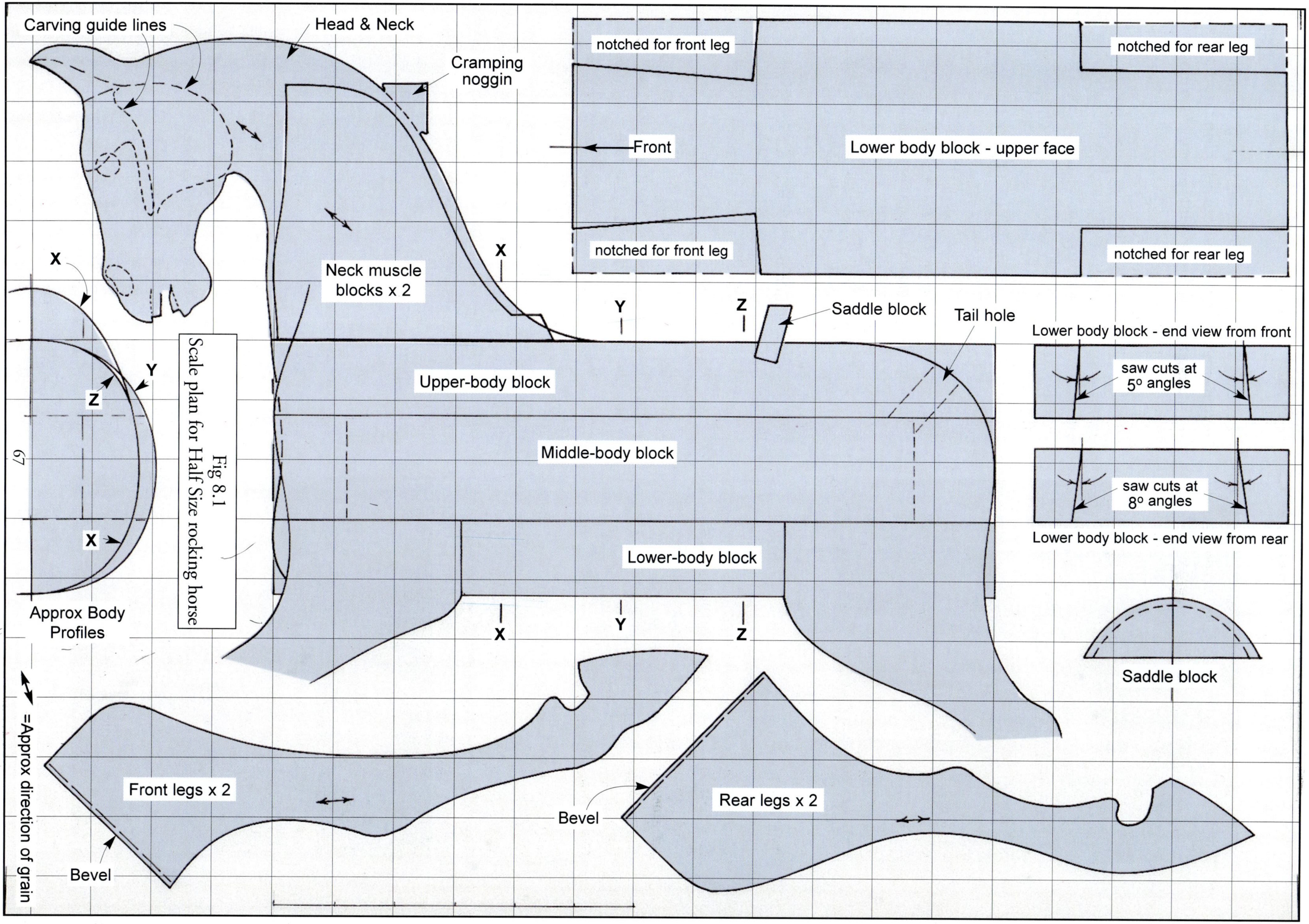

Fig 8.1
Scale plan for Half Size rocking horse

Plates 8.4 Using a coping saw to separate the ears. Note the pencilled guidelines that have been drawn on.

Half Size horse, but please refer to Chapters 13 and 14 for more information on finishing and dappling, fitting hair and saddlery. It is advisable to have the accessories (saddle, bridle, hair etc) to hand now so that you can understand how they are to be fitted and make the necessary preparations: there are different types with different methods of fitting, but they all come with instructions.

Half Size horses are normally fitted with manes and forelocks on thin strips of hide which will be simply nailed onto the neck with 1/2in (13) gimp pins. The tail hole is drilled through into the hollow middle of the body with a 1/2in (13) bit.

Plate 8.5 Starting the carving with a 1inch gouge.

Make and fit the saddle block so that it is set into the upper body block approximately 3/8in (10) in the middle and runs smoothly into the horse's back at either side.

To cut the hoof notches place the horse on a flat surface and if it wobbles (as it surely will), tuck a wedge of wood under the hooves until it stands level and without wobbling. Place the hoof rails against the insides of the hoofs and use a pair of compasses open to about 1/4in (6) to mark out for the hoof notches and carefully saw them out.

The horse will be secured to the hoof rails with a 5/32in (4) bolt at each hoof, but it is a good idea to screw the horse onto temporary rails or scraps of wood now, to aid painting. For details of stand construction see Chapter 11.

Half Size horse painting and dappling are done in the same manner as for the larger ones, but you will need a very fine pencil brush (we have one with only a very few hairs) for the fine detail of the eye lashes, and a steady hand. The dappling pad is a small piece of sponge wrapped around the end of a thin piece of dowel to hold it with. Leather tack is initially secured with 1/2in (13) gimp pins and decorated with 1/4in (6) diam brass dome nails.

The reins are riveted onto the bit rings and the rest of the bridle is nailed on. The bit is held in place in the mouth by the top bridle strap (which is taken over the top of the head just behind the base of the ears) folded under and through the rings and nailed in each side. The rest of the bridle is made up of short lengths of strapping nailed in position with 1/4in (6) diam brass dome nails. Damp the leather strap before fitting to persuade it to conform to the curves of the head.

When the completed horse is mounted on its stand it is ready to rock; a delightful decorative artifact which will complement any collection of dolls or teddy bears - and give them something to play with during the long winter evenings.

Plates 8.6 to 8.17 Opposite page
Stages in assembling and carving the Half Size horse.
Also study the pictures accompanying the Small Horse, because the finished look is very similar. A key differnce is that the Half Size horse has no additional eye and ear pieces or leg muscle blocks, so more is carved away to thin the head and legs.

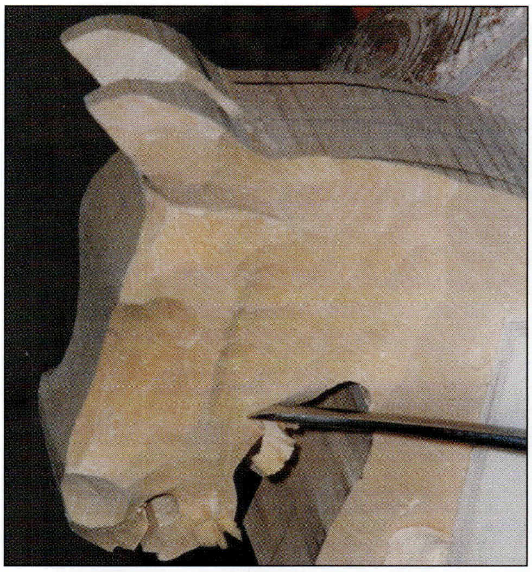
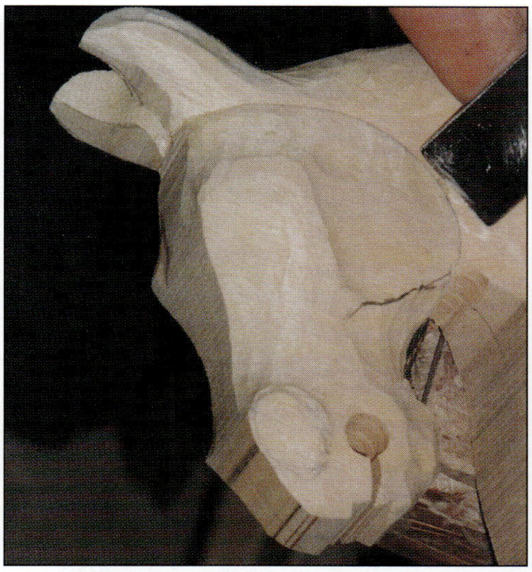

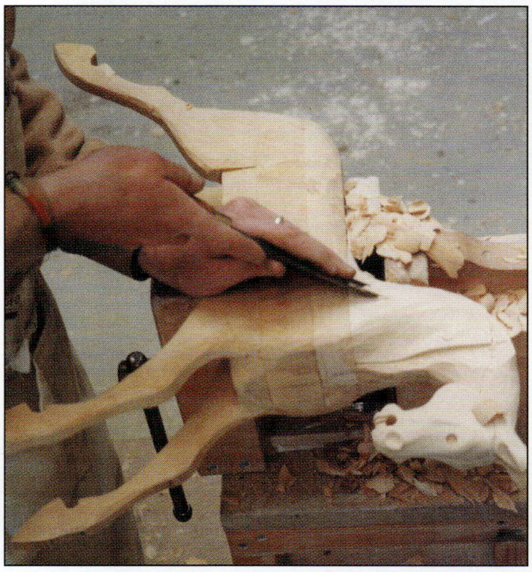

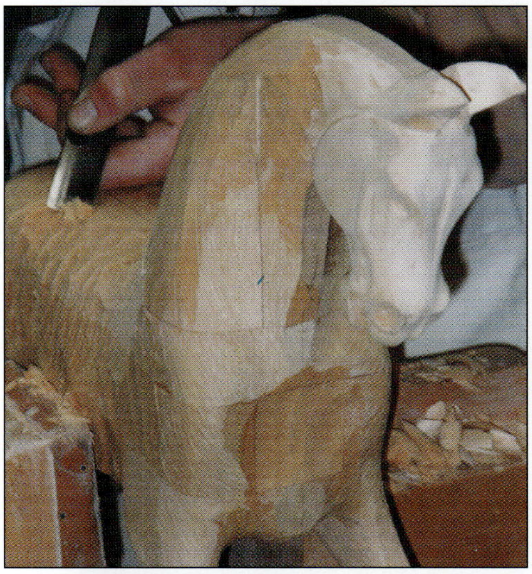

Plate 9.1 (above) The completed Small Carved Horse with traditional dapple grey paintwork, fitted with removable bridle & nailed on saddle, mounted on a dark stained ash stand.

Plate 9.2 (right) Stained & polished version of the Small Carved Horse, this one fitted with removable bridle, saddle & martingale. This horse is made of mahogany, the stand is clear varnished oak.

CHAPTER 9

SMALL
TRADITIONAL CARVED ROCKING HORSE
for mounting on a safety stand

In our experience children will normally be 2 to 2½ years old before they are big enough to climb unaided onto a fully carved rocking horse of any size; smaller children may well need assistance both to mount and to keep their balance. This design for a fully carved traditional Victorian style horse has a body 18in (457) long, which is about the smallest size that can actually be ridden by children, and it is suitable for riders up to about five years old or so. Apart from being a rideable plaything, this rocking horse is a delightful and decorative artefact which will enhance any room - and it is a fascinating project.

PREPARATION
Before starting, read Chapter 1 and study the following method carefully. The horse is made in the following order: selecting and planing timber; preparing patterns of all shaped parts; drawing patterns onto the timber and cutting out parts (all of which is already done if you use a timber pack, see Appendix); gluing ear and eye pieces to head; carving the head; fixing head and neck to upper body block; rough carving legs; gluing up the rest of the horse; carving the body and neck.

HOW TO MAKE IT
Position the patterns carefully on the timber and pencil round them, then bandsaw out the shapes, keeping the sawcut on the waste side of your pencil line. Make sure that you leave the cramping noggins in place on the neck and neck muscle blocks - these are to aid the assembly later. The upper and middle body blocks are not bandsawn or shaped at all prior to assembly.

Plate 9.3 Eye & ear pieces are glued & cramped to the head.

CUTTING LIST

	Thickness x width x length Inches	*Thickness x width x length* Millimetres
Head & Neck	1 3/4 x 8 3/4 x 16	45 x 222 x 406
Neck Muscle Blocks (both)	1 3/4 x 5 3/4 x 19	45 x 146 x 483
Eye & Ear Pieces (both)	3/8 x 2 3/4 x 9	10 x 70 x 230
Lower & Upper Body Blocks (x 2)	1 3/4 x 5 3/4 x 18	45 x 146 x 457
Middle Body Blocks (sides) (x 2)	1 3/4 x 3 1/4 x 18	45 x 83 x 457
Middle Body Blocks (ends) (x 2)	1 3/4 x 3 1/4 x 2 3/4	45 x 83 x 70
Legs (all four)	7/8 x 5 3/4 x 48	22 x 146 x 1220
Leg Muscle Blocks (all)	3/8 x 4 3/4 x 24	10 x 121 x 610
Saddle Block	3/4 x 1 3/4 x 5	19 x 45 x 127

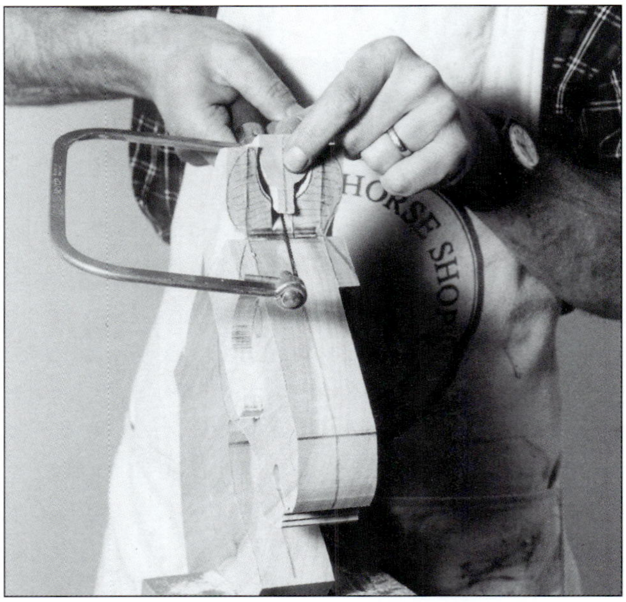

Plate 9.4 Separating the ears with a coping saw.

Plate 9.5 Shaping ears with large shallow gouge & mallet.

Plate 9.6 Carving away corners above nostril.

Glue the eye and ear pieces to the head, one at each side. The head is carved before it is fixed to the rest of the horse - it is easier to handle like this. Pencil in some guidelines - a centreline, the outline of the ears looking from the front, the approximate positions of the eyes and nostrils and the curve of the cheek. Carry the top line of the cheek, on either side on to the front and across to join in the middle - this line marks the bottom of the ears. With the coping saw cut along this line at each side, through the ear and eye piece, almost to the glue line. Also with the coping saw cut away the waste around the ears. It is wise to cut well on the waste side: you can always trim more off later, and avoid making the ears sharp.

When carving you must cut *with* the grain of the wood. You can also cut across the grain, but not against it, because the cutting edge will want to follow the grain and will dig in too deep. If this happens (and sometimes it is difficult to tell at a glance which is the best way to cut), you should withdraw the gouge and try from another angle. If you do not do this and try to force the gouge against the grain, the cutting edge will continue to dig deeper and the wood may split. Carve steadily, a little from each side in turn to keep the symmetry. Hold the gouge firmly, but not too tight, and guide the cutting edge, pushing it across the wood with your thumb in a slicing action that removes small clean slivers with each cut.

Secure the head so it is looking up at the ceiling, take up the 1in (25) shallow gouge and carve the fronts of the ears so that they angle back at each side. If you cut downwards from the tips of the ears, towards the line and sawcut at the base of the ears, you will be cutting with the grain and the wood will cut away cleanly. Shape the ears at the sides so that they curve in to meet the glue line. Then, cutting up towards the base of the ears, remove the corners and round over at each side of the forehead.

Cut away the corners for the nostrils, which angle back at each side. Pencil in the oval shape of the nostrils and carve back all round; above them the corners are rounded up to the eye, rounding more near the nostril than near the eye, so that when viewed from the front the head tapers from the

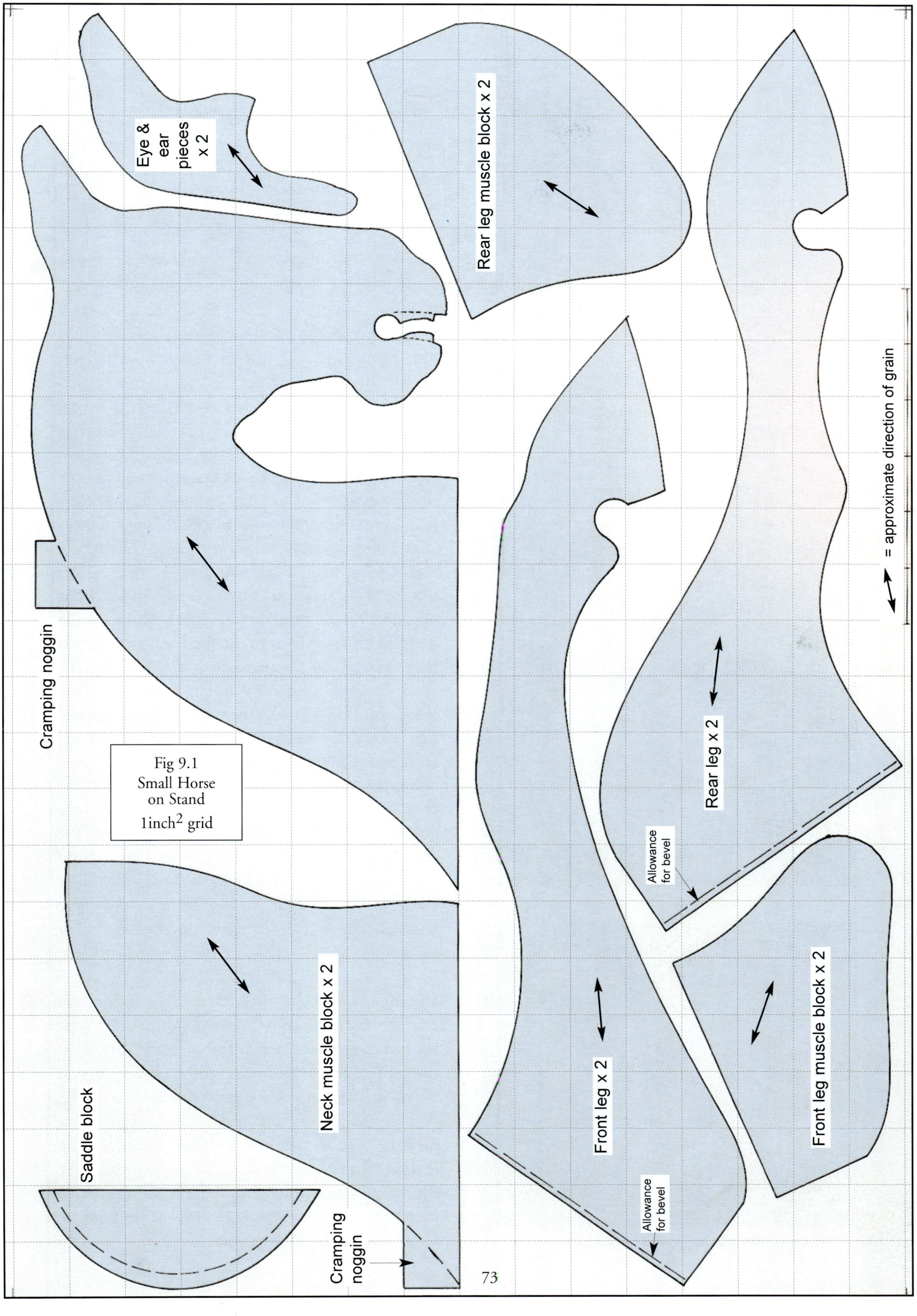

Fig 9.1
Small Horse
on Stand
1inch^2 grid

Fig 9.2
Lower Body Block
of Small Horse -
right & below
showing where corners
are notched to receive
legs at the approriate
angles.

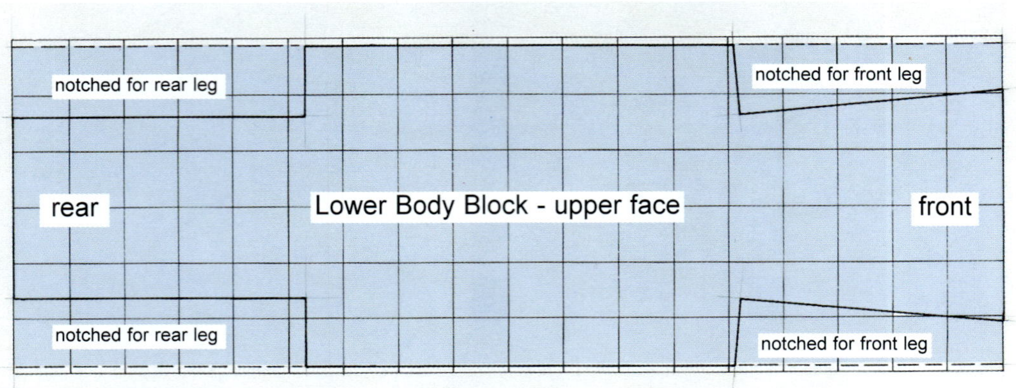

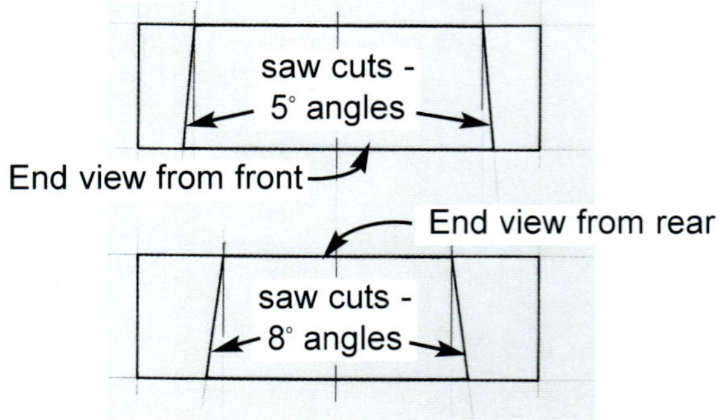

Plate 9.7 Tapering head and defining nostril.

Plate 9.8 Paring down cheek bone with spoon gouge.

widest part at the eyebrow to the narrowest part near the mouth, with just the nostrils sticking out.

Turn the head on one side and cramp it to the bench. Pare back the area above the eye until it meets the glue line at the top of the cheek, and pare back the 'cheekbone' so that it is proud of the surrounding wood by only about 1/8in (3). Now with a straight chisel make a series of cuts at right angles into the wood along the curved line of the cheek, from base of ear round to the neck. Then use the lin (25) gouge again to cut the waste from outside this line, leaving the cheek proud of the neck by about 1/8in (3) near the top, 3/8in (10) at the lower end by the neck.

With the No. 5 gouge carve back below the line that marks the lower part of the cheek, and carry on paring down to the mouth and lower jaw. When finished, the mouth will be about 1 1/2in (38) wide, or slightly less. Use the No. 9 deep gouge to carve round the lower jaw and under the cheek, and to cut back the corner of the eye piece where the eye socket will later be positioned. The head should now be taking on a recognisably horselike shape; turn it over and carve the other side to match.

Use the spoon gouge to cut along either side of the cheekbone so that it runs smoothly into the surrounding wood, and the straight chisel to carefully carve away around the mouth to reveal the teeth. The tops of the ears are shaped with the No. 5 gouge, and when you have achieved a pleasing overall appearance, the head can be sanded smooth with 120 grit abrasive. Finally, use the spoon gouge to slightly hollow the insides of the ears and nostrils, and the head is finished, as far as it needs to be at this stage.

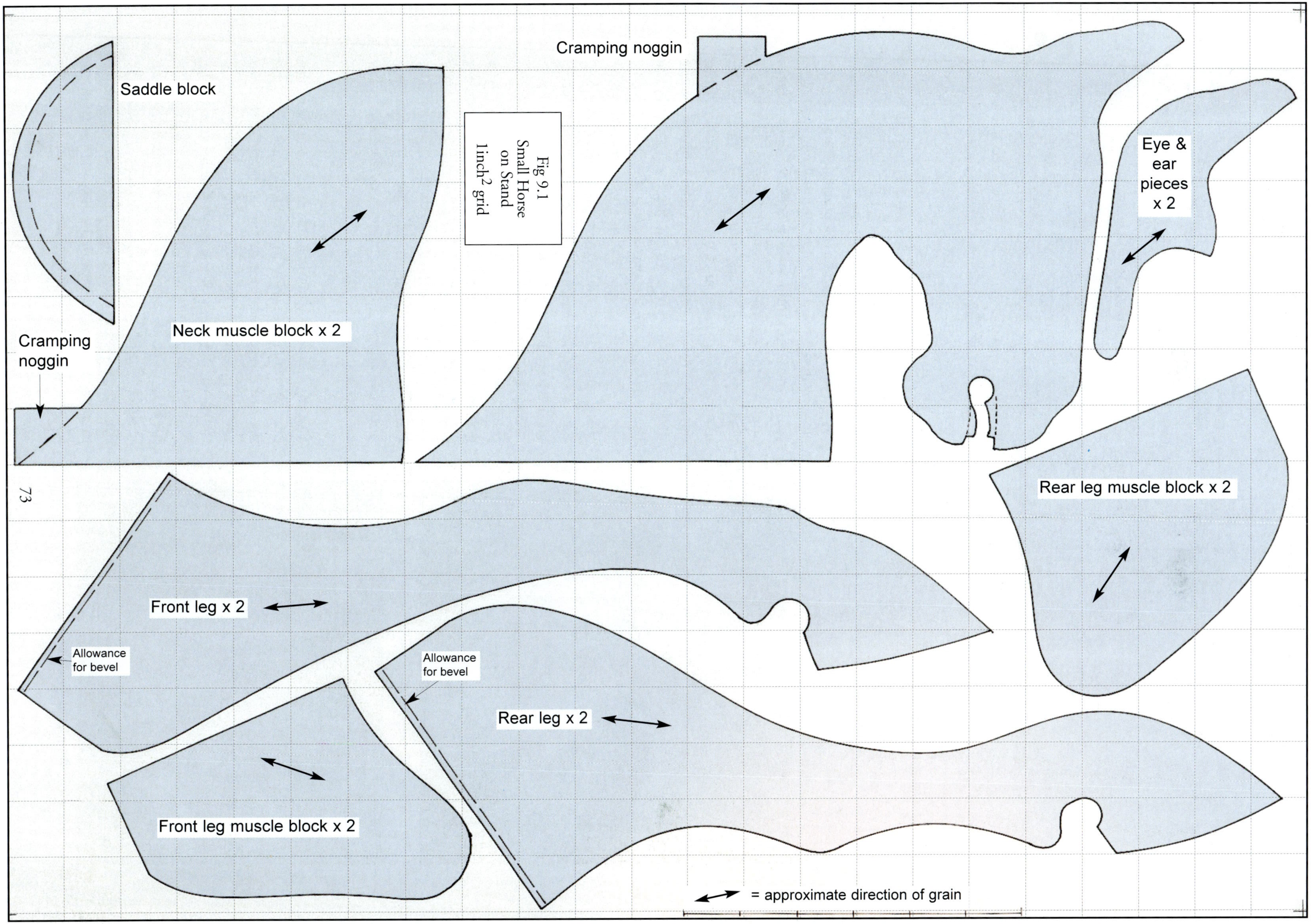

Fig 9.1
Small Horse
on Stand
1inch^2 grid

Fig 9.2
Lower Body Block of Small Horse - right & below showing where corners are notched to receive legs at the approriate angles.

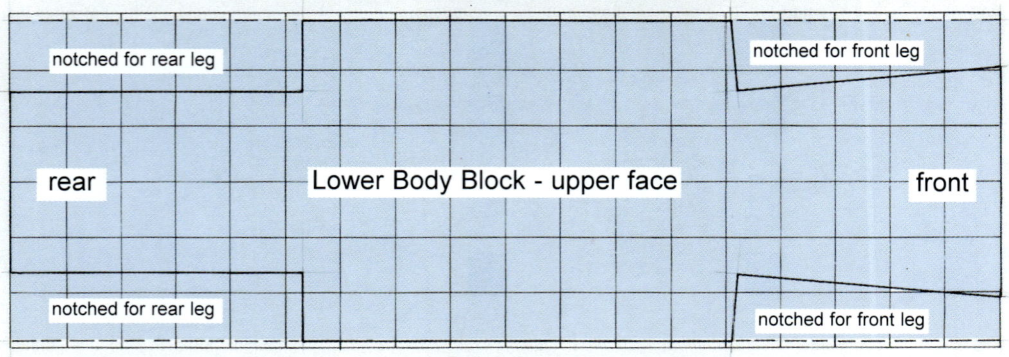

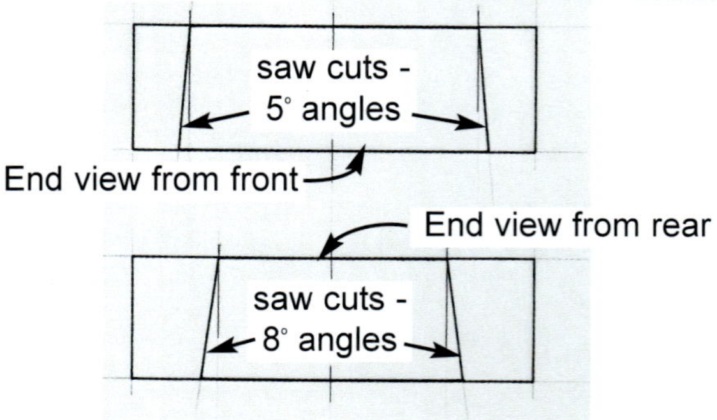

Plate 9.7 Tapering head and defining nostril.

Plate 9.8 Paring down cheek bone with spoon gouge.

widest part at the eyebrow to the narrowest part near the mouth, with just the nostrils sticking out.

Turn the head on one side and cramp it to the bench. Pare back the area above the eye until it meets the glue line at the top of the cheek, and pare back the 'cheekbone' so that it is proud of the surrounding wood by only about 1/8in (3). Now with a straight chisel make a series of cuts at right angles into the wood along the curved line of the cheek, from base of ear round to the neck. Then use the 1in (25) gouge again to cut the waste from outside this line, leaving the cheek proud of the neck by about 1/8in (3) near the top, 3/8in (10) at the lower end by the neck.

With the No. 5 gouge carve back below the line that marks the lower part of the cheek, and carry on paring down to the mouth and lower jaw. When finished, the mouth will be about 1 1/2in (38) wide, or slightly less. Use the No. 9 deep gouge to carve round the lower jaw and under the cheek, and to cut back the corner of the eye piece where the eye socket will later be positioned. The head should now be taking on a recognisably horselike shape; turn it over and carve the other side to match.

Use the spoon gouge to cut along either side of the cheekbone so that it runs smoothly into the surrounding wood, and the straight chisel to carefully carve away around the mouth to reveal the teeth. The tops of the ears are shaped with the No. 5 gouge, and when you have achieved a pleasing overall appearance, the head can be sanded smooth with 120 grit abrasive. Finally, use the spoon gouge to slightly hollow the insides of the ears and nostrils, and the head is finished, as far as it needs to be at this stage.

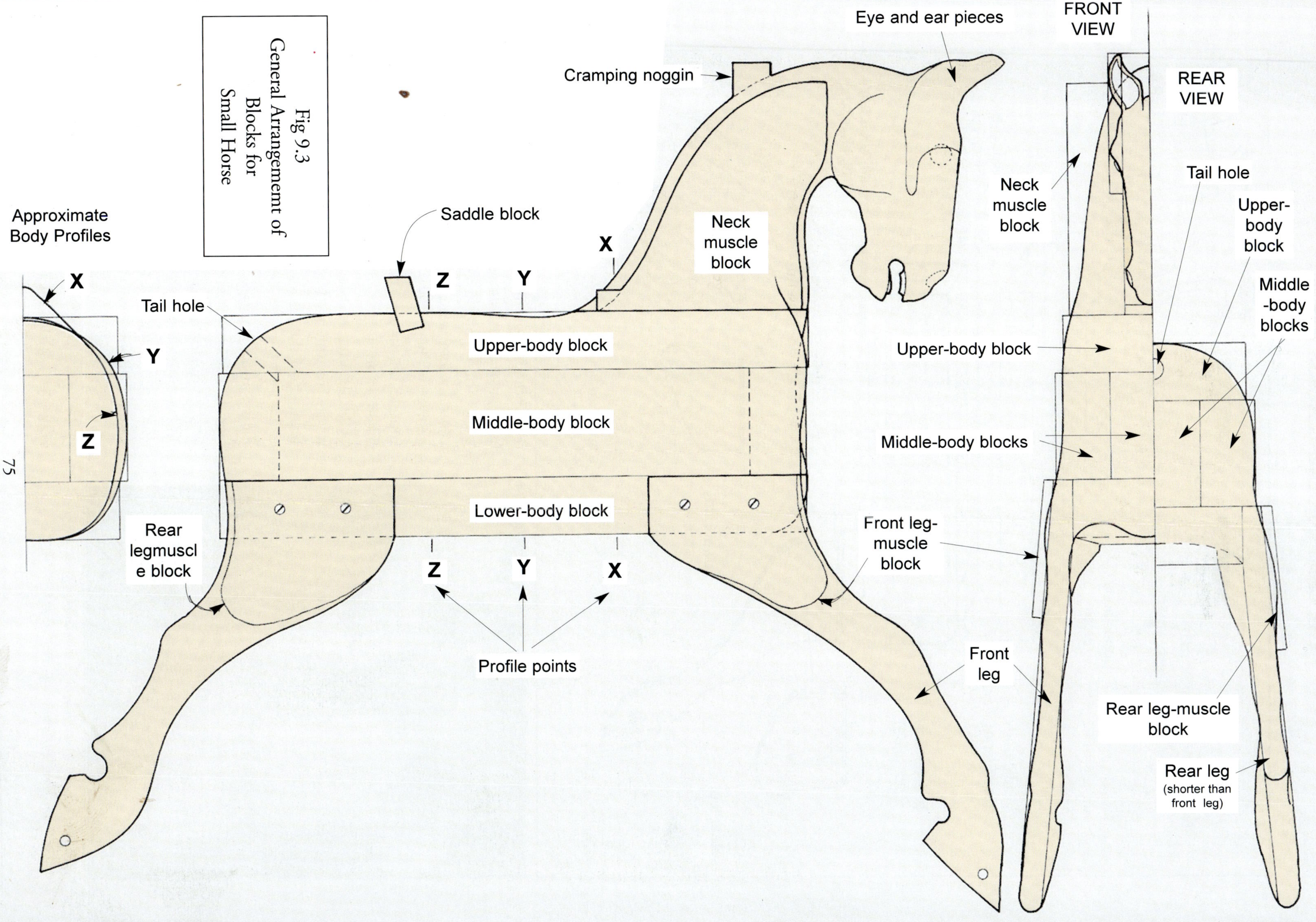

Fig 9.3
General Arrangememt of
Blocks for
Small Horse

Fig 9.4
Exploded drawing of parts for the Small Horse

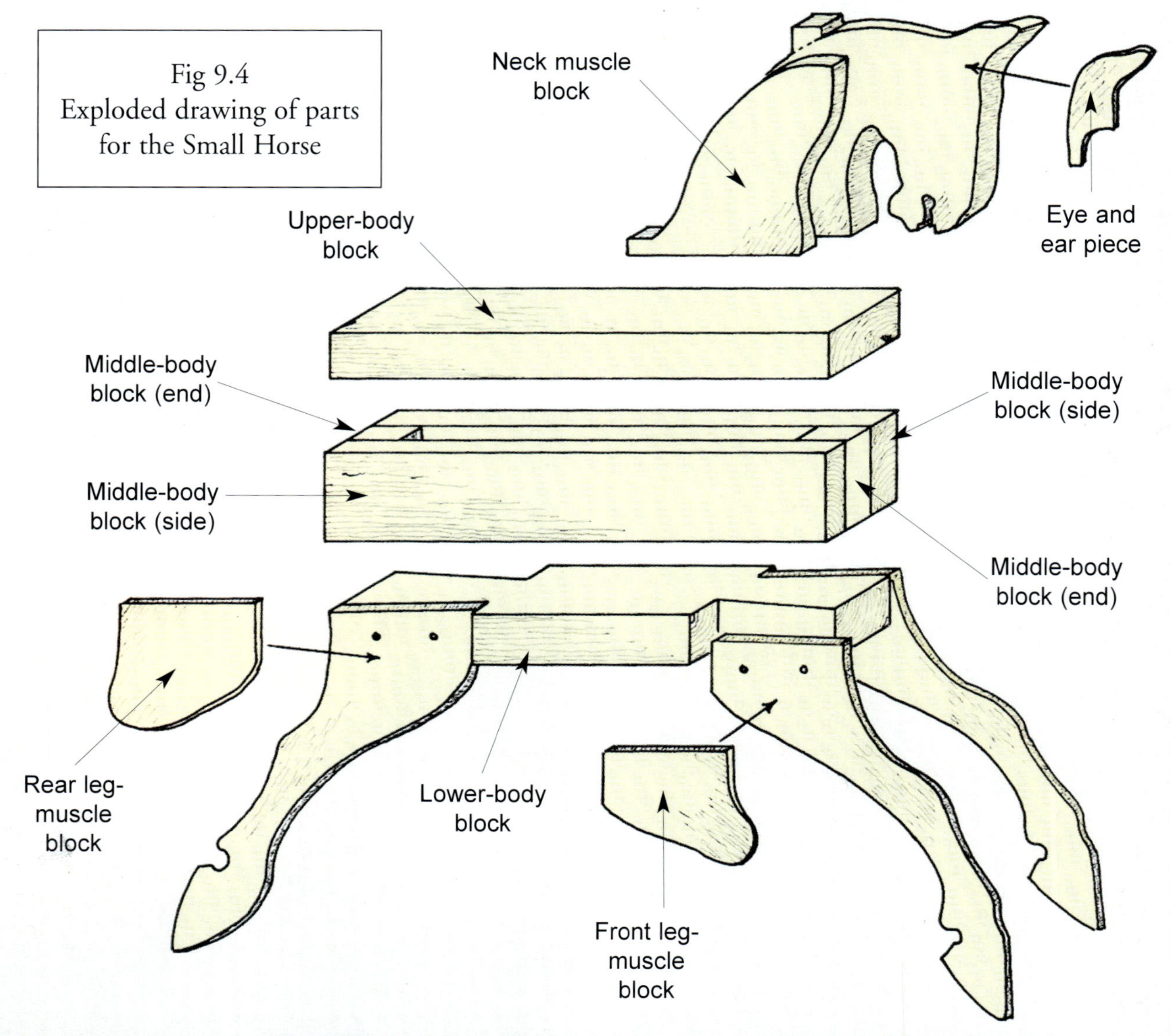

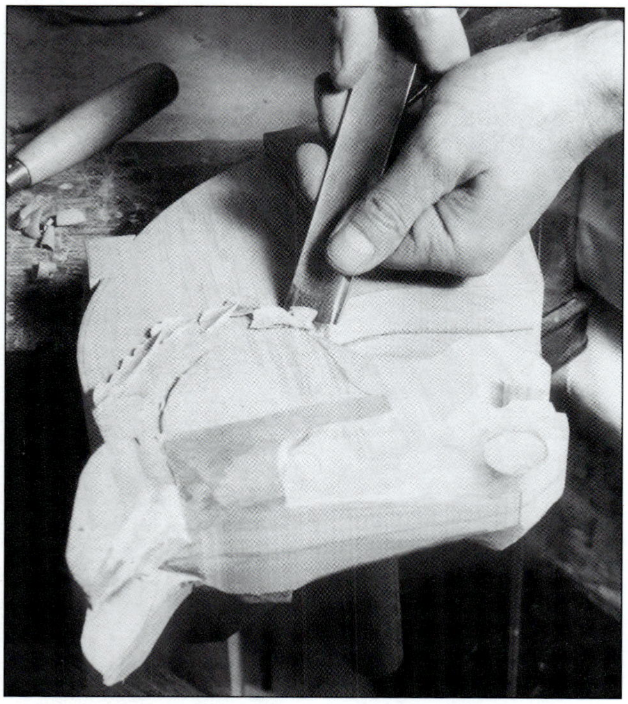

Plate 9.9 Cutting back along the curve of the cheek, note how the cheek line runs into the base of the ears.

Plane the bottom of the neck flat and square and, using two fluted dowel pegs, glue it down to the upper body block. Make sure it is positioned centrally and use the noggin on the neck for the cramps. When this joint has set, the two neck muscle blocks can be glued on, one each side. There is no need to use dowel pegs for these, but before gluing ensure that the muscle blocks fit neatly to the neck and upper body block by planing off their bottoms.

Now you can rough carve the lower parts of the legs. It is easier to do this before assembly, using a rasp or Surform to round over the corners. Drill and countersink the legs for the screws that will be used to fix them to the lower body block - 8 x 1½in (38mm) No.10 countersunk woodscrews will be needed for this, 2 for each leg. The legs are glued and screwed onto the notches bandsawn from each corner of the lower body block. Note

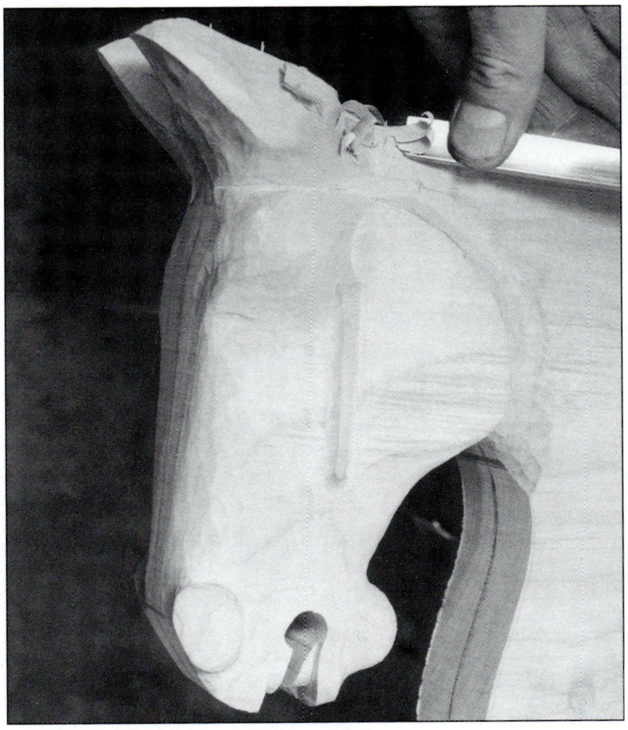

Plate 9.10 Shaping top of neck and ears.

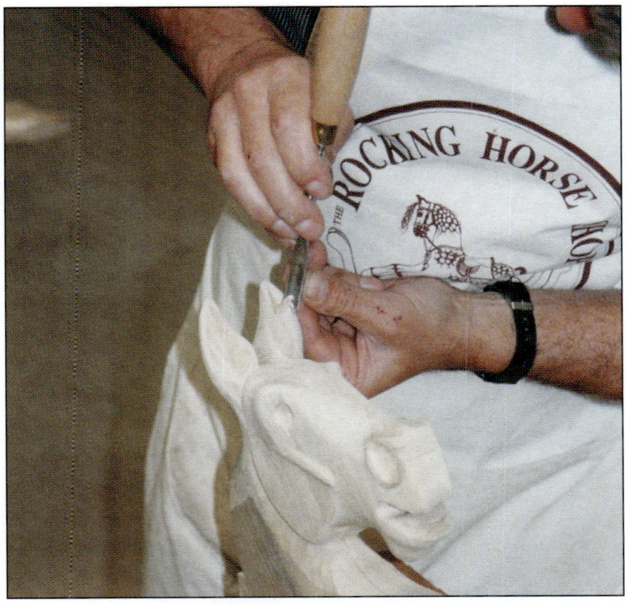

Plate 9.11 After rough sanding down the head, the nostrils & ears are hollowed out using a spoon gouge.

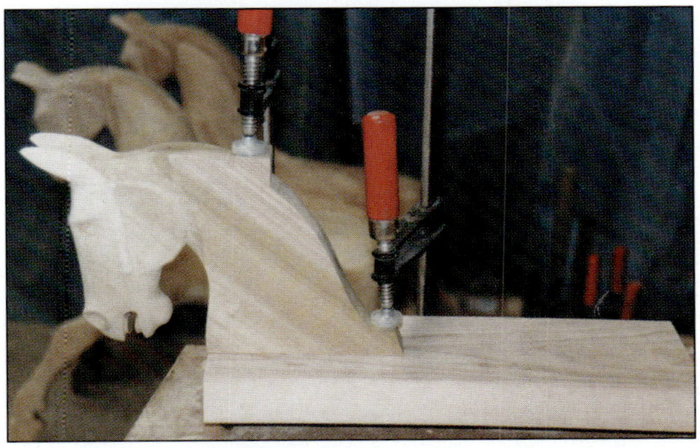

Plate 9.12 Cramping neck to upper body block.

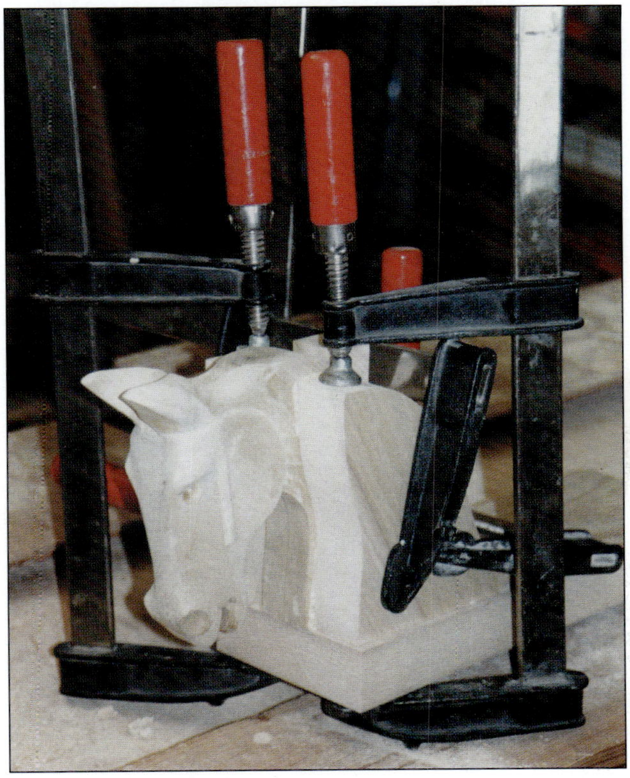

Plate 9.13 Gluing on neck muscle blocks.

the splay of the legs as shown on the plan and true up the surfaces to be joined, by planing to ensure a good joint before gluing them.

The leg muscle blocks are glued on over the tops of the legs, and will conceal the leg fixing screws. Again, make sure that they will be a good fit before gluing. Use a 4in (100) G-cramp to cramp each one to its leg, and sliding F-cramps across the tops in conjunction with the waste pieces sawn from each corner of the lower body block. To prevent the leg muscle blocks from sliding about while you are cramping them nail them on - leave the nail heads proud - to be removed later and the nail holes filled. After fixing the legs to the lower body block, the hooves should be the same distance apart front and rear - but do not worry if they are not; this will not affect the ability of the horse to rock. Nor does it matter if the hooves do not stand four square on a flat surface - they rarely do - and this will be easily corrected later. The front legs are slightly longer than the rear so that the horse is tilted up slightly at the front, giving the finished horse a slightly prancing appearance.

The legs and leg muscle blocks are glued on so that their tops are flush with or slightly proud of the top of the lower body block, which can now be planed flat to receive the middle body blocks. You may need to plane a little from the inside of the

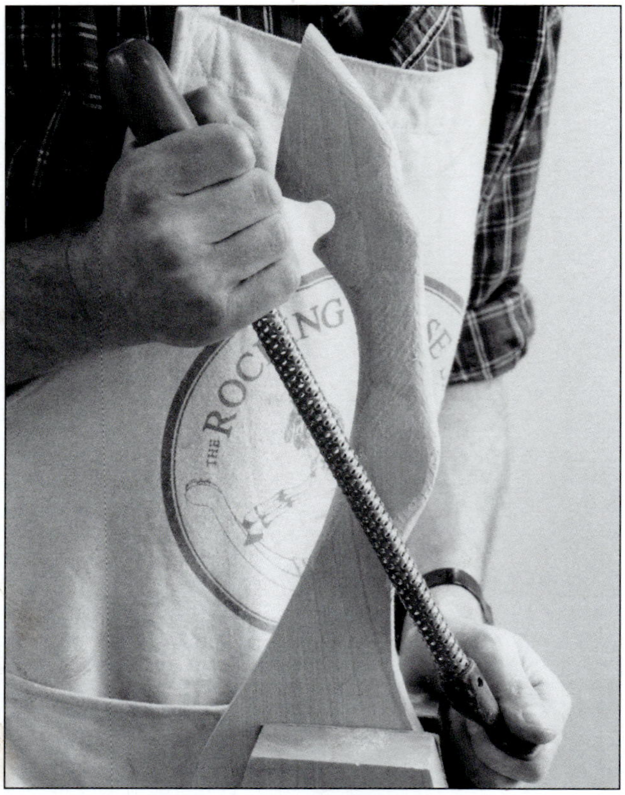

Plate 9.14 Rough shaping leg with a Surform

Plate 9.15 Glue & screw legs to the lower body block....

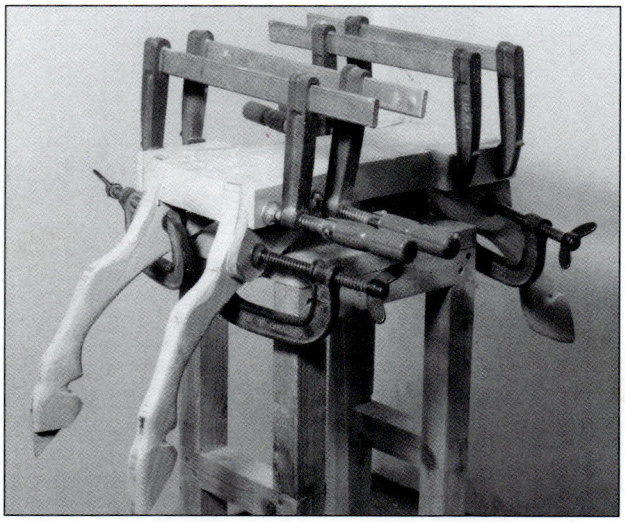

Plate 9.16 ...and cramp the leg muscle blocks in place until the glue sets.

middle body block sides to let them fit neatly to the ends. Even so the middle body block sides will overhang the lower body block by about $^1/_4$in (6) at each side - this is to allow for the swell of the horse's belly. Place the middle body blocks on the lower body block and pencil mark their positions so that you can replace them precisely, and drill for the fluted dowel pegs. Use three dowel pegs each side and avoid drilling into the leg fixing screws. There is no need for dowels in the end blocks. If you have enough cramps you will be able to glue and cramp up all the middle body blocks at the same time.

The last operation in the assembly is to glue and dowel peg the upper body block (with head and neck attached) to the middle body blocks (with lower body and legs attached). Again, make sure they fit true before glueing and use four dowel pegs, two each side. Place them towards the inner edges of the middle body blocks so that there is little chance of exposing them later when you are carving the body.

Pencil in a centre line along the horse's back, down the rear end and the chest, to help you to keep it symmetrical. For the rough carving of the body and neck, use the large deep alongee gouge and, if you have one, a drawknife. Put the horse on its side and start by removing the top corners from the neck muscle blocks at each side. The neck tapers from base to top, and at the top will be rounded over. Avoid making the top of the neck too narrow and pointed; the mane has to go on

Plate 9.17 Fitting middle body blocks. Ensure you have sufficient cramps to hold all joints tight.

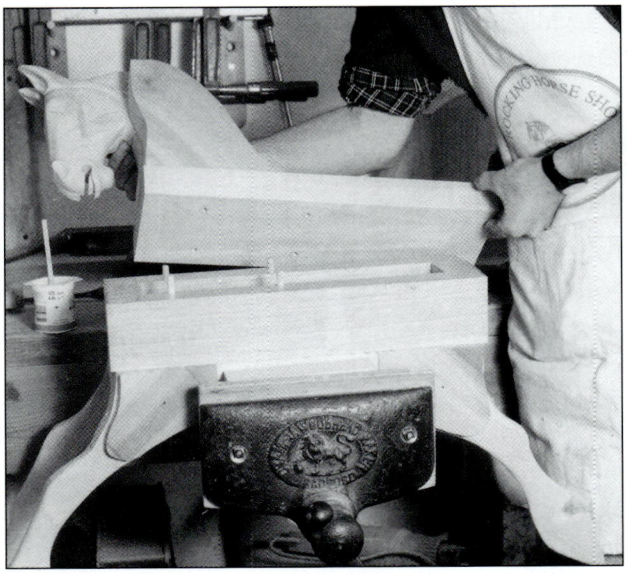

Plate 9.18 Fitting upper body block. The four dowel pegs are placed near the inside edges of the middle body blocks.

Plate 9.19 With the blocking up complete, and the glue dry, you can turn your mind to the carving.

there. Carve off any bits of the leg muscle blocks that jut out, and cut them back so that they taper down and merge into the legs. Pencil in the curve of the rump - you can saw off the triangular waste piece. Also saw off the cramping noggin on the neck.

With the horse on its side, pencil a cross near the centre of the middle block to indicate the highest point of the swell of the belly. Viewed from above, three areas of the body will remain wide: below the neck, at the rump and at the middle of the body. Between these areas, that is from behind the front leg round to the base of the neck, and in front of the rear leg round to the top, the body is shaped thinner. The body is well rounded over the rump and in the middle, where the saddle will fit, and rounded along the lower edges also, though to a lesser extent; the actual underside of the body remains flat.

Before you start to round the body and it becomes more awkward to hold securely, turn the horse upside down so that you can get at the areas between the legs. With the alongee gouge and a Surform or rasp, shape the insides of the legs so that they are rounded and run smoothly into the lower body block. At the front the lower body block is carved to leave a bulge in the middle, while at the rear a 'valley' between the legs curves up towards the tail. English rocking horses do not normally have any carved details between the rear legs since we are traditionally coy about such matters; anyway, they are all geldings (or mares).

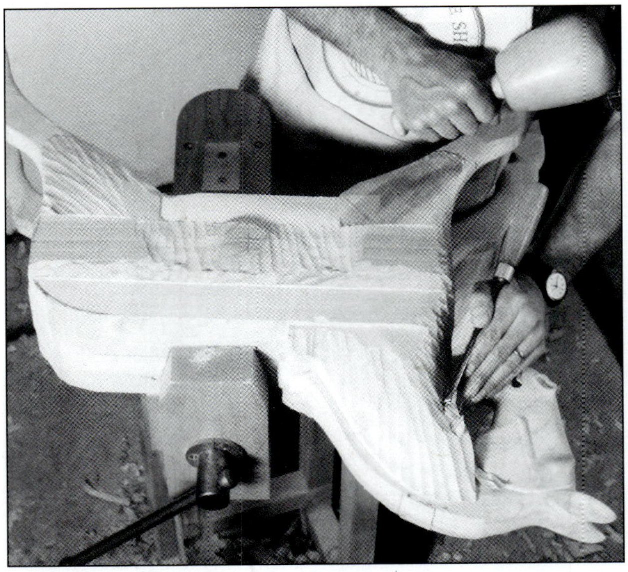

Plate 9.20 Rough shaping with the largest gouge & mallet.

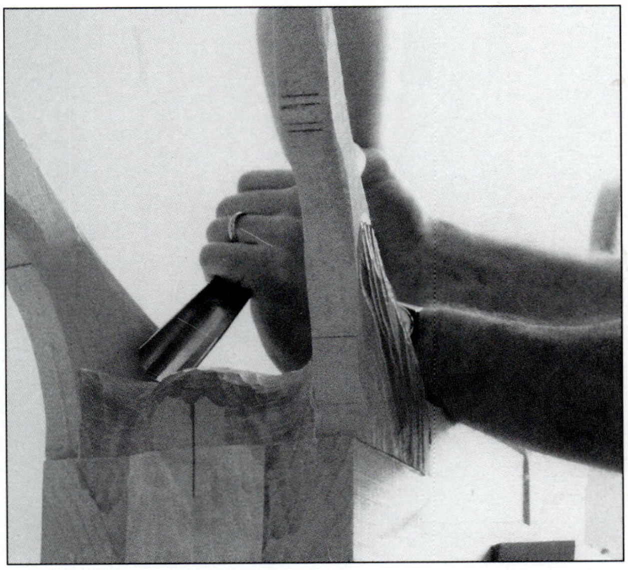

Plate 9.21 Shaping between the front legs.

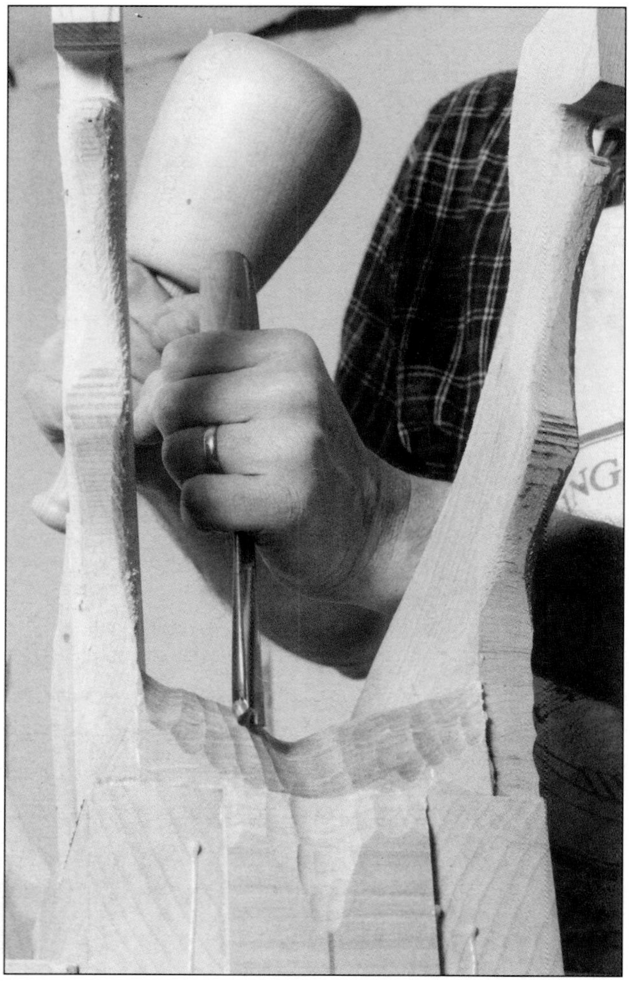

Plate 9.22 Hollowing a valley between the rear legs.

Carving is three dimensional: bear in mind as you carve that any wood you remove from one area will alter the appearance when viewed from any other angle. So keep altering your angle of view to see how the shape is changing. The most common fault of novice carvers is to be too tentative and fail to remove enough wood, leaving parts of the horse still looking rather square and box-like. There are no corners on a horse; the shaping on the body and neck should produce slow gentle curves that invite people to run their hands over them.

The shoulders are rounded, but left proud of the area above them, which is cut back towards the neck. Below the shoulders the corners of the middle body blocks are rounded in towards the chest. The chest is one of the more difficult areas to carve, since you have to contend with carving across the ends of the body blocks towards the middle. The chest finishes up concave in the middle, above the bulge at the centre of the lower body block. The shape of the base of the neck at the glue line where it joins the upper body block is that of an almost pointed egg, big end towards the front. Keep carving a little from each side in turn so that the shape remains symmetrical about the centreline of the horse's body.

Plate 9.23 Shaping body with drawknife - note gouge marks over rest of body. The drawknife is a fine traditional tool & is good to use for slicing away the waste wood, but there is a knack to using it.

The deep alongee gouge leaves marked ripples, the high points of which you can remove with the shallower 1in (25) gouge and Surform, Microplane or rasp, particularly good for achieving smooth curves. You may also find a spokeshave useful for smoothing the curves of the rump and neck. Each maker's horse comes out a little different from every other: carve until you feel you want to go no further, and then stop.

If you are going to gesso and paint there is hardly any need to sand because a rough surface will provide a good key for the gesso. But if you intend going for a natural wood finish, then you will need to sand down with progressively finer papers - 120, 180, 240, and 360 grit - to remove all the blemishes and scratchmarks. Drum sanding attachments for your electric drill and pad sanders will be useful, but there will be some areas where the details just have to be sanded by hand. Drill a 3/4in (19) diameter hole for the tail - this hole can go right into the hollow middle of the horse. Now you can think about bringing your horse to life by fitting the glass eyes, and painting and finishing it. For details of these techniques, turn to Chapters 13 and 14.

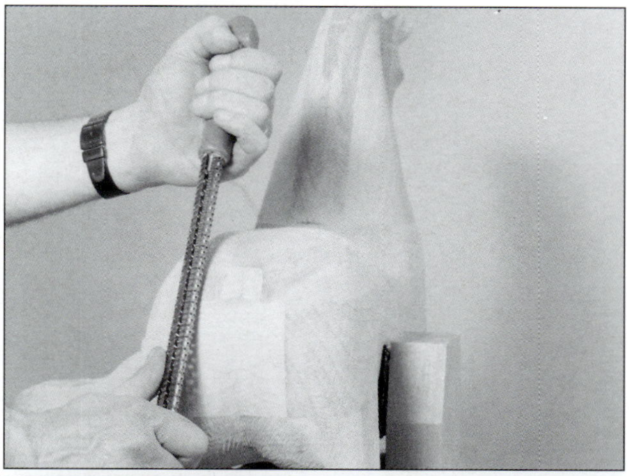

Plates 9.24 & 25 Using Surform (top) & Microplane..

Plate 9.26 The carving is complete and this Small horse, which is made of pine, is ready for the next stage.

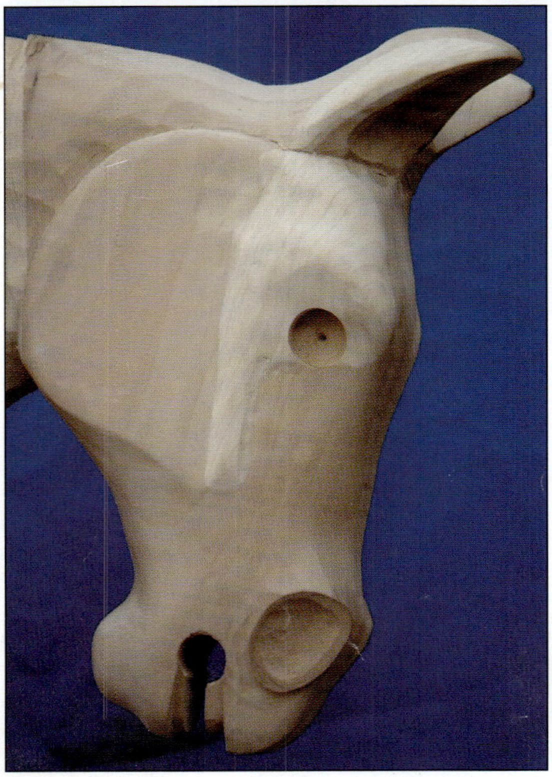

Plate 10.1 (above)
Large & Medium horses complete.
Note the extra carving on the Medium.

Plate 10.2 (left)
Medium head, carved with 'basic' features.

Plate 10.3 (right)
Medium head.
On this one more detail has been carved & the mouth is opened to make room to carve a tongue, & teeth, as in the Medium pictured above.
Note what a difference an eye makes.

CHAPTER 10

MEDIUM & LARGE

TRADITIONAL CARVED ROCKING HORSES

for mounting on safety stands

Whilst the Small rocking horse described in the last Chapter is an excellent woodworking project, and fine for smaller children, the Medium Size horse described here is considerably bigger and will be good for riders of pretty well any age. It will even take an adult's weight; when my children were small they would often ride our Medium Size rocking horse, with their mother. The Medium is by far the most popular size. The Large rocking horse is bigger again, and is for the woodworker who has the houseroom for what is, potentially, the finest of rocking horses.

PREPARATION

The method of making the Medium and Large horses is broadly similar to that for the Small horse, so you should read Chapter 9 thoroughly before starting one of these. But the Medium and Large designs involve some modifications to the

CUTTING LIST for MEDIUM	*Thickness x width x length*	*Thickness x width x length*
	Inches	**Millimetres**
Head	2¾ x 7 x 10½	70 x 178 x 267
Neck	2¾ x 8¾ x 11	70 x 222 x 279
Ear & Eye Pieces (both)	½ x 3¾ x 14	13 x 95 x 356
1st Neck Muscle Blocks (both)	1¾ x 8¾ x 26	45 x 222 x 660
2nd Neck Muscle Blocks (both)	1¼ x 8¾ x 16	32 x 222 x 406
Lower Body Block	2¾ x 8¾ x 24	70 x 222 x 610
Middle Body Block (sides x 2)	2¾ x 3¾ x 24	70 x 95 x 610
Middle Body Block (ends x 2)	2¾ x 3¾ x 3½	70 x 95 x 90
Upper Body Block	1¾ x 8¾ x 24	45 x 222 x 610
Legs (all four)	1¼ x 7¾ x 62	32 x 197 x 1574
Leg Muscle Blocks (all four)	½ x 7¾ x 29	13 x 197 x 737
Saddle Block	⅞ x 2 x 7	22 x 50 x 178

CUTTING LIST for LARGE	*Thickness x width x length*	*Thickness x width x length*
	Inches	**Millimetres**
Head	2¾ x 7¾ x 12½	70 x 197 x 318
Neck	2¾ x 9¾ x 12	70 x 248 x 305
Ear & Eye Pieces (both)	½ x 4½ x 16	13 x 114 x 406
1st Neck Muscle Blocks (both)	1¾ x 9¾ x 30	45 x 248 x 762
2nd Neck Muscle Blocks (both)	1¾ x 8¾ x 18	45 x 222 x 457
Lower Body Block	2¾ x 9¾ x 27¾	70 x 248 x 705
Middle Body Block (x 2)	2¾ x 4¾ x 27¾	70 x 121 x 705
Middle Body Block(x 2)	2¾ x 4¾ x 4½	70 x 121 x 114
Upper Body Block	1¾ x 9¾ x 27¾	45 x 248 x 705
Legs (all four)	1⅜ x 8¾ x 76	35 x 222 x 1930
Leg Muscle Blocks (all four)	½ x 8 x 32	13 x 203 x 813
Saddle Block	⅞ x 2¾ x 8	22 x 70 x 203

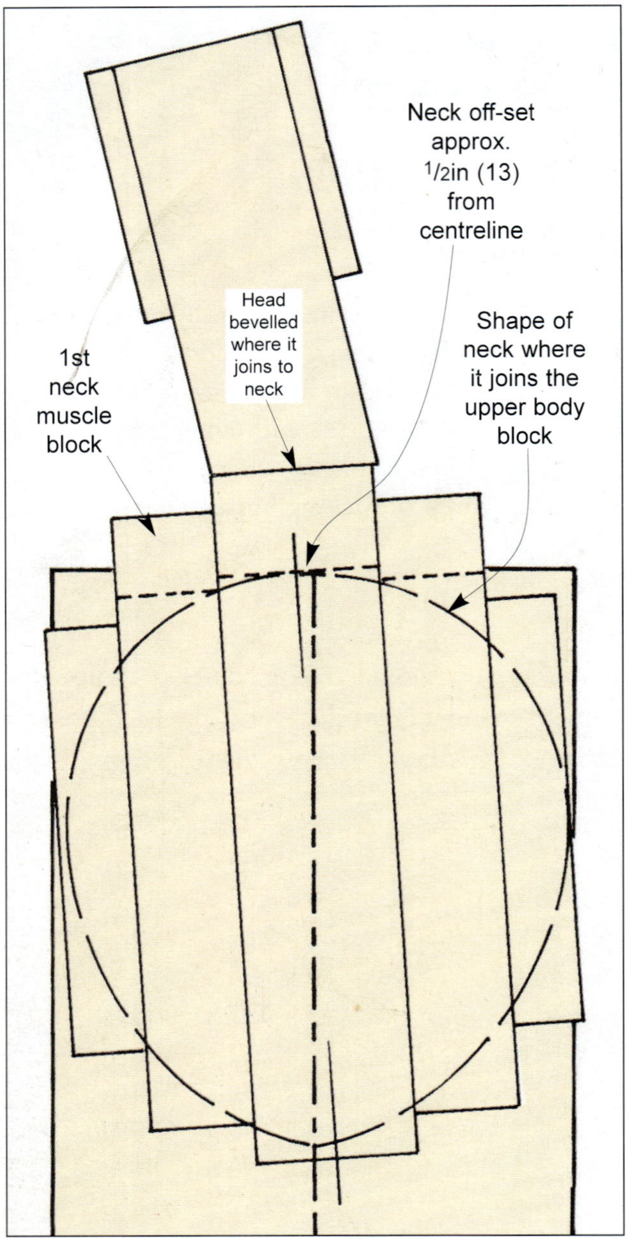

Fig 10.1 The angling of the head to one side is enhanced by off-setting the neck a little from the centreline.

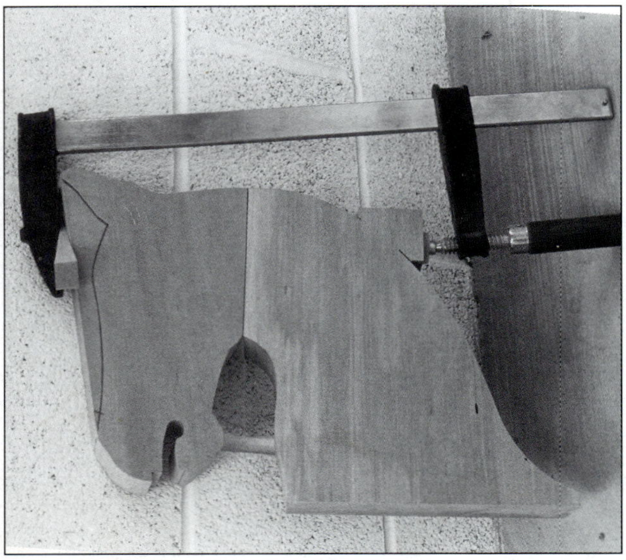

Plate 10.4 Glue & F cramp head to neck, using the cramping noggin & the waste piece sawn from the front of the head.

construction method and the carving of detail. These are intended to enhance and add interest to the projects, because they mean that each horse is different from the others in configuration and character, as well as in size. The principal differences are as follows:

The head and the neck are cut from separate pieces of timber. The head is bevelled where it is joined to the neck, which has the effect of angling the head to one side. The Medium and Large horses both have two neck muscle blocks glued either side of the neck rather than just the one for the Small horse. The neck is set at a slight angle to the upper body block, thus accentuating the angling of the head mentioned above. This angling of the head and neck to the left or right (it doesn't matter which) gives the horse a dynamic touch of life which is lacking in horses built all in a straight line, and is well worth the small extra effort.

HOW TO MAKE IT

When bandsawing out the shaped parts, note that you need to allow 1/2in (13) for the bevel on the head where it is to join to the neck, and 1/4in (6) for the bevels on the straight top edges of the legs. The bevels are planed off. The angle of the bevel between head and neck need not be precise; the important thing is to make a good joint. Strengthen the joint with two fluted dowel pegs and cramp together using the cramping noggin on the neck and the waste piece cut from the front of the head. The eye and ear pieces are glued on at either side and the head is ready to carve. The head is normally carved virtually to completion prior to fixing the neck to the upper body block since it is easier to turn and work on. Examine the accompanying series of photographs to see the shapes and contours involved. If you feel you would like additional guidance a step by step video is available in which the carving process is demonstrated, see Appendix.

The neck is fixed down to the body, and this joint is strengthened by three fluted dowel pegs. The timber is not wide enough to cut out all of the neck in one piece, leaving a small triangular piece at the base of the neck which can be glued on after the neck has been fixed down. The neck muscle blocks are glued on either side, and you will find

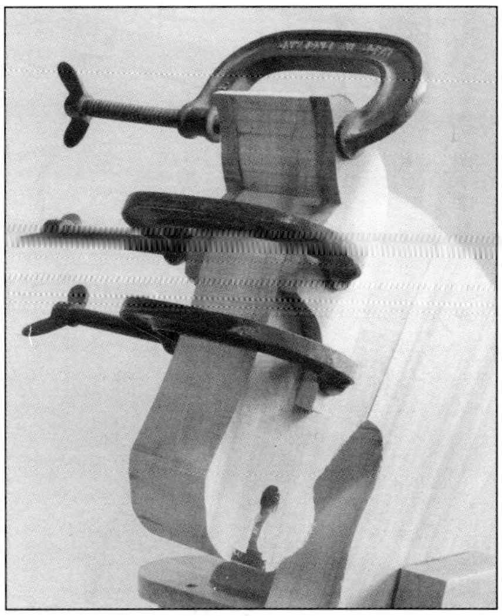

Plate 10.5 Gluing on eye & ear pieces.

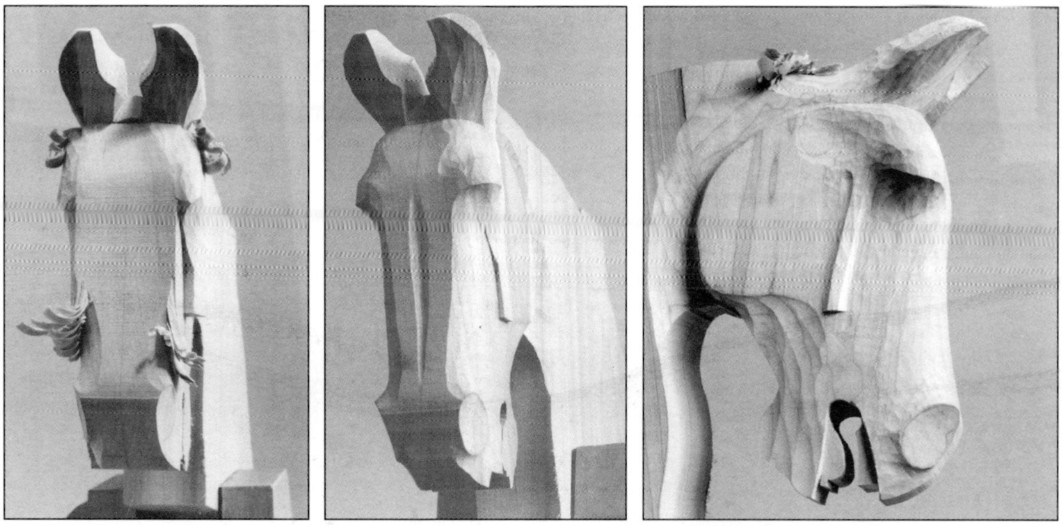

Plates 10.6, 7 & 8 Carving ears, nostrils, eyebrows & cheek of a Large head.

Plates 10.9, 10 & 11 Continue to round the lower jaw & cheek, define the teeth, hollow ears & nostrils, sand off & drill eye sockets.

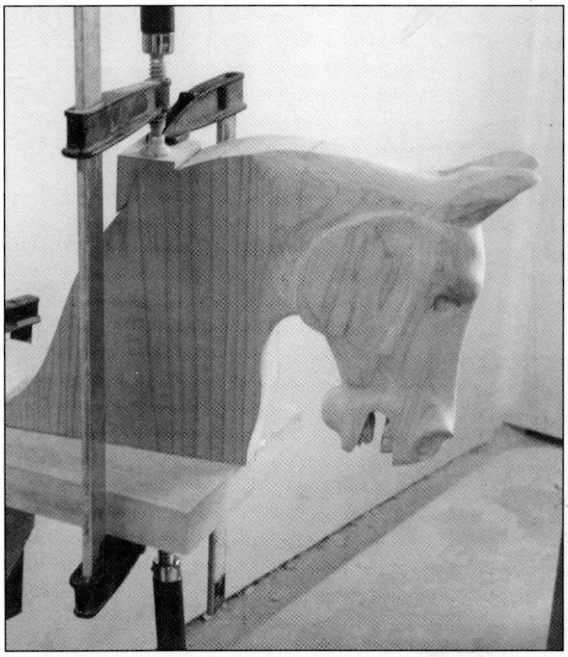

Plate 10.12 Fixing neck to upper body block.

Plate 10.13 Neck muscle blocks glued on, legs rough shaped & fixed to lower body block.

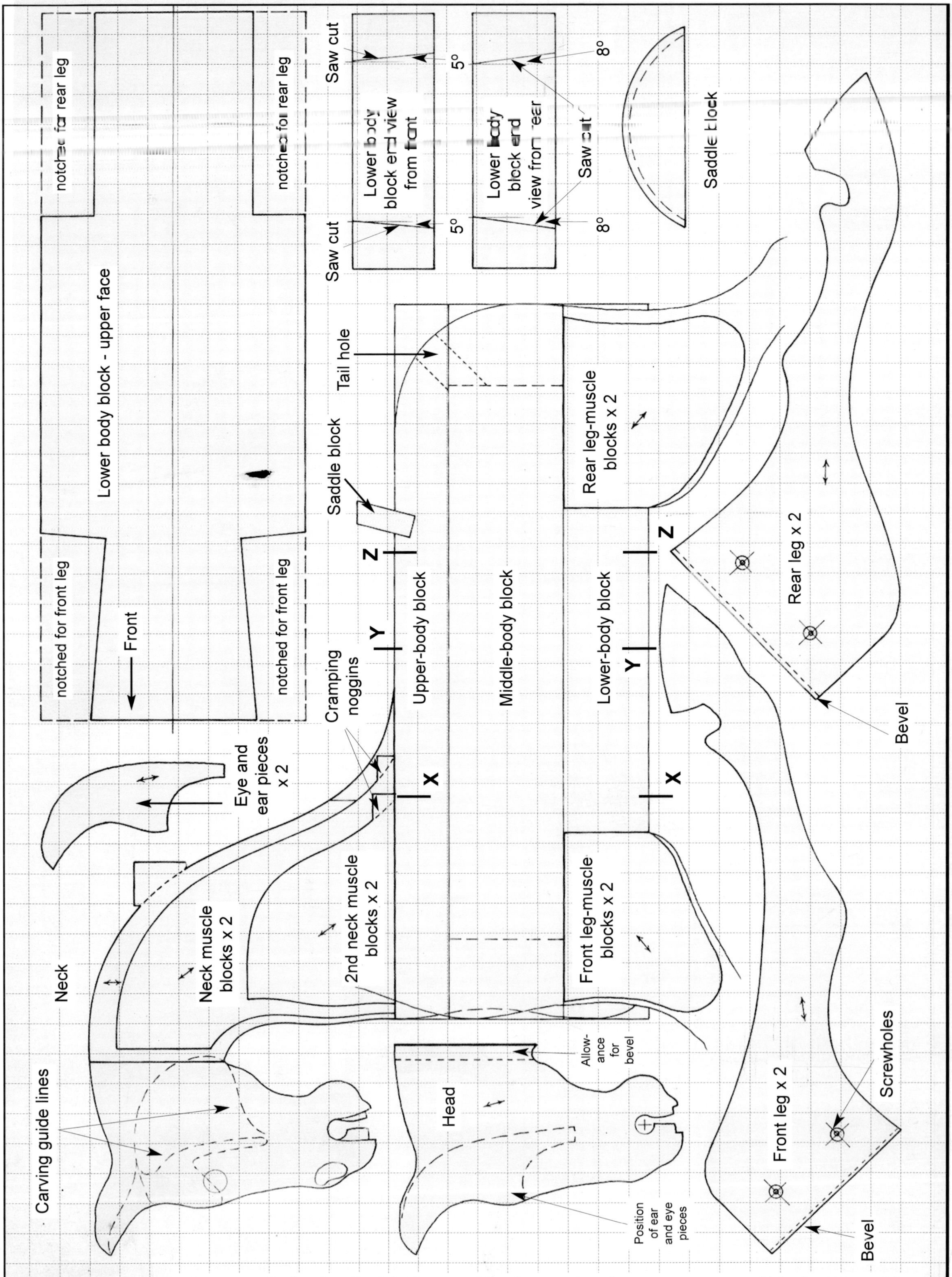

= Approximate direction of grain

Fig 10.2 Scale plan for Medium rocking horse, showing arrangement of blocks (1in² grid).

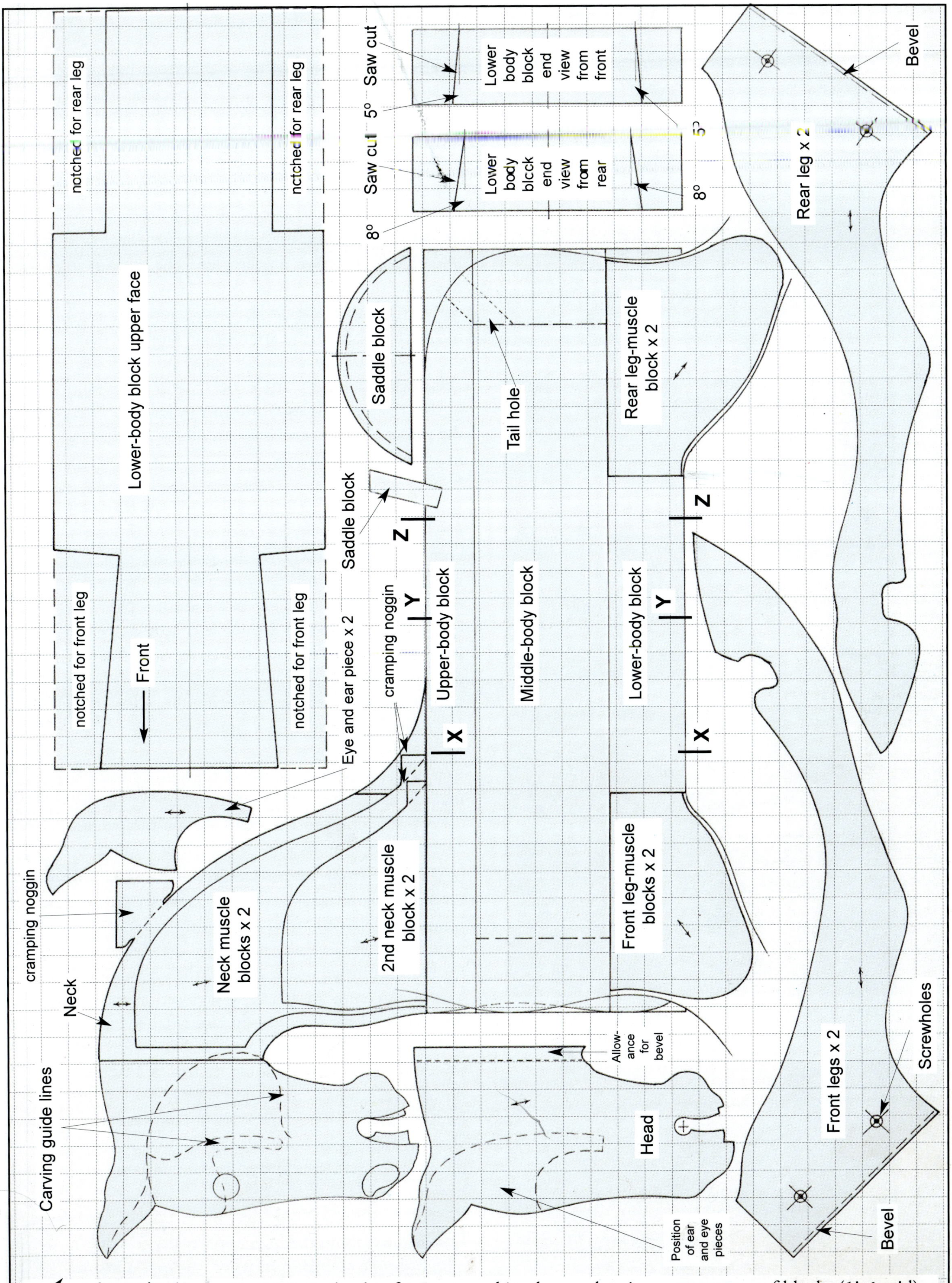

Fig 10.3 Scale plan for Large rocking horse, showing arrangement of blocks (1in² grid)

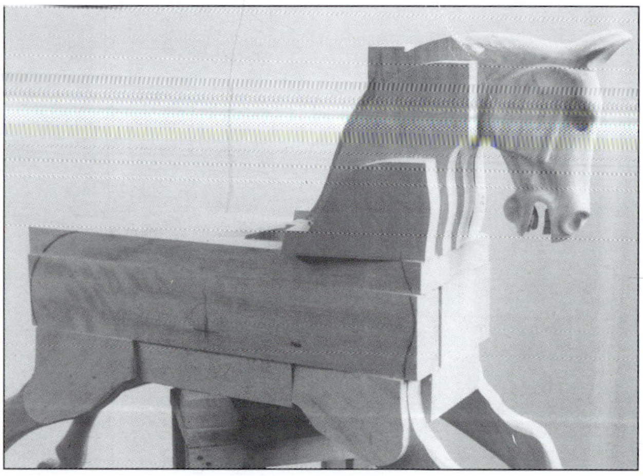

Plate 10.14 Blocked up, ready to start carving neck & body.

Plate 10.15 Mental & physical exercise & concentration ...

Plate 10.16 ... the traditional mallet & gouge approach.

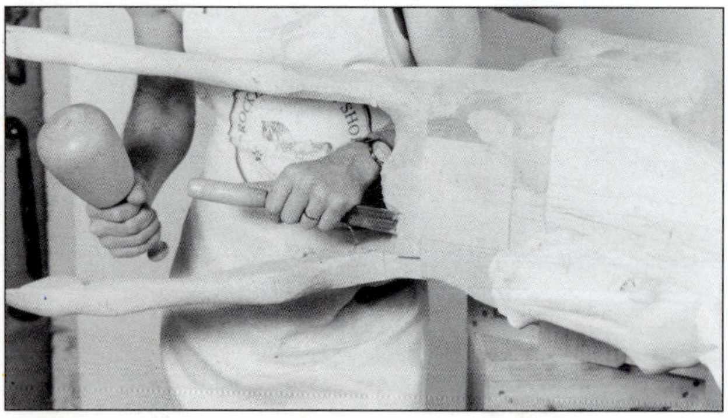

Plate 10.17 Defining the bulge at the lower chest.

that because of the angling of the neck they tend to stick out at what appear to be peculiar angles. Do not worry about this, you will lose all these jutting out bits in the carving.

Notching out the lower body block at the appropriate angles to receive the legs needs a little thought. Mark out the upper face of the lower body block as shown on the plan. The sawcuts in from the sides are vertical. If you have a bandsaw with a table that will tilt both ways you only need to tilt the table to the appropriate angle to make the cuts in from the ends. Do make sure your saw-cuts angle the right way (it is easy to get it wrong) so that the legs will splay out from the body. Keep the pieces cut from each corner, they will help you in cramping on the legs.

If you do not have a tilting table bandsaw then you need to mark the angles on the ends of the lower body block as shown on the plan, and saw the notches out by hand. Do not worry if the angles you cut in the lower body block are not precisely spot-on. If the hooves do not end up exactly the same distance apart front and back, or if the legs do not stand four square on a flat surface, these can be corrected later by adjusting the swing irons and when cutting the hoof notches.

Rough carve the lower parts of the legs. Make sure that the leg joints are good by cleaning up the lower body block notches with a smoothing plane. The straight top edges of the legs should be bevelled (5° front, 8° rear), either by handplaning or on the bandsaw. Glue and screw the legs in position so that the tops are slightly proud of the upper face of the lower body block. Glue on the leg muscle blocks, which conceal the screws in the legs, and cramp in place. When set, plane the upper face of the lower body block flat to receive the middle blocks which are glued in place with three fluted dowel pegs along each side. Place the dowel pegs towards the inside edge of the middle body blocks. Insert a message for posterity and glue on the upper body block, using four fluted dowel pegs, and you are ready for the body and neck carving.

I mentioned above that it is unnecessary to achieve a high degree of precision when cutting joints, so

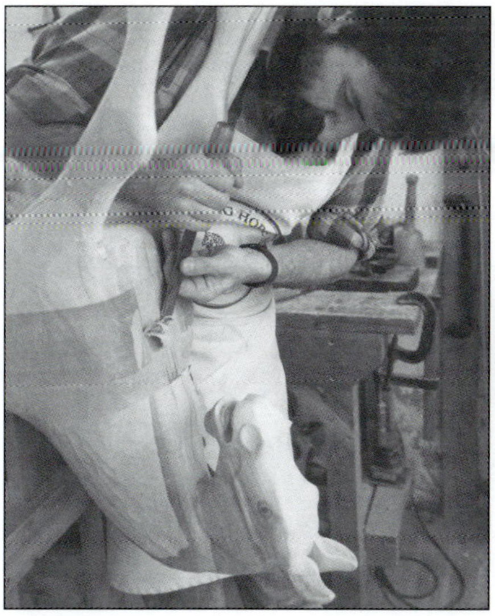
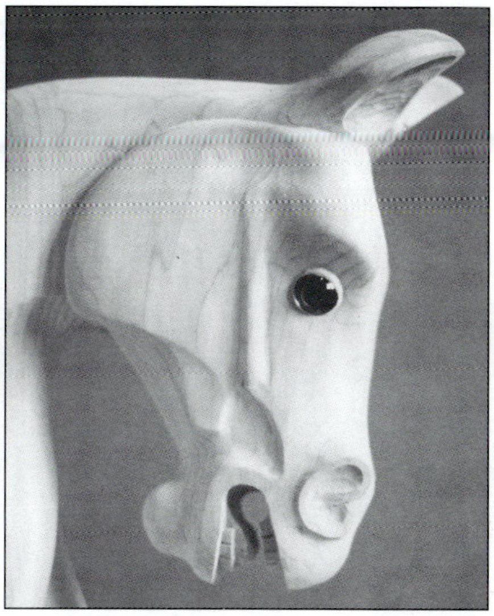
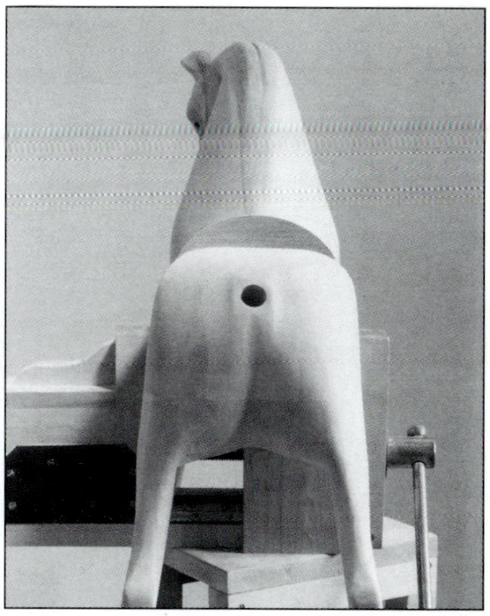

Plates 10.18, 19 & 20 Hollowing the middle of the chest, an awkward area; a finished Medium head; rear view with tail hole.

long as they are good and strong. Similarly carving is not a precise art. People with, for example, an engineering background who are used to dealing with tolerances in the order of thousandths of an inch, often express some concern about the relative imprecision of woodcarving. But it is not sensible to aim for accuracy in a job such as this. Do not say to yourself, "This is going wrong; I must get it correct". Rather, stand back periodically, look carefully at what you are doing, and say to yourself, "Can I enhance the shape and form by carving more off here, rounding over more there?". If you become frustrated with it, if the wished-for shape does not seem to be coming, leave it alone for a while. When you come back to it you may well be able to see your way forward with fresh eyes. It will come good eventually.

When making the Medium or Large rocking horse you may wish to aim for rather more detail in the carving than was described for the Small horse. You will see from the pictures that a tongue may be carved, and teeth marked by V cuts made with a straight chisel. Further shaping suggests the muscling around the mouth, on the neck and crest (the top of the neck), which is carved with a deep gouge. Although the head has been angled off to one side, the neck should be carved so that the base of the neck is central, both at the front where it runs down towards the chest, and at the rear where the saddle will be placed.

Larger gouges are used for roughing out, smaller gouges for picking out the details. Surform, Microplane or rasp and spokeshave are for smoothing off the curves, followed by hand and power sanding. Drill a 1in (25) hole for the tail. We're getting there! Turn to Chapter 11 for details of hoof notching and stand making, and Chapters 13 and 14 for finishing, painting and tacking up.

Plates 10.21 & 22 Master carvers! Sam Glass (left) & the author, in the workshop at The Rocking Horse Shop.

Plate 11.1 Large carved horse on swing iron safety stand.

CHAPTER 11

SWING IRON SAFETY STANDS

Since it was developed well over a hundred years ago, the swing iron safety stand has become the most popular mechanism for rocking horses. It takes up less space than the same size horse mounted on bow rockers, and yet has a very effective rocking action. As the horse rocks forward the back rises; as it rocks back the head rises. The disposition of the swing irons ensure that there is a limit to the extent of the movement, and although if rocked very vigorously the stand can be made to lift a little off the floor, stand mounted horses do not tend to 'travel' in the way that bows mounted rocking horses can.

PREPARATION

The swing iron stands described here have been designed to suit the horses in this book: the Half Size stand is for the horse in Chapter 8, the Small stand fits the Small carved horse in Chapter 9 as well as the Swinger in Chapter 5 and the Little Red Rocker in Chapter 6. The Medium and Large stands are for the Medium and Large carved horses described in Chapter 10. The construction method is similar for each of the four sizes.

We generally use ash, a hardwood which is tough and attractive, but other timbers such as maple or oak may be used, even pine. In the cutting lists overleaf, actual finished dimensions are given, after planing and cutting exactly to length, except that the timber for the posts is rough sawn to size, for turning.

HOW TO MAKE A STAND

The top rail and hoof rails are rounded at the ends, and the top and bottom rails and the two cross pieces are chamfered at 45° all around their top edges. The hoof rails may also be chamfered, but these chamfers should be stopped about 1½in (38) before the swing iron holes (or ¾in(19) for the Half Size). Figure 11:1 overleaf also shows an alternative style of hoof rail which you may like to use with the large stand.

The posts are normally turned, with pegs or spigots which fit through corresponding sized holes in the top and bottom rails. The lower end post peg passes through both the bottom rail and the centre of the cross piece. The cross and end pieces are glued and screwed onto the bottom rail, see Figure 11:2. The posts are secured by gluing and driving wooden wedges into two saw cuts along the pegs, taken to about 1/8in (3) from the shoulder. It is important to ensure that the wedges

Plate 11.2 Fitting an unfinished Half Size horse onto its swing iron stand. The stand and rails are yet to be varnished.

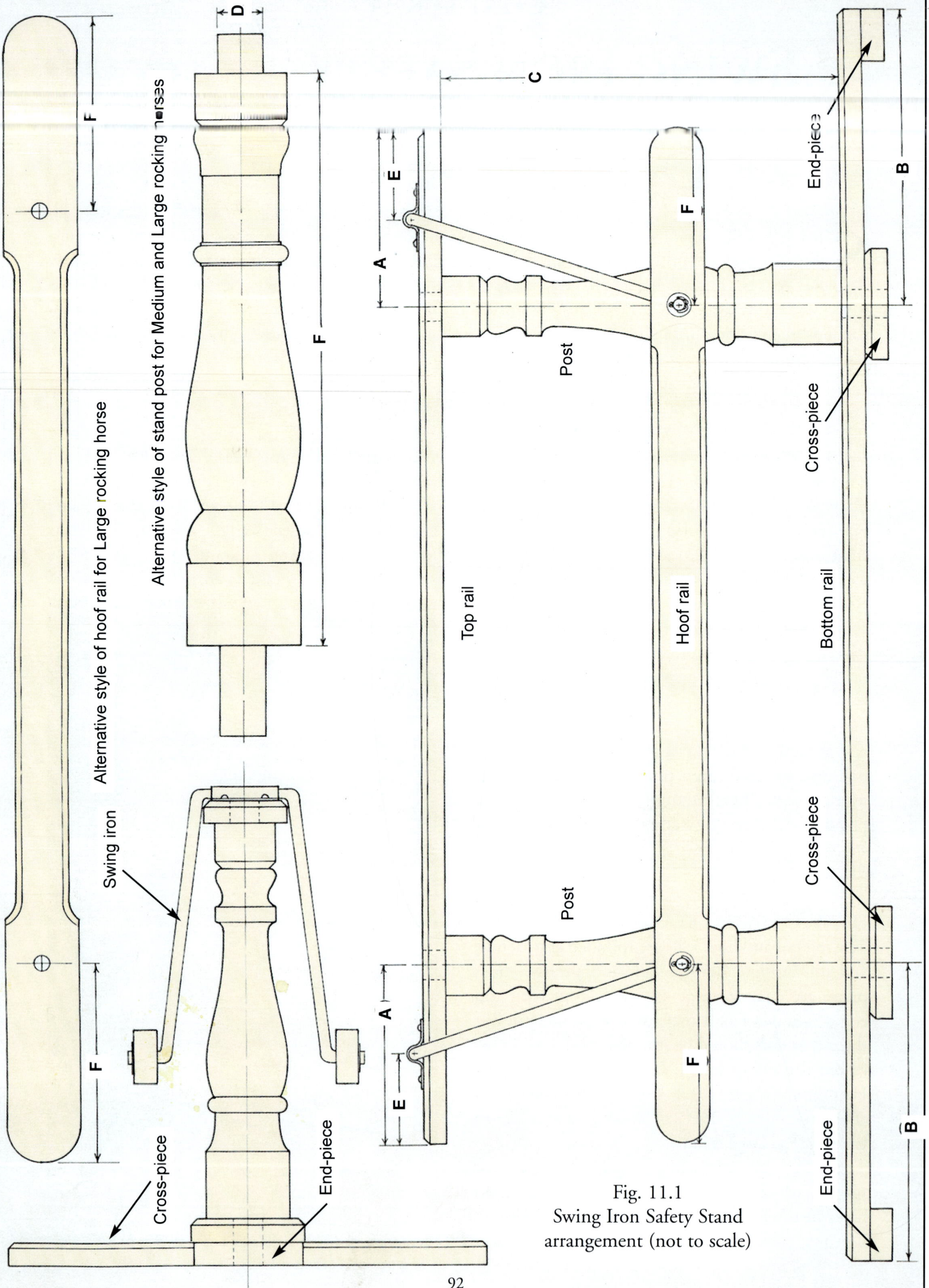

Fig. 11.1
Swing Iron Safety Stand
arrangement (not to scale)

CHAPTER 11

SWING IRON SAFETY STANDS

Since it was developed well over a hundred years ago, the swing iron safety stand has become the most popular mechanism for rocking horses. It takes up less space than the same size horse mounted on bow rockers, and yet has a very effective rocking action. As the horse rocks forward the back rises; as it rocks back the head rises. The disposition of the swing irons ensure that there is a limit to the extent of the movement, and although if rocked very vigorously the stand can be made to lift a little off the floor, stand mounted horses do not tend to 'travel' in the way that bows mounted rocking horses can.

PREPARATION

The swing iron stands described here have been designed to suit the horses in this book: the Half Size stand is for the horse in Chapter 8, the Small stand fits the Small carved horse in Chapter 9 as well as the Swinger in Chapter 5 and the Little Red Rocker in Chapter 6. The Medium and Large stands are for the Medium and Large carved horses described in Chapter 10. The construction method is similar for each of the four sizes.

We generally use ash, a hardwood which is tough and attractive, but other timbers such as maple or oak may be used, even pine. In the cutting lists overleaf, actual finished dimensions are given, after planing and cutting exactly to length, except that the timber for the posts is rough sawn to size, for turning.

HOW TO MAKE A STAND

The top rail and hoof rails are rounded at the ends, and the top and bottom rails and the two cross pieces are chamfered at 45° all around their top edges. The hoof rails may also be chamfered, but these chamfers should be stopped about 1½in (38) before the swing iron holes (or ¾in(19) for the Half Size). Figure 11:1 overleaf also shows an alternative style of hoof rail which you may like to use with the large stand.

The posts are normally turned, with pegs or spigots which fit through corresponding sized holes in the top and bottom rails. The lower end post peg passes through both the bottom rail and the centre of the cross piece. The cross and end pieces are glued and screwed onto the bottom rail, see Figure 11:2. The posts are secured by gluing and driving wooden wedges into two saw cuts along the pegs, taken to about 1/8in (3) from the shoulder. It is important to ensure that the wedges

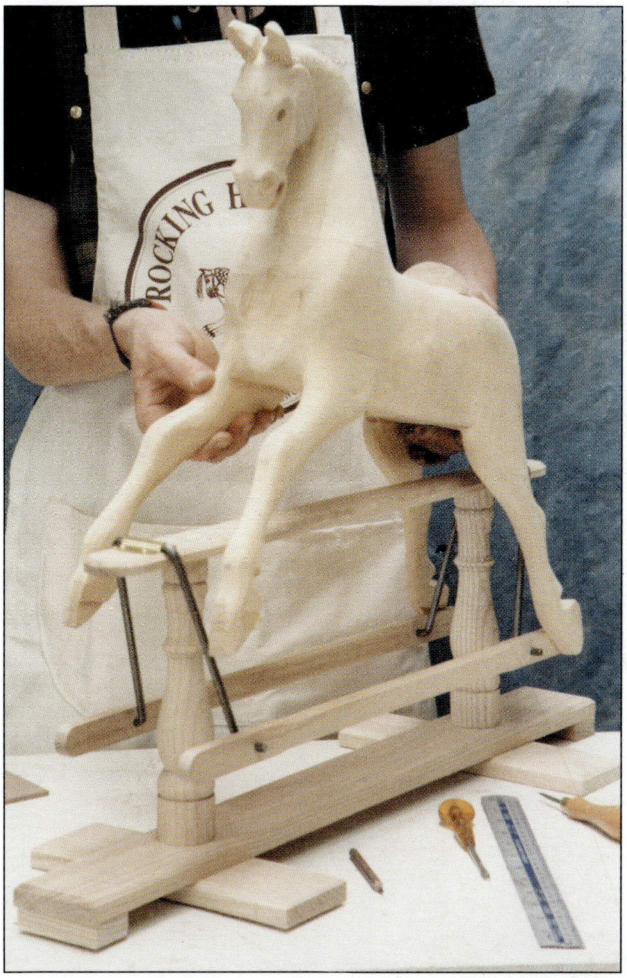

Plate 11.2 Fitting an unfinished Half Size horse onto its swing iron stand. The stand and rails are yet to be varnished.

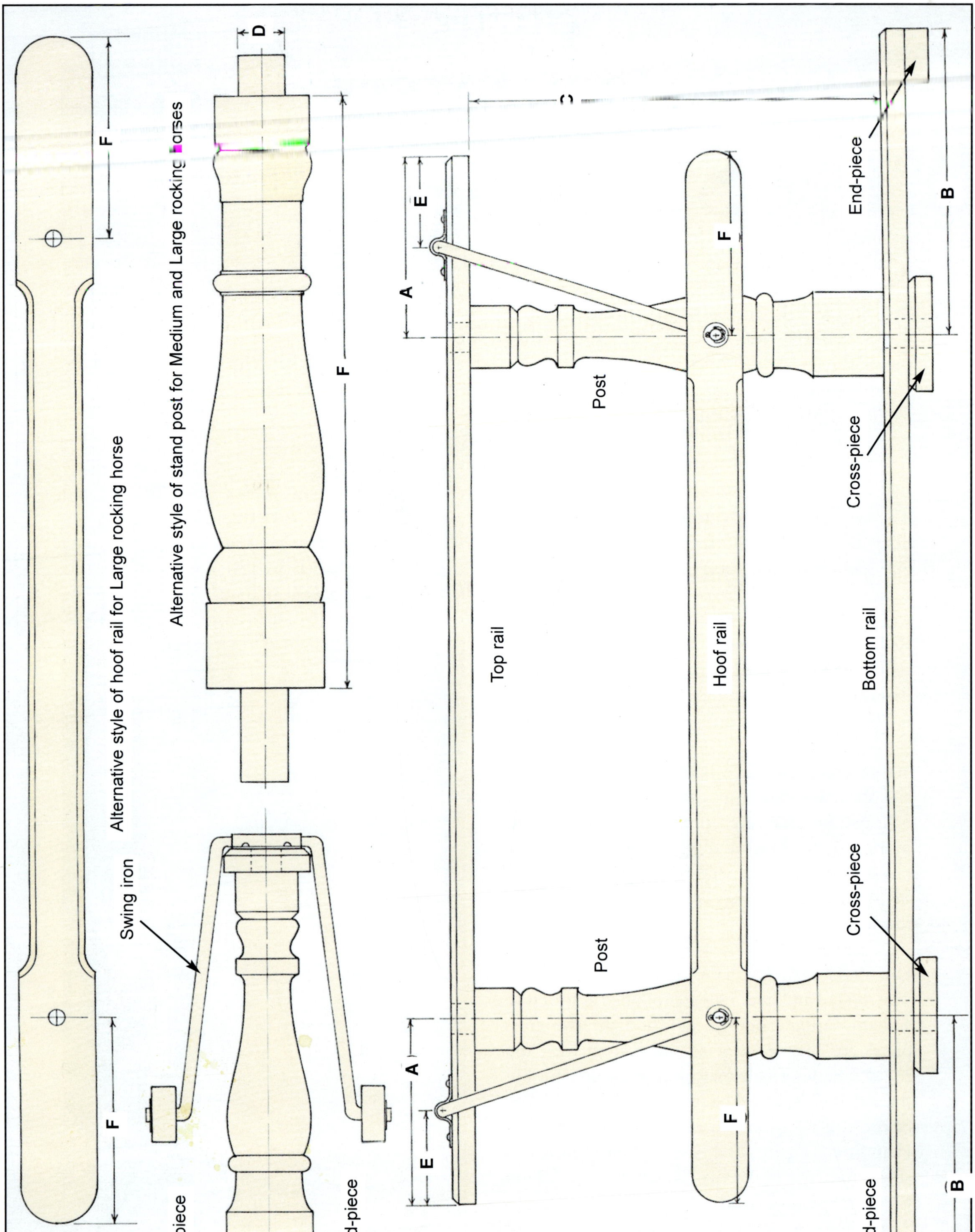

Fig. 11.1
Swing Iron Safety Stand
arrangement (not to scale)

CUTTING LIST - HALF SIZE STAND for Half Size Horse

	Thickness x width x length Inches	*Thickness x width x length* Millimetres
Top Rail	3/8 x 1 3/4 x 23	10 x 44 x 584
Bottom Rail	5/8 x 2 3/4 x 26 1/2	16 x 70 x 674
Cross Pieces (x 2)	5/8 x 2 3/4 x 9 1/8	16 x 70 x 230
End Pieces (x 2)	5/8 x 1 1/4 x 2 5/8	16 x 32 x 68
Posts (x 2)	1 1/2 x 1 1/2 x 10	38 x 38 x 254
Hoof Rails (x 2)	3/8 x 7/8 x 21	10 x 22 x 533

CUTTING LIST - SMALL STAND for Swinger, Little Red Rocker and Small Horses

	Thickness x width x length Inches	*Thickness x width x length* Millimetres
Top Rail	3/4 x 2 3/4 x 34	19 x 70 x 864
Bottom Rail	3/4 x 3 3/4 x 42	19 x 95 x 1066
Cross Pieces (x 2)	3/4 x 3 3/4 x 16	19 x 95 x 406
End Pieces (x 2)	3/4 x 1 3/4 x 3 1/2	19 x 45 x 89
Posts (x 2)	2 3/4 x 2 3/4 x 16	70 x 70 x 406
Hoof Rails (x 2)	3/4 x 1 3/4 x 34	19 x 45 x 864

CUTTING LIST - MEDIUM SIZE STAND for Medium Size Horse

	Thickness x width x length Inches	*Thickness x width x length* Millimetres
Top Rail	7/8 x 3 3/4 x 46	22 x 95 x 1168
Bottom Rail	1 1/4 x 5 3/4 x 53	32 x 146 x 1346
Cross Pieces (x 2)	1 1/4 x 5 3/4 x 18	32 x 146 x 457
End Pieces (x 2)	1 1/4 x 1 3/4 x 5 1/2	32 x 45 x 140
Posts (x 2)	3 x 3 x 20	75 x 75 x 508
Hoof Rails (x 2)	7/8 x 1 3/4 x 42	22 x 45 x 1067

CUTTING LIST - LARGE SIZE STAND for Large Size Horse

	Thickness x width x length Inches	*Thickness x width x length* Millimetres
Top Rail	7/8 x 3 3/4 x 52	22 x 95 x 1321
Bottom Rail	1 1/4 x 5 3/4 x 60	32 x 146 x 1524
Cross Pieces (x 2)	1 1/4 x 5 3/4 x 21	32 x 146 x 533
End Pieces (x 2)	1 1/4 x 1 3/4 x 5 1/2	32 x 45 x 140
Posts (x 2)	4 x 4 x 23 1/2	100 x 100 x 600
Hoof Rails (x 2)	7/8 x 2 3/4 x 52 1/2	22 x 70 x 1334

TABLE of STAND MEASUREMENTS as indicated in Figure 11.1

	Stand for Half Size Horse	Stand for Swinger, Little Red Rocker & SmallHorse	Stand for Medium Horse	Stand for Large Horse
A Post centres, from ends of top rail	3 3/4" (95)	6" (152)	7 1/2" (190)	8" (203)
B Post centres, from ends of bottom rail	5 1/2" (140)	10" (254)	11" (279)	12" (305)
C Length of post between rails	8 (203)	13" (330)	15 1/2" (394)	19" (483)
D Diameter of post pegs, and post peg holes	5/8" (16)	1" (25)	1 3/8" (35)	1 3/8" (35)
E Swing iron, from ends of top rail	1 1/2" (38)	3" (76)	3" (76)	3" (76)
F Swing iron holes, from ends of hoof rails	3" (76)	6" (152)	6" (152)	7 1/4" (184)

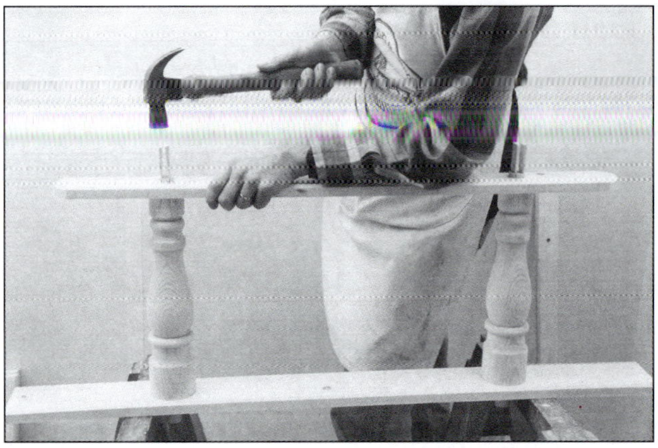

Plate 11.3 Wedges are glued and hammered in firmly. They must be placed so that they are at right angles to the direction of grain in the surrounding timber

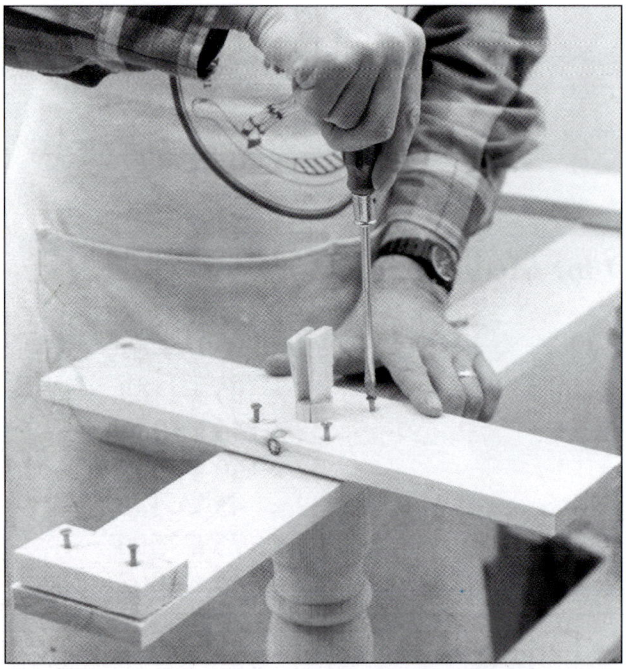

Plate 11.4 Cross and end pieces are glued and screwed to the bottom rail. Note the wedges in the post spigot, at right angles to the grain of the cross piece

Plate 11.5 Sawing off the waste from the top of the spigot. A piece of thin card protects the top rail.

Fig 11.2
Stand fixings,
view from below

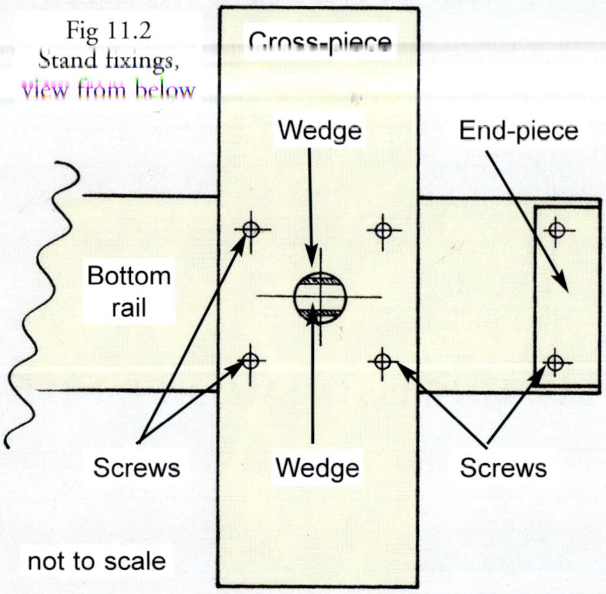

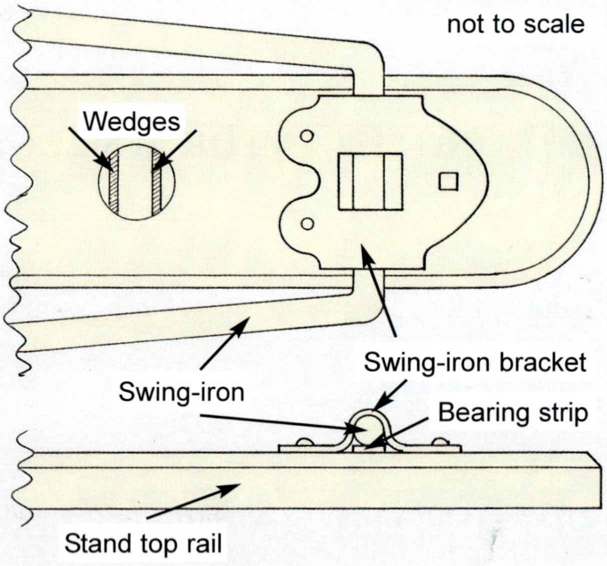

Fig 11.3 Detail showing swing iron arrangement.

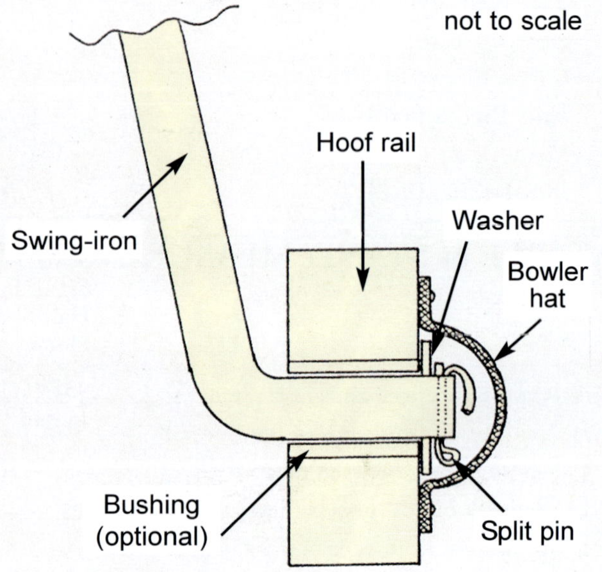

Fig 11.4 Detail of lower end of swing iron & hoof rail.

are placed at right angles to the direction of grain of the surrounding timber. Figure 11:1 shows an alternative traditional 'Ayres' style of post which may be used on medium and large stands. If you do not have a lathe, posts can be purchased ready turned, (as indeed can all stand parts, see Appendix) or may be made up from square or rectangular section timber, appropriately jointed (ie morticed) into the top and bottom rails.

The swing irons are made from bright mild steel rod, 1/4in (6) diameter for the Half Size, 3/8in (10) diameter for the Swinger, Little Red Rocker and Small horses, 7/16in (11) diameter for the Medium and Large horses. They are 6 1/4in (160) long for the Half size, 9 1/4in (235) long for the Swinger, Red Rocker and Small horse, 12 1/2in (318) long for the Medium, and 14 1/2in (368) long for the Large horse. This is the longest practicable in order to give a good rocking action, while allowing sufficient clearance over the top rail that a child's fingers could not get trapped.

The lower ends pass through holes in the hoof rails which should be drilled fractionally larger than the diameter of the swing irons so that they will pivot freely. It is not really necessary to bush these holes since in normal use they suffer surprisingly little wear, even over many years of use. However, if we are making a horse for a school or hospital where it is likely to come in for exceptionally hard usage then we do insert bushes, which we cut from brass or copper pipe.

It will almost certainly be the case that the right and left hooves of your horse will be different distances apart front and back, and it is important that the swing irons are adjusted to fit them properly. Using a vice to hold them firm, push the ends of the swing irons closer together or pull them further apart so that when the horse is lifted onto its rails the ends of the irons protrude just far enough to accommodate the securing washers and split pins which will be covered by four brass bowler hats secured with small brass screws. On the Half Size horse, instead of split pins, star-lock washers secure and finish the swing irons. The horse's legs should not be put under any strain by ill-fitting swing irons. The steel swing irons can then be primed and painted.

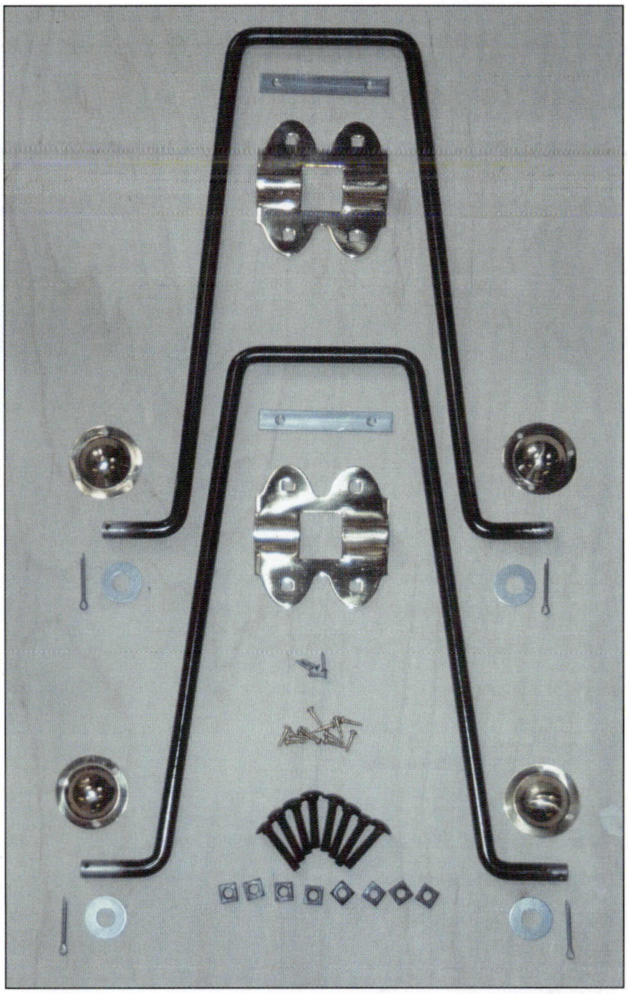

Plate 11.6 Steel swing irons (painted), solid brass brackets and bowler hats, and all bolts, screws, washers, split pins etc

Plate 11.7 Brass bowler hat conceals washer and split pin.

Plate 11.8 Bracket for Small horses, Swinger and Little red Rocker. Solid brass, fixed with a bolt and two screws.

Plate 11.9 Solid brass bracket for Medium and Large horses, secured with four bolts, this one on a stained ash stand.

Plate 11.10 Chrome plated version of Medium and Large bracket, this one on a varnished maple stand.

A bearing strip made of $\frac{1}{2}$in (12) wide steel will be screwed onto the top rail of the stand for the swing iron to bear upon. The swing irons are held in position on the top rail by polished brass, chrome plated or painted steel brackets, secured with $\frac{1}{4}$in (6) diameter carriage bolts (bolts and woodscrews in the case of the small brackets). Mark the positions of the bearing strips and brackets and drill the bolt holes. Half Size stands do not need bearing strips and the little brass brackets are secured with small round head brass screws. Before fitting on the metalwork give the stand and hoof rails a final sand down and varnish. We favour a satin or matt varnish finish, two or three thin coats, gently rubbed down between each coat. Stands may be stained to a darker shade, according to your preference, or they may be painted a colour: traditionally stands were often painted green (presumably to represent grass). When the paint or varnish is dry fit all the metalwork, adding a dab of grease under the brackets and to the lower ends of the swing irons. The stand is now complete, ready for the horse to be lifted on and secured to the hoof rails. Ready to rock!

Plate11.11 Completed Large Horse, this one mounted on a pine swing iron stand.

Plate11.12
Some makers like to fix a plate to the stand which will be a permanent indication of the horse's origin. This plate is cast solid brass, but brass plates can also be engraved, with the maker's name, & perhaps the date & the name of the recipient(s); a nice personal touch.

Fig 11.13 Large & Medium horses on ash stands, Small on a pine stand with steel brackets & swing irons painted black.

Plate 12.1 Completed Medium Size Horse, on stained and varnished ash bow rockers.

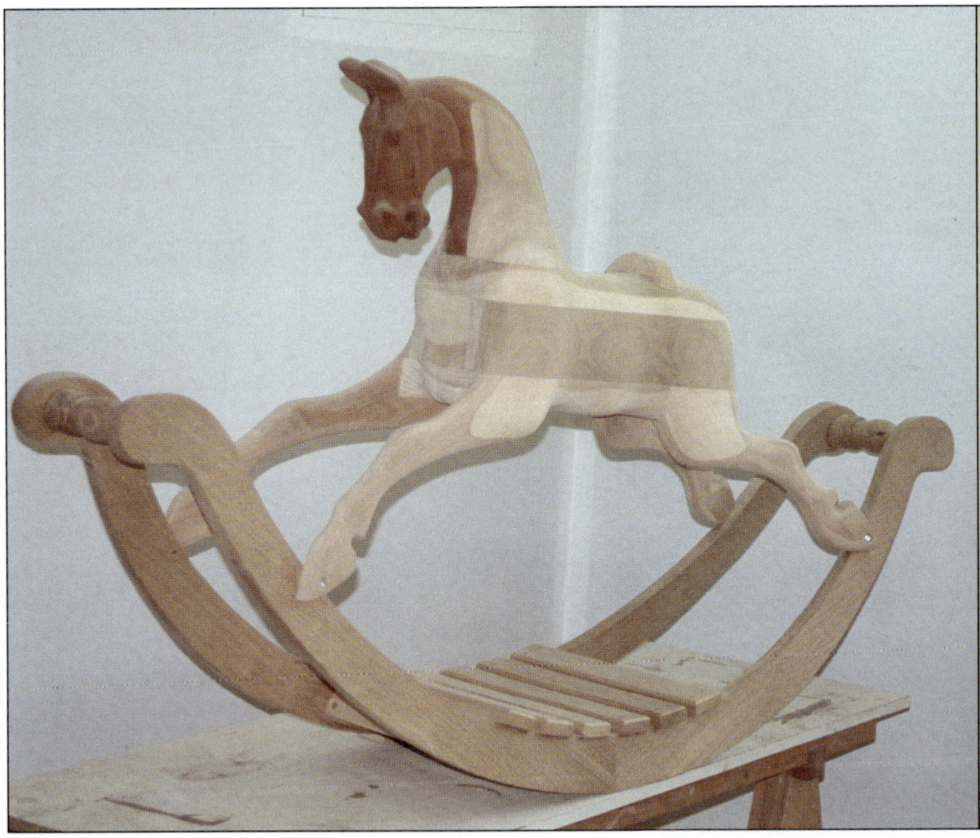

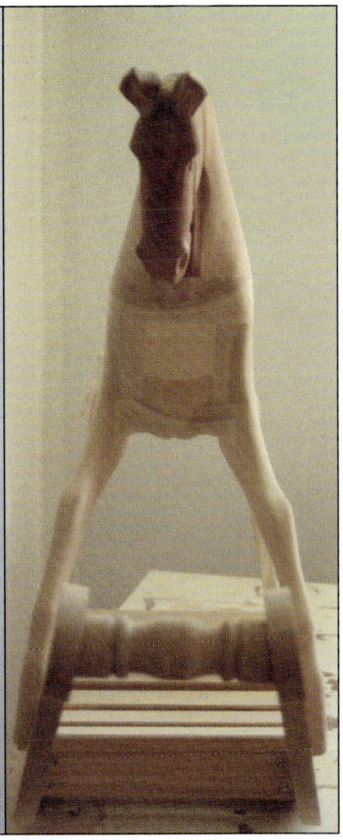

Plates 12.2 and 12.3 A Small Horse mounted up on its bow rockers and ready for finishing.

CHAPTER 12

Bow Rockers
FOR TRADITIONAL CARVED ROCKING HORSES

Wooden toy horses were mounted on bow shaped rockers long before the swing iron safety stand was developed, and many people still regard bows as the 'proper' form of the rocking horse. This chapter covers bows for Half Size, Small and Medium rocking horses. They do indeed look superb and have an excellent rocking action, despite some disadvantages, including a tendency to 'travel' when ridden. Also, a bows mounted horse takes up much more space than the same size of stand mounted horse. Bows for the Large horse are not given here since they are not often called for - you would need a very large house to accommodate one (and a nanny to supervise its use).

PREPARATION
Except for the configuration of the legs, horses for mounting on bows are constructed in exactly the same manner as the Half Size, Small and Medium horses in Chapters 8, 9 and 10 respectively. The legs are different in that when horses are mounted on bow rockers the legs are more stretched out to the front and rear in a galloping or jumping stance, while the stand mounted horse has its legs in a more upright position in order to ensure that there is sufficient space between the hooves and belly to accommodate the swing irons.

With the exception of the legs and leg muscle blocks therefore, as detailed below, use the appropriate cutting lists in Chapters 8, 9 and 10 to prepare the timber for all parts of the horses. Note that the jointing of the legs to the lower body block is done in a similar manner, but the angles at which the lower body block is notched to receive the legs for a bows mounted horse are greater, that is $7\frac{1}{2}°$ for front and 15° for rear legs, in order to achieve a greater splay, as shown in the Figures in this chapter.

The assembly and carving is accomplished in the same manner as for the stand mounted horses described in Chapters 8, 9 and 10 and all the instructions given for those horses concerning assembly and carving apply to these.

HOW TO MAKE THE BOW ROCKERS
Bow rockers are most often made from ash, for its springy quality, strength and appearance, but oak, beech or other hardwood may also be used. Each side of the bow is made from two pieces joined at

	Thickness x width x length	*Thickness x width x length*
	Inches	**Millimetres**
CUTTING LIST for Legs for Half Size on Bows		
Legs (all four)	7/8 x 4 x 36	22 x 100 x 914
CUTTING LIST for Legs for Small on Bows		
Legs (all four)	7/8 x 5 3/4 x 54	22 x 146 x 1372
Leg Muscle Blocks (all)	3/8 x 5 3/4 x 28	10 x 146 x 711
CUTTING LIST for Legs for Medium on Bows		
Legs (all four)	1 3/8 x 7 3/4 x 72	35 x 197 x 1830
Front Leg Muscle Blocks	3/4 x 6 3/4 x 16	19 x 171 x 406
Rear Leg Muscle Blocks	1/2 x 7 3/4 x 18	13 x 197 x 457

	Thickness x width x length	*Thickness x width x length*
	Inches	**Millimetres**
CUTTING LIST for Bow Rockers for Half Size Horse		
Bow Rockers and Frame (x 2)	3/8 x 4 3/8 x 42 1/2	10 x 110 x 1100
Slatted Platform (x 11)	3/8 x 7/8 x 8 3/4	10 x 22 x 222
End Pieces (x 2)	1 x 1 x 4 1/2	25 x 25 x 115
CUTTING LIST for Bow Rockers for Small Horse		
Bow Rockers and Frame (x 2)	3/4 x 6 1/2 x 65	19 x 159 x 1651
Slatted Platform (x 6)	5/8 x 1 3/4 x 12 1/2	16 x 45 x 318
End Pieces (x 2)	1 3/4 x 1 3/4 x 6	45 x 45 x 152
CUTTING LIST for Bow Rockers for Medium Horse		
Bow Rockers and Frame (x 4)	3/4 x 8 1/2 x 42 1/2	19 x 216 x 1080
Slatted Platform (x 11)	5/8 x 1 3/4 x 17 1/4	16 x 45 x 438
End Pieces (turned) (x 2)	1 3/4 x 1 3/4 x 9	45 x 45 x 229

the centre to each side of a rectangular frame around which the rockers are assembled. The frame sides and cross members are cut from the same piece of timber as the bows.

The widths given for the rockers are the minimum needed, and if you can obtain wider boards you will be able to economise on the length. In any case you should position the patterns carefully, bearing in mind that the rockers and rocker frame sides have bevelled edges towards the middle and due allowance must be made for these, so study the drawings before cutting out. Instead of hardwood, some makers have used plywood or MDF for the rocker sides and frame. In this case it may be possible to cut each side of the rocker in one piece and dispense with the join in the middle, which makes the assembly easier although the wastage will be greater.

The distinctive boat shaped appearance, in which the rockers are closer together at the ends than in the middle, is formed by angling the two rockers, at 10° from the vertical, towards each other. They are not steamed or bent. The edges of the rockers are bevelled so that they sit flat to the floor

Fig 12.1
Bow rocker arrangement
(not to scale)

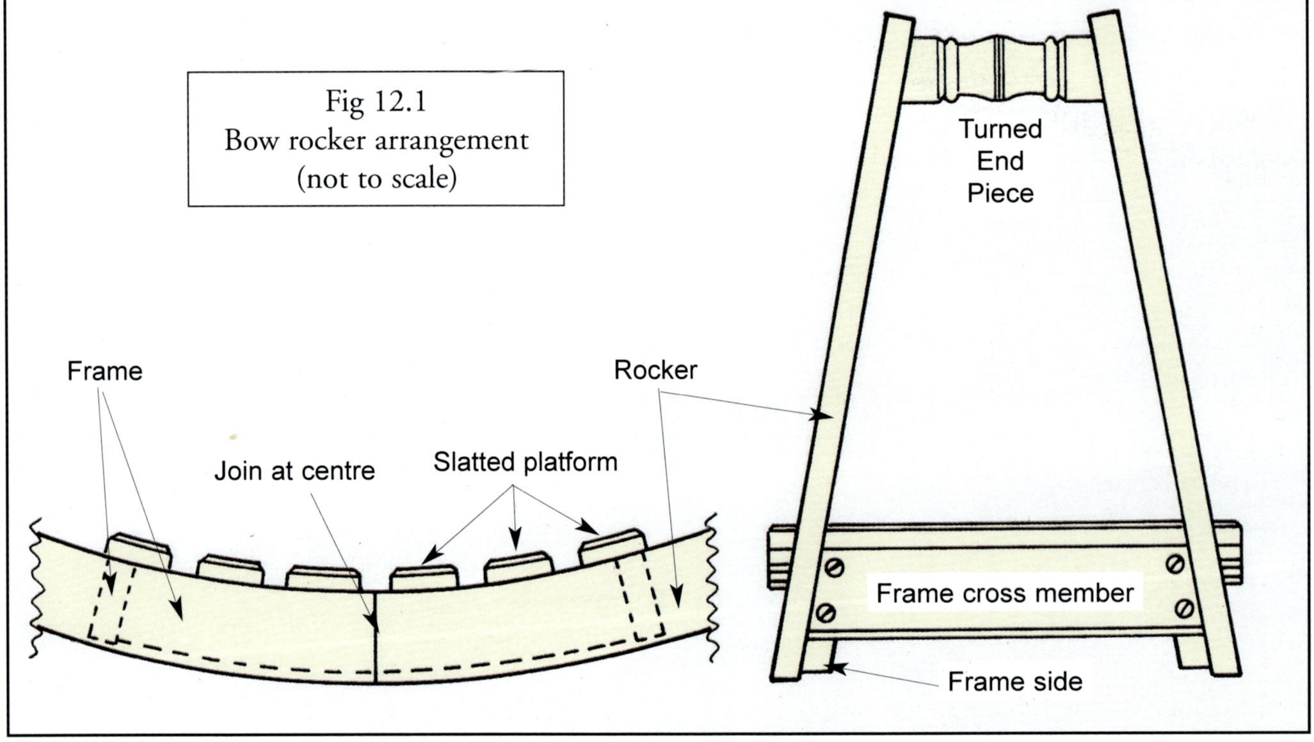

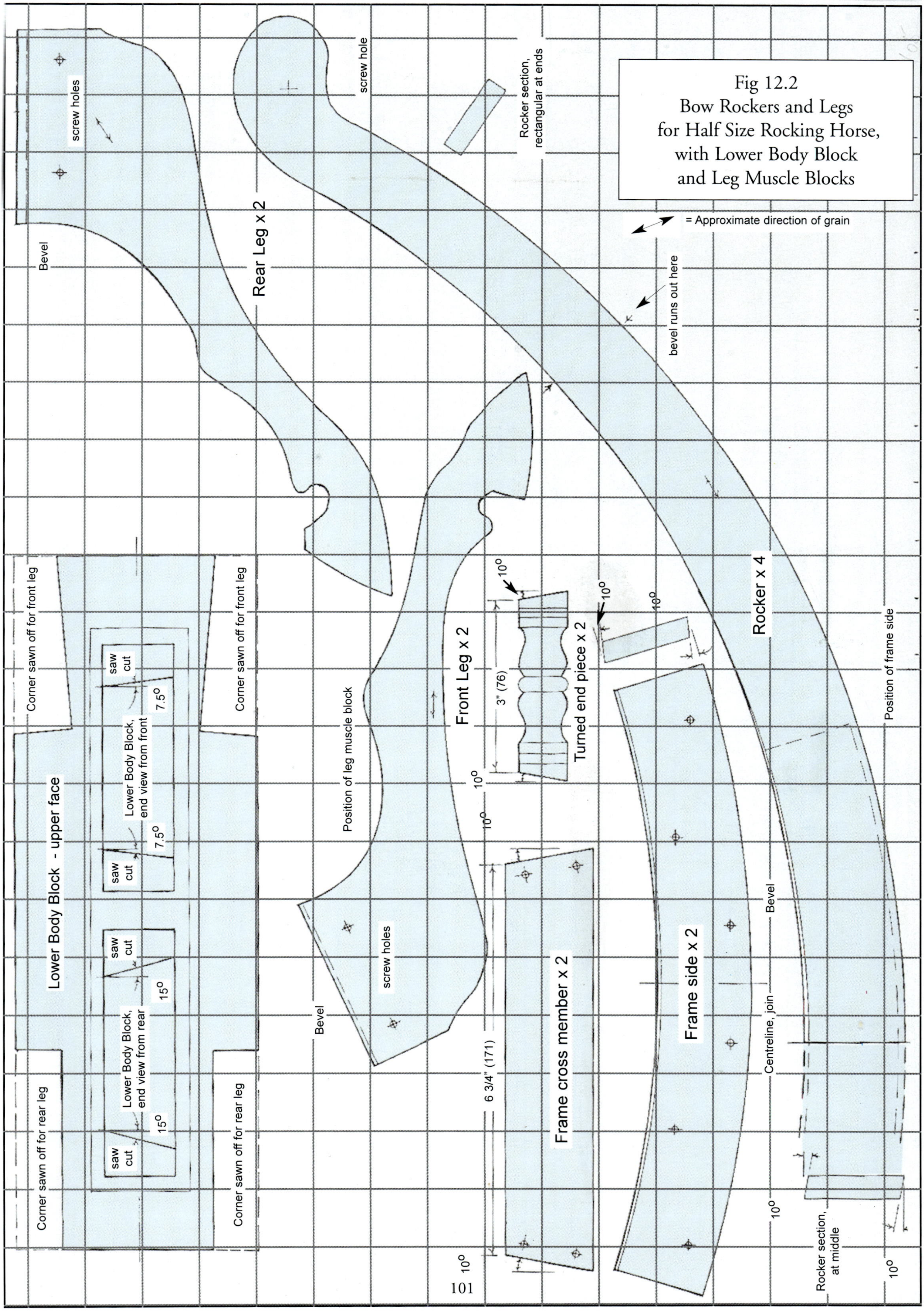

Fig 12.2
Bow Rockers and Legs
for Half Size Rocking Horse,
with Lower Body Block
and Leg Muscle Blocks

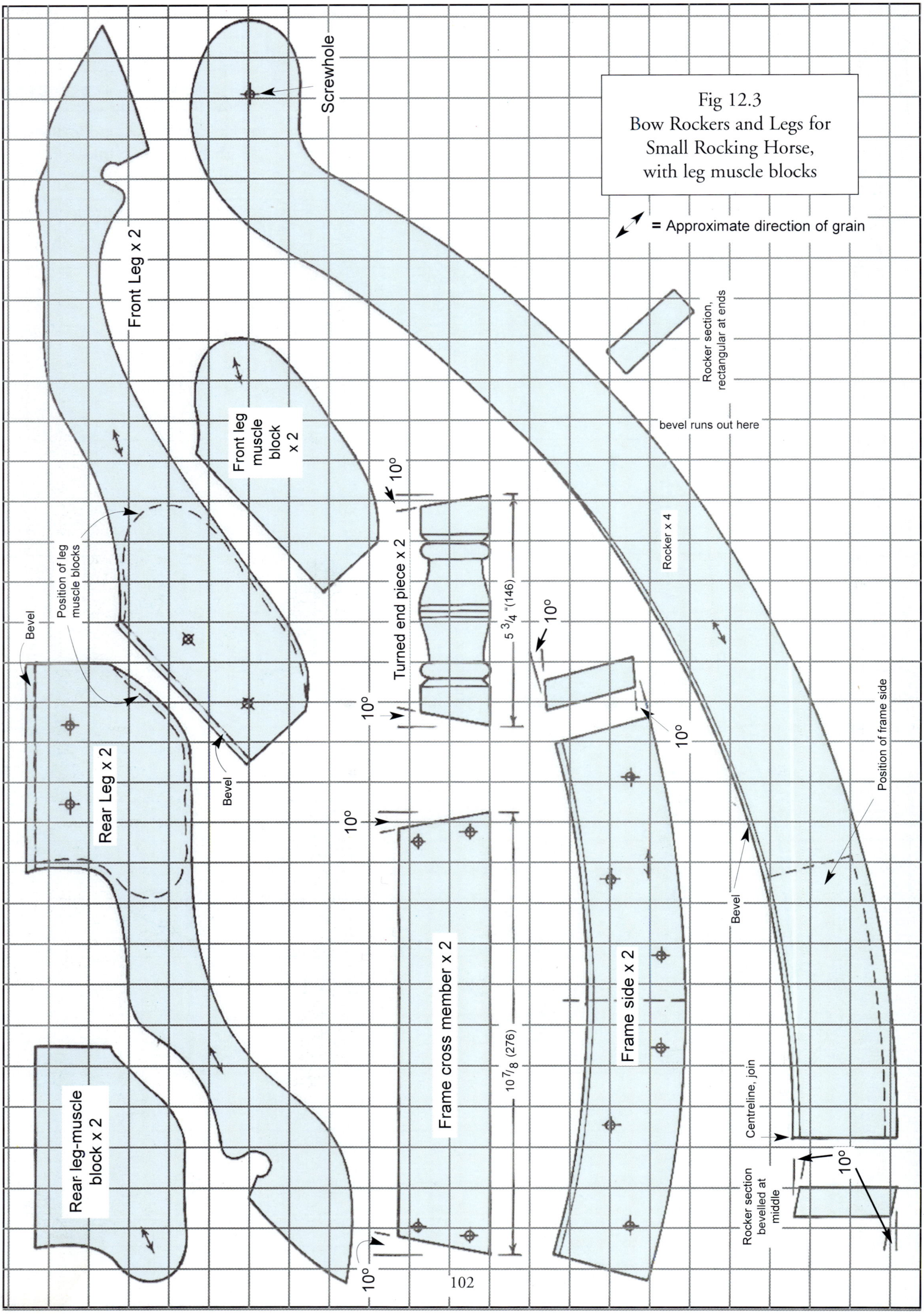

Fig 12.3
Bow Rockers and Legs for Small Rocking Horse, with leg muscle blocks

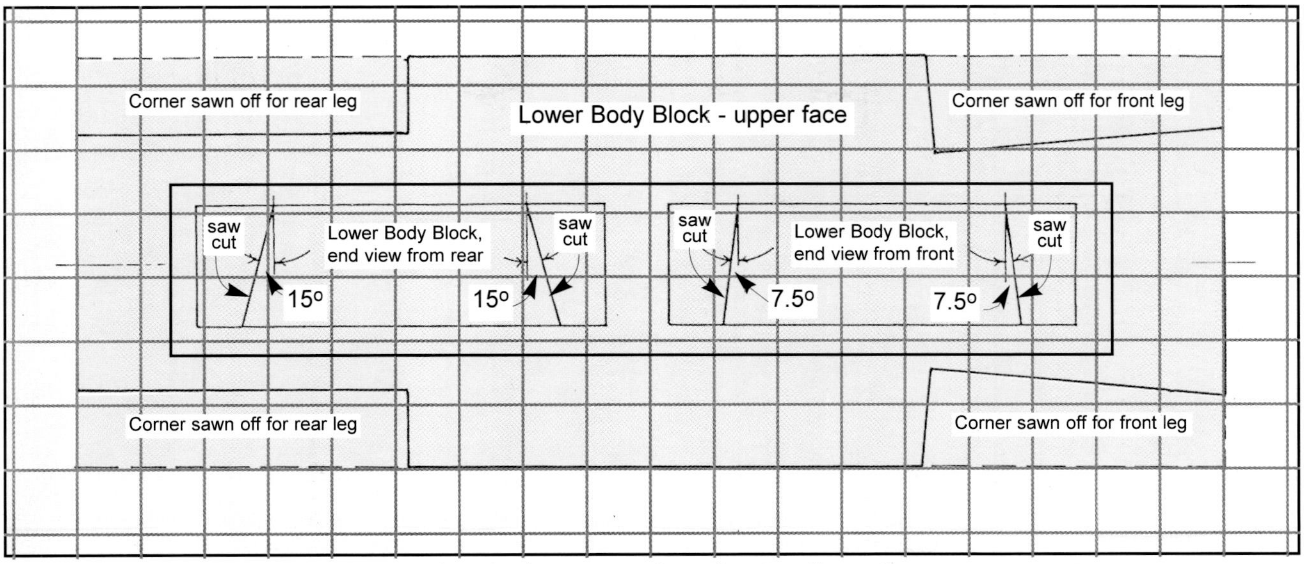

Fig 12.3a Lower Body Block - upper face, for Small Rocking Horse on Bows
showing (inset) end views of the Lower Body Block from the front and rear.

underneath and so that the slatted platform will sit flat on top of them, but this bevelling runs out before the ends of the rockers where they become rectangular in section. The two curved frame sides are also bevelled at 10° top and bottom. If you have a bandsaw on which the table can be tilted to 10° you will be able to bandsaw the bevels. If not, the bevels will have to be cut by hand with a spokeshave, and due allowance should be left for them when cutting out. Take particular care when marking and cutting out the timber that the bevels angle the correct way.

The two pieces that form each side of the bow rocker are simply butted together and secured by glueing and screwing on the frame sides with 1 1/4in (32) wood screws, or 5/8 (16) for the Half Size. We have made up a jig to help to ensure that the rockers are assembled correctly. It consists simply of a drawing of the full rocker on a piece of board with scraps of wood screwed on at intervals round the edges, so that the rocker parts can be wedged in position while they are glued and screwed together. It is not really necessary to go to the trouble of making a special assembly jig if you are making only one horse, but you must ensure that the bevels correspond, that the pieces are drawn as close together as possible, and most important, that you get a smooth curve across the join (or it will click when it rocks). The rocker frame cross members are glued and screwed onto the ends of the frame sides, thus joining together the two bows which angle in towards each other. The ends of the cross members, particularly on the Medium, may be bevelled to ensure a good fit (shown on Fig 12.4). Before the glue has dried place a straight 'winding stick' across each end of the bow rockers then stand back and sight across them. The winding sticks should be parallel - if not, pull at the rockers until they are and then let the glue dry.

The ends of the rockers are joined together with turned end pieces. If you do not have a lathe they can be purchased, or may be made square or octagonal. The ends are sawn off at 10° angles. The easiest way of fixing them in place is to drill a 3/16in (4) countersunk hole through each rocker end, prick-mark the centres of the end pieces, spread glue on them and secure with woodscrews. You may need to cramp them also. When the glue has set, you may remove the screws and enlarge the holes to 3/8 inch (10) - let the drill penetrate at least an inch (25) into the end piece. Put some glue into the holes and drive in 3/8 inch (10)

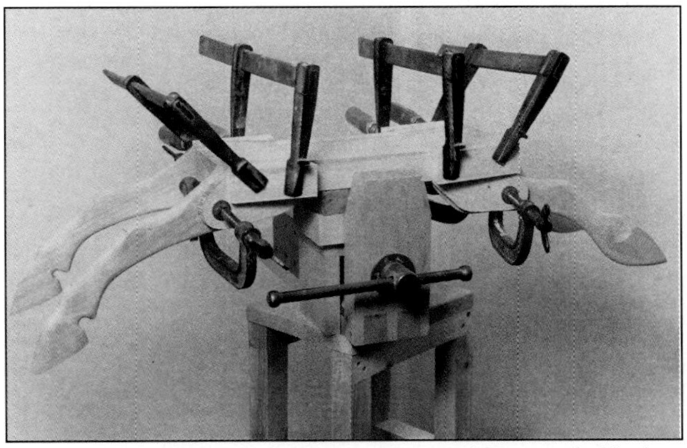

Plate 12.4 Gluing and cramping legs and leg muscle blocks.

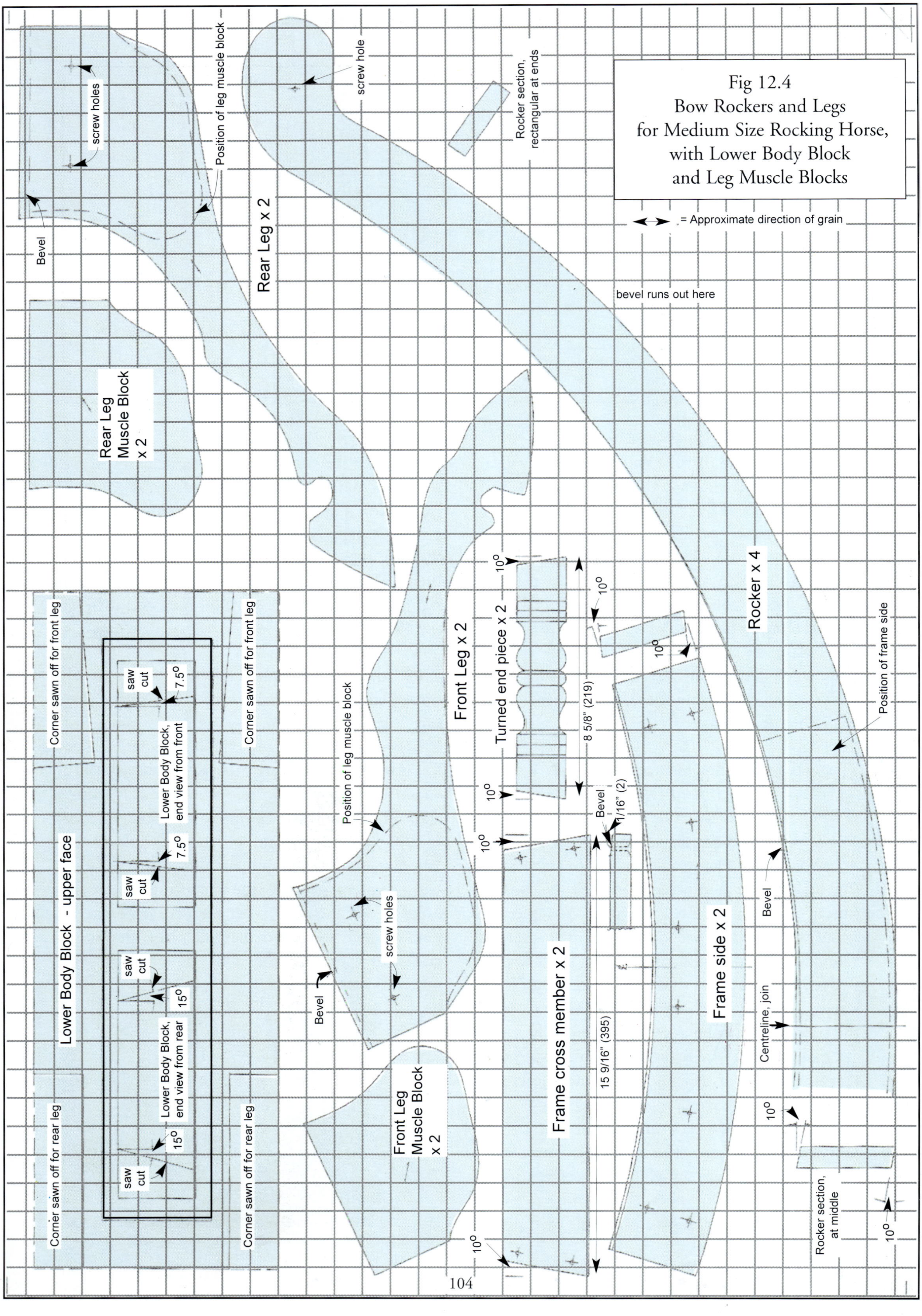

Fig 12.4
Bow Rockers and Legs
for Medium Size Rocking Horse,
with Lower Body Block
and Leg Muscle Blocks

diameter dowel pegs. Saw off the waste ends of the dowel pegs and sand smooth. Alternatively the screws may be left, and covered with a small turned cap to conceal the screw heads. Or, if you are concerned about the possibility of the ends pulling apart, and want to make a really strong construction that will never come apart, you can insert a length of threaded steel rod right through the middle of the turned end piece and secure with nuts at each end. The nuts are concealed under turned wooden caps. It may surprise you to know that in the good old days rockers were invariably fixed to the turned end pieces by the simple means of glue and cut nails (but this simple fixing does tend to come apart over a period of time).

The tops of the pieces for the slatted platform are chamfered all round and fixed onto the rockers at each side with adhesive and either woodscrews or brass pins. Make sure that they overhang equally at each side and space them apart evenly, by eye.

FITTING THE HORSE TO THE ROCKERS

Before giving the rockers a final sand down and varnishing, the hoof notches can be marked and cut ready for the horse to be fitted on. Wedge some scrap wood under the rockers to stop them moving and lift the horse on to the rockers so that each hoof rests on the outer edge of the rockers and the horse is not tilting to one side. It is good to have someone to help you to position the horse and steady it, in case it slips and falls off.

Because the fully carved horse is quite heavy, especially the medium size one, we have found that the hoof notches can be fitted at that stage in the construction of the horse when the legs are secured to the lower body block, but before the rest of the body and head are fixed; it is so much lighter and easier to handle then. By carefully marking and cutting away a little at the inside of each hoof with saw and chisel, the hooves are notched so that they drop down to overlap the rockers by about an inch (25).

Notching the hooves for fixing to the bow rockers is probably the trickiest part of making this horse because of the odd angles involved. You may well have to lift it on and off several times before getting the notches to fit just right and sometimes

Plate 12.5 Small Horse ready for mounting. Note the way the legs are stretched out to front and rear for bows mounting.

Plate 12.6 Gluing and screwing a frame side, which joins the two rockers together, using a home made assembly jig which positions the rockers correctly. A piece of paper under the join prevents the work from becoming stuck to the bench.

Plate 12.7 A straight piece of scrap wood is placed on the ends of the rockers. These "winding sticks" should be parallel.

Plate 12.8 Assembling a set of Half Size bow rockers

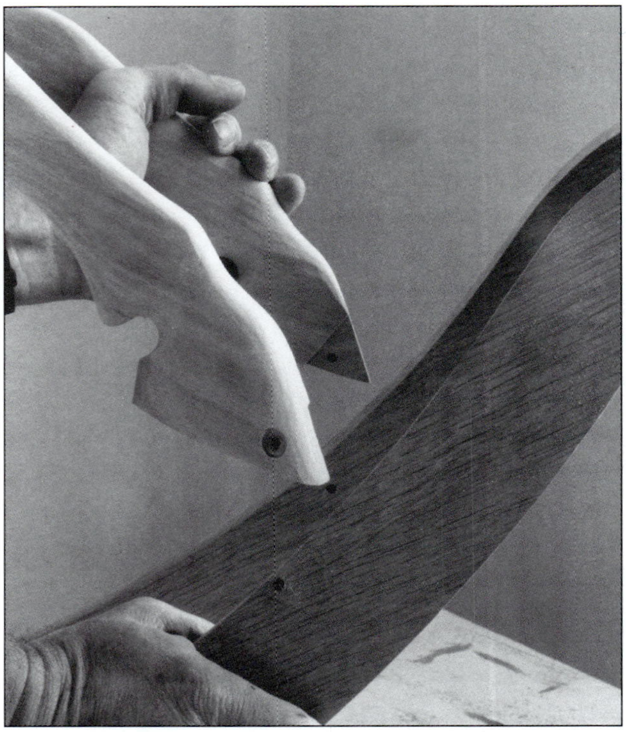

Plate 12.9 Fitting hooves to bow rockers

it is necessary to glue a packing piece onto the inside of a hoof. Once the horse fits neatly on the rockers you can drill the bolt holes. Angle them downwards through solid timber. Although only four bolts and nuts are used to secure the horse to its rockers, experience has shown that this is quite sufficiently strong. Remove the rockers and screw a scrap of wood on to each hoof, to prevent them being chipped, and turn to Chapter 13, for finishing and painting the horse.

Fig 12.10
Completed Medium and Small Horses on bow rockers.
The Small is fitted with "Black Beauty" accessories with removable saddlery.

Plate12.11 Bows mounted horses have an exciting rocking action; the rider is in control!

Plate 13.1 Large & Medium horses with traditional dapple grey paintwork, Small with stained & varnished finish.

are usually hung from giant staples hammered securely into the horse. Determine the position of these stirrup staples by placing the saddle on the horse's back, lifting up the skirts, and pencilling round the two oval holes in the flaps. With the large gouge hollow out a recess about 3/8in (10) deep at each oval. These recesses will allow the stirrup leather buckle to be run up close to the stirrup staple and lie more or less flat to the side of the horse so that it does not cause an unsightly bulge and, since it is then tucked underneath the skirt, does not rub on the rider's leg. Drill 1/8in (3) pilot holes for the stirrup staples and hammer them in, ensuring that you leave sufficient gap underneath to enable the stirrup leather to be threaded through. Actually, you may leave hammering in the staples until after the saddle cloths have been fixed (see Chapter 14), avoiding having to cut the saddle cloth from around them.

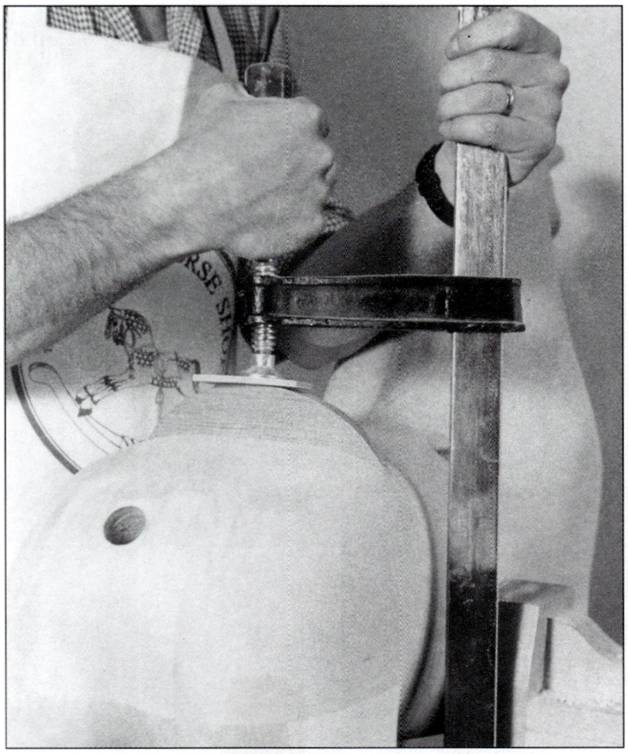

Plate13.9 Glue & cramp the saddle block in place.

Half Size and Small horses are not fitted with stirrup staples since the stirrup leather fixing does not require them. Some rocking horse saddles simply buckle on with a girth strap (see Chapter 14). If you are planning on using one of these buckle on saddles it is not necessary to fit either stirrup staples or a saddle block.

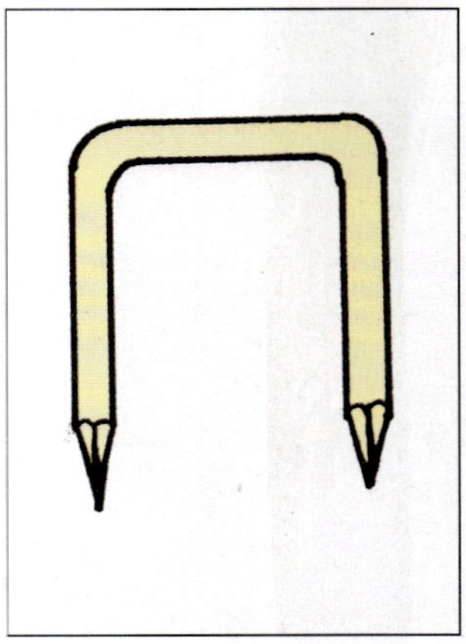

Fig 13.1
Stirrup staple.

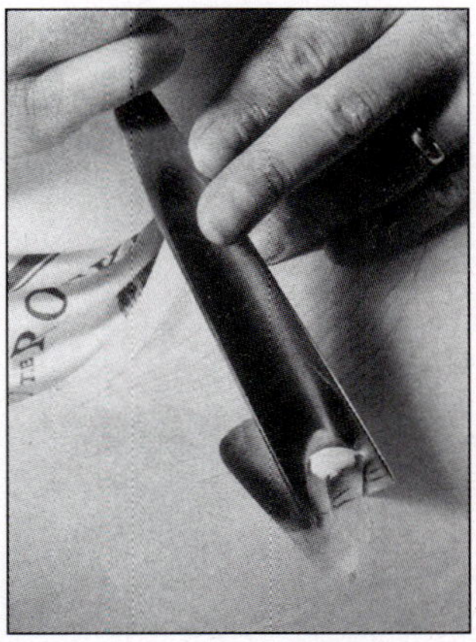

Plate 13.10 Gouging recess for stirrup staple.

HOOF NOTCHES

Rocking horses made for mounting on swing iron stands have their hooves notched so that they fit neatly over the hoof rails of the stand, to which they are secured. Place the horse on a flat surface and under each hoof tuck a piece of scrap wood about 1/4in (6) thick. You may well find that the horse leans to one side or wobbles due to unequal leg lengths. If so, tuck further pieces of scrap wood under the hooves until the horse stands upright and without wobbling. Take the hoof rails and place them on the flat surface against the inside of the hooves, and use a pencil and a pair of compasses open to about 1/4in (6) for the half Size, 3/8in (9) for the Swinger, Little Red Rocker and Small carved horse, 1/2in (13) for Medium or Large horses, to mark and scribe for the hoof notches.

Carefully saw out the hoof notches and then drill each hoof for the bolt or woodscrew that will hold the horse onto the hoof rails. Smaller horses can be

Plate13.11 Hammering in stirrup staple.

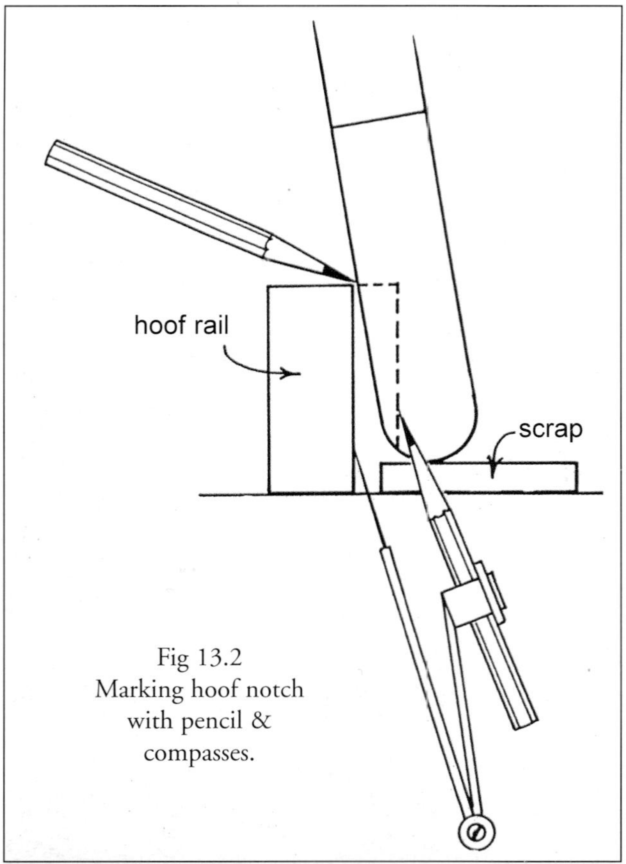

Fig 13.2
Marking hoof notch
with pencil &
compasses.

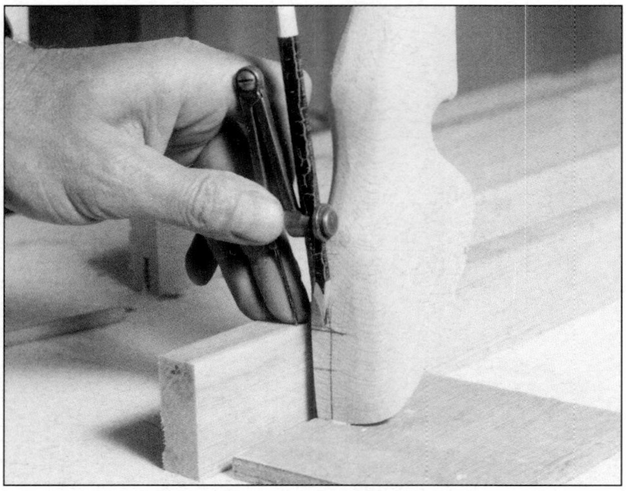

Plate 13.12 Marking hoof notch.

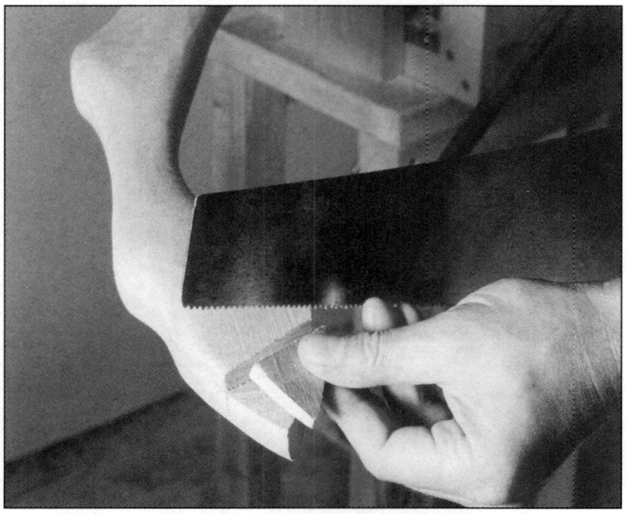

Plate 13.13 Sawing out hoof notch.

secured to the hoof rails with woodscrews or 3/16in (5) bolts and nuts, but for the Medium or Large rocking horses use 1/4in (6) carriage bolts and nuts. Angle the drill downwards a little so that the holes will not be too close to the top edge of the hoof rails. Then screw on blocks of scrap wood or temporary hoof rails, which serve to prevent the hooves getting chipped as you move the horse around, and also enable you to paint all round the visible part of them.

GESSO

The traditional way of preparing the wood for painting is to use gesso. This is a mixture of rabbit skin glue and gilder's whiting, brushed hot onto the bare wood. It acts as a grain filler and obliterates rasp marks and other minor blemishes, so if you are going to apply gesso there is no need to sand the surface much, if at all. In fact a rougher surface is better, providing a key for the gesso. After it has dried, gesso is easily sanded to leave a hard, beautifully smooth surface on which to paint.

Also, because the gesso remains slightly flexible even after it has set hard, it will tend to take up slight movements in the underlying timber and minimise cracking of the painted surface. This flexibility is, however, only very slight; if the underlying timber does move it will probably crack the paintwork anyway, in spite of the gesso. The only way to minimise any tendency to crack is to have used properly dried timber and to have good joints.

Some makers do not use gesso, regarding it as messy and bothersome. They simply sand the surface smooth and then use a primer and several coats of paint straight onto the wood, rubbing down between each coat to achieve a good finish. But if you decide you would like to do the traditional thing and gesso your horse, the method is as follows:

Soak 3¼ozs (80gms) of crushed rabbit skin glue overnight in just under two pints (1.1 litres) of cold water, then heat. Do not apply the heat directly but use a glue kettle - a Pyrex bowl over a saucepan of boiling water will serve the purpose. Heat the liquid, which is called size, until it begins to steam and you can hardly bear to dip in a finger.

Then put it on one side for several hours to cool down to room temperature; when it will set to a khaki coloured jelly.

Divide the jelly and re-heat half of it. In this way you can add more to the mix as and when you need it, and if you find you will not finish the gessoing in one session, then the remaining jelly can be kept for later use. It will keep quite happily for several days - preferably in a fridge if the weather is warm. Use a 2in (50) flat brush and brush the first coat of the size onto the bare wood, all over the horse. You may also wish to use scrim (fine weave cotton plasterer's scrim) which is stuck over the joints, particularly those at the tops of the legs which are most likely to crack. Scrim also helps to minimise any tendency to cracking, but is awkward to use and we have found its beneficial effects to be minimal; we no longer bother with it.

Gently stir in some of the gilder's whiting to give the size body. The consistency of the mix is that of a thin coffee cream which runs easily from the brush. Brush on five or more coats in quick succession, one after the other, and try to alternate the direction of the brush strokes to give an even build-up. Gesso right over the eyes. After it has dried you can easily scrape it off with a craft knife and clean up the glass eyes with a damp rag. Keep the mixture hot and stir it from time to time as you use it. If the mix seems thin you can thicken it up by adding a little more whiting, but avoid applying the gesso thickly over the lower legs, or the head, where it can obliterate the detail of your careful carving.

As you use the gesso you will lose some of the water through evaporation and it may be necessary to add a drop or two more. If it is too strong, too concentrated, it will set too hard and will crack. Do not add too much water, though, because if it becomes too weak, too dilute, the gesso will be too soft and will clog your abrasive. Over-dilution can be rectified by adding some more glue soaked in very little water.

After gessoing allow the horse to dry out thoroughly for several days before sanding smooth with 150 grit abrasive. It is not unusual to find that a few hairline cracks have appeared as the

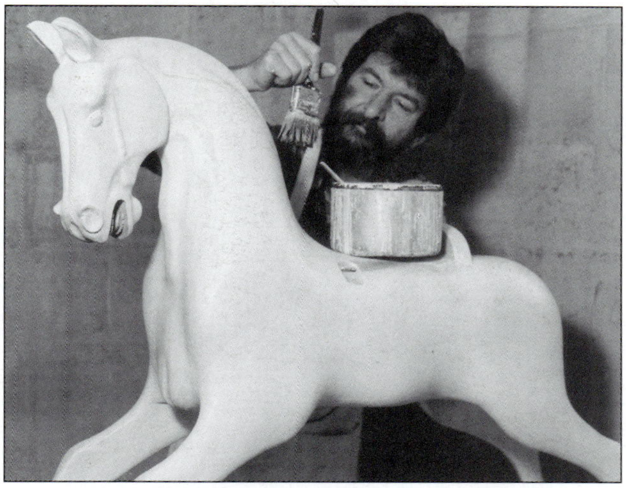

Plate13.14 Applying gesso - slap it on with a big brush!

Plate13.15 Gessoed & base coated, ready for dappling. The horse takes on a rather drab appearance at this stage, but is revitalised when the eyes are scraped off, & by the dappling.

Plate13.16 A Half Size horse being dappled. The dappling pad is foam rubber wrapped round the end of a stick, & the black dappling is applied with a dabbing action.

gesso dries but do not worry about this; just work in some soft woodfiller before sanding down.

PAINTING AND DAPPLING

The painted dapple grey is the characteristic traditional finish for a rocking horse, and remains the most popular. The horse is painted all over with a basecoat which is either white or pale grey. We usually start with white paint and mix in a touch of black to make pale grey - a little more black if we (or the customers) fancy a darker shade. Three or four coats should be sufficient, allowing the paint to dry and giving it a gentle rub down with fine abrasive between coats.

You can paint right over the glass eyes. Then, when the paint has dried, run the point of a craft knife round the eyes and peel off the paint, which does not stick too well to glass. Use red paint to rim the eyes, to paint the insides of the ears, nostrils and mouth, and to delineate the teeth. Carefully paint in the eyelashes with black; you will need a very thin pencil brush for this, and a steady hand. Black is also used for the hooves, and for the dappling.

Plate 13.17 A Half Size dapple grey.

Plate 13.18 Painting in the eye detail.

Traditional style dappling is applied freehand with a dappling pad made from a piece of sponge rubber around which may be wrapped a piece of stockinette which leaves an interesting 'hairy' appearance. Squeeze some black paint onto a scrap of wood or an old tile and dip the dappling pad into it, then dab it onto the horse. Start near the top of the neck and keep dabbing until the dabs form a circle with an area of the base coat showing in the middle, then move on to dab another circle, and so on.

Some makers will start with one circle then put five or six more circles around the first one to form a sort of flower pattern, gradually fading out. Others put the dappled circles in lines or have a more random pattern. Practice your dappling technique on a piece of scrap wood or card before attacking the horse. It is important to use a dabbing action; do not smear the paint or you will make a mess of it. The first dabs will leave a lot of black, but as the paint is used up the dabs become lighter so that you can vary the intensity of the dappling to achieve an interesting gradation. The dappling should be roughly symmetrical on both sides of the horse.

It is possible to pre-determine the positions of the dapples by sticking circles cut from thin card onto the horse with double sided masking tape or Blutack. Traditional style dappling can also be applied with a short bristle stencil brush (keep it almost dry), or air brush or spray. As above, test out your dappling technique on a piece of scrap before attempting the horse.

After the dappling, rocking horses are usually varnished all over with a clear matt or satin varnish. The varnish softens the appearance of the dappling and protects the surface from finger marking.

'ANTIQUE' PAINT

Old rocking horses often have a slightly yellow appearance, the original varnish having mellowed with age. You can suggest this by simply adding a dash of yellow to your final varnish coat. For a more authentic looking antique finish you can apply an antique glaze, after the dappling has dried but before the final varnish.

The antique glaze is a mixture of varnish, linseed oil and turpentine (approx. proportions 4:1:½) and a dash of Vandyke brown. It is brushed liberally all over the horse and then, before it has dried, ragged off with a clean cotton cloth. Interesting variations in colour can be achieved by wiping more glaze off the high spots. The glaze may take several days to thoroughly dry out before you can apply the final coat of varnish.

ALTERNATIVE FINISHES

You may prefer a paint finish other than the traditional dapple grey, for example piebald, palomino, black or white. It is usual to give them socks and a blaze in a contrasting colour. Bear in mind though, that an all over plain colour will show up every imperfection. This is a major advantage of the dapple grey in that the dappling breaks up the surface and helps to mask imperfections, and probably accounts for the popularity of dappling among traditional rocking horse makers, apart from the obvious fact that it looks good.

You may opt for a natural wood finish. Why cover the natural beauty of the wood, and all your careful carving, with paint? In our experience painted rocking horses are preferred by children while natural wood has a more adult appeal. Since many rocking horses are regarded as prized artifacts and pieces of furniture as well (I hope) as children's playthings, a natural wood finish is an attractive proposition, either stained and lacquered or varnished and polished, or simply oiled. You will have to prepare the surface by very thorough sanding with progressively finer grit papers. You will also want to make sure that your joints are as good as can be, since all mistakes or blemishes will be seen. However beautiful your horse is though, I do hope you will let children ride it, because that is what it's for!

Plate 13.19 Completed Medium Size dapple grey. A very pale grey base coat has been used, the dappling has the 'flower' pattern, & then a satin sheen over varnish.

Plate 13.20 On this Medium Size horse the base coats are white, it has been given a light antique glaze & the over varnish has been slightly tinted to give it a mellow look.

Plate 14.1
Small Carved Horse
fitted with buckle on bridle,
nailed on martingale &
synthetic hair mane.
Note ribbon rosette
on chest.

CHAPTER 14

LEATHER TACK AND HAIR FOR CARVED HORSES

Rocking horse tack is traditionally uncomplicated, practical and attractive. It can consist simply of leather strapping nailed on to look like a bridle and martingale, and a padded leather saddle, also nailed on, all enhanced with decorative brass nails and rosettes. It may be more elaborate and realistic: removeable buckle-on bridles and martingales may be used, particularly on bigger horses, and saddles can also be removeable - some are just like miniature real ones. I tend to favour a combination of buckle-on bridle, which children can enjoy in their play, and a nailed on saddle which cannot slip when in use, all made with top quality leather in attractive colour combinations.

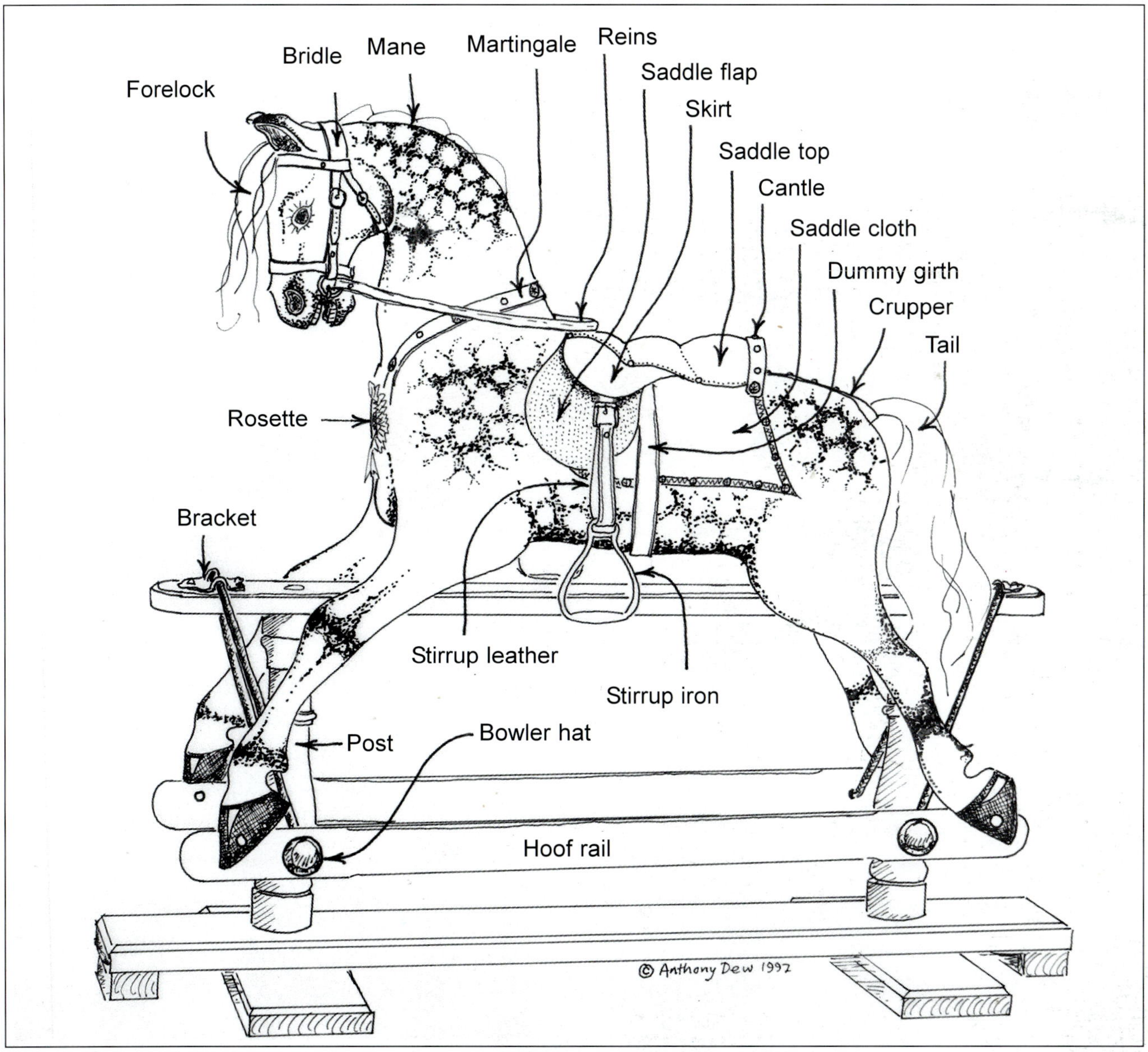

Fig 14.1 Rocking horse tack.

Dimensions for nail-on saddles for each of the four sizes of carved horse:								
	Half Size Horse		Small Horse		Medium Horse		Large Horse	
Dimension A	8in	(203)	13in	(330)	16in	(406)	18in	(457)
Dimension B	2³/4in	(70)	4¹/4in	(108)	5¹/4in	(133)	6¹/4in	(159)
Dimension C	4¹/4in	(108)	6¹/2in	(165)	7³/4in	(197)	9in	(229)
Dimension D	4³/4in	(121)	7in	(178)	9¹/2in	(241)	11in	(279)
Dimension E	4¹/2in	(114)	7in	(178)	10¹/2in	(267)	13in	(330)
Dimension F	2³/4in	(70)	6in	(152)	6¹/2in	(165)	8in	(203)
Cantle Strap	5in	(127)	8in	(203)	9¹/2in	(241)	11in	(279)

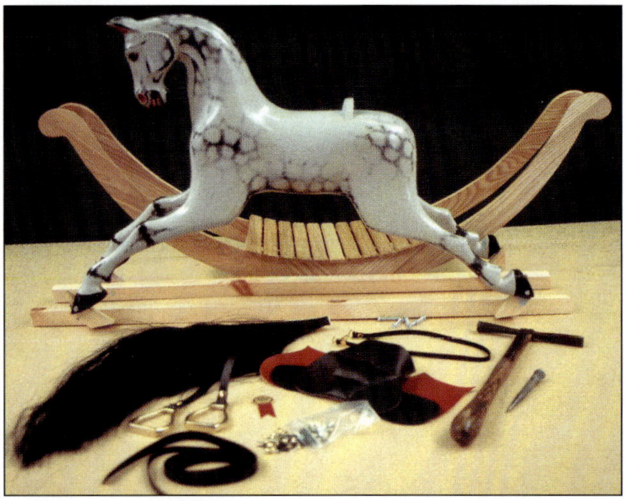

Plate14.2 Accessories ready for tacking up a Half Size horse.

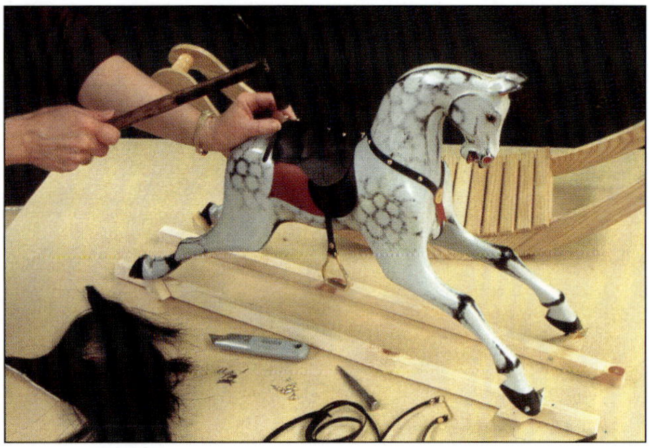

Plate14.3 Fixing saddle to the Half Size horse.

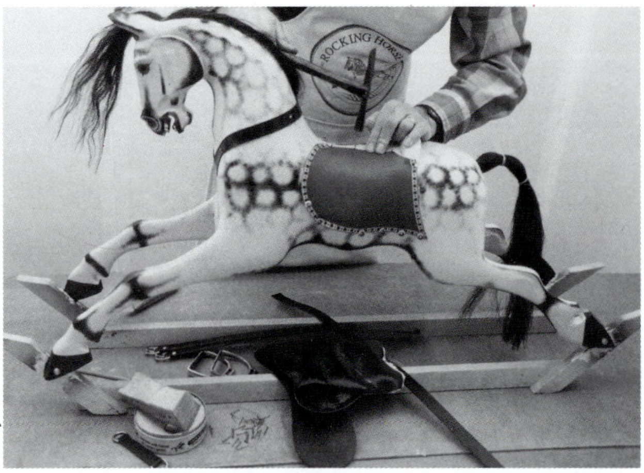

Plate14.4 With nail-on saddles, the saddle cloths are fixed first. This is a Small horse for mounting on bows. Note the temporary rails that have been screwed to the hooves.

Leather bridles, saddles, martingales and strapping, for nailing or buckling on, and manes and tails in real or synthetic hair, are available ready to fit in a wide choice of styles and colours, see Appendix.

NAIL-ON SADDLES

These nail-on saddles are based on a typical traditional Victorian style. The saddle is made from a high quality vegetable tanned leather and the seat, generally a softer leather, perhaps in a complimentary colour, is padded with cotton wadding or foam rubber. The skirts are usually stitched to the seat which is enhanced by additional stitching across it. Saddle cloths are made from thin leather or coloured leathercloth with a decorative woven braid stitched round the edges. The main dimensions for each of the four sizes of horse are given in the table above, which refers to drawings Fig 14.2 and 14.3 opposite.

Half Size saddlery is secured with 1/2in (13) gimp pins and decorated with 1/4in (6) brass dome nails. Small, Medium and Large saddlery is fixed in place with 1in (25mm) round wire nails, with 1/2in (13) dome or daisy head nails driven in close alongside to conceal the wire nails.

Saddlecloths are fitted first. The back of the saddle cloth lines up with the back of the saddle block and the top edges will be concealed under the saddle top. Pull the saddlecloths as tight as you can over the contours of the horse before hammering home the nails. On Medium and Large horses the saddlecloths may have covered the stirrup staples, so with a sharp knife or scissors cut the saddle cloth material along the line of the stirrup staples, and nail the cut edges in behind the staples. If you have not yet hammered in the stirrup staples, this should be done now.

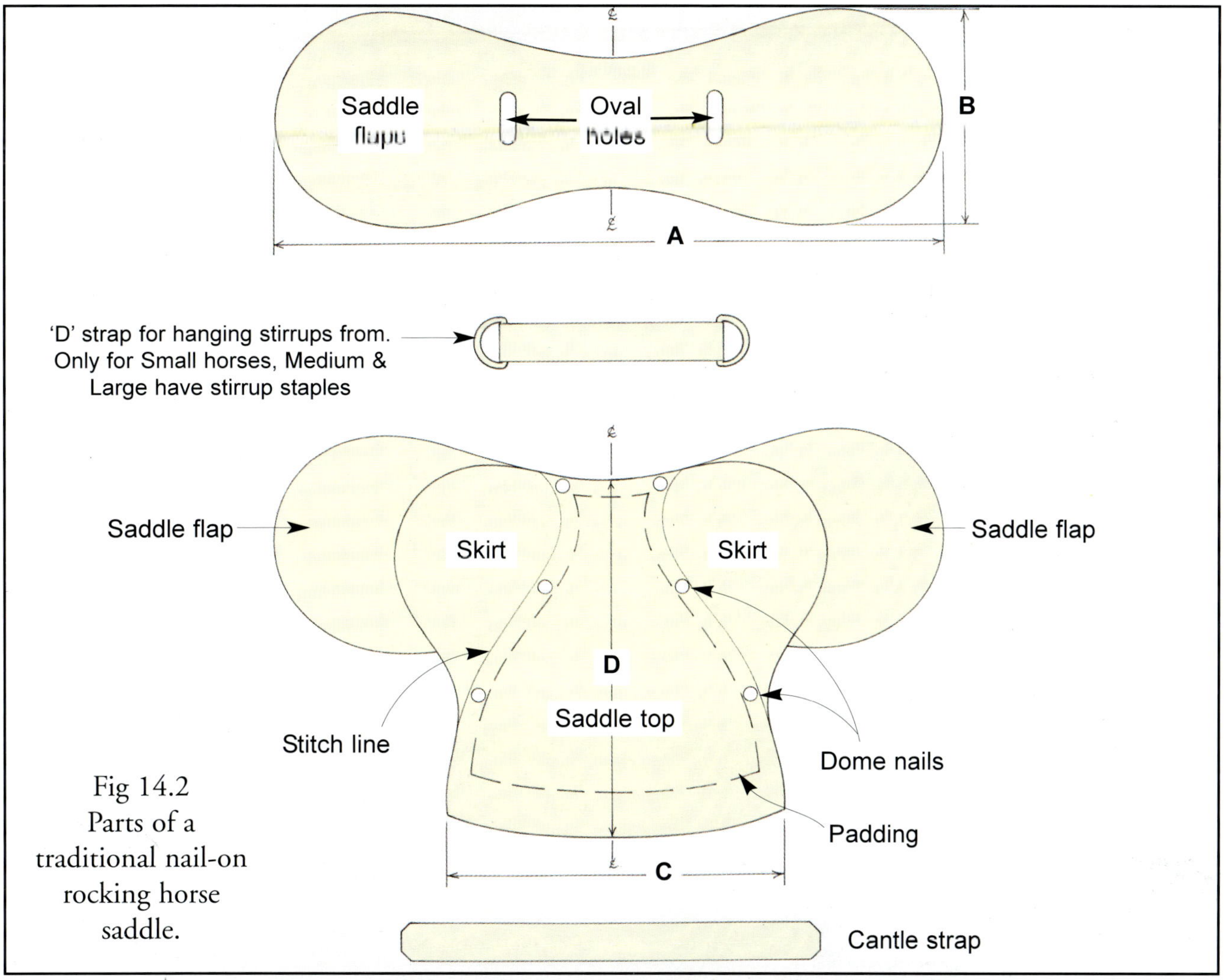

Fig 14.2
Parts of a traditional nail-on rocking horse saddle.

Next fit a dummy girth by taking a length of strapping right round the horse's body at the fattest part. Pull it tight and nail in place at the top middle. A nail underneath the belly at either side will hold the dummy girth firmly in place.

The saddle flaps are fixed in place with a couple of nails in the middle so that the flaps hang down either side. If you damp the leather before fitting you will be able to pull and stretch it so that it follows the contours of the horse. On Medium and Large horses the flaps have oval holes each side which should align with the stirrup staples. You can then thread the stirrup irons onto the leathers, which are made from 3/4in (19) wide strap, and lead them round the stirrup staples, taking the end in through the oval hole, up under the staple and back out through the oval hole to the buckle on the outside. The buckle can then be moved up to rest close to the stirrup staple and the skirts, when they are fitted, will cover them so that the young rider's legs do not rub against the buckle. Small horses have a D strap instead of stirrup staples: this

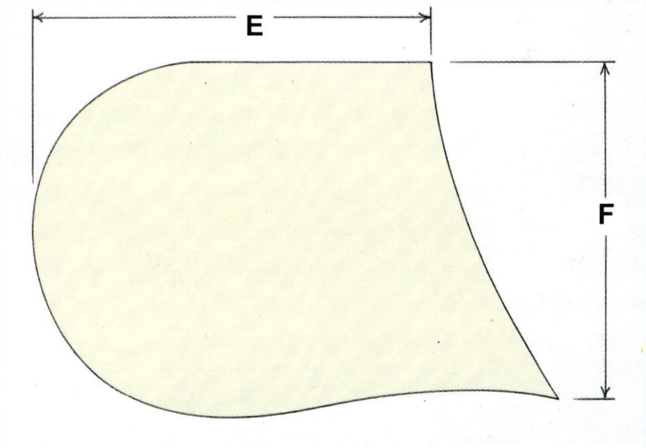

Fig 14.3 Saddle cloth, usually edged with fancy braid.

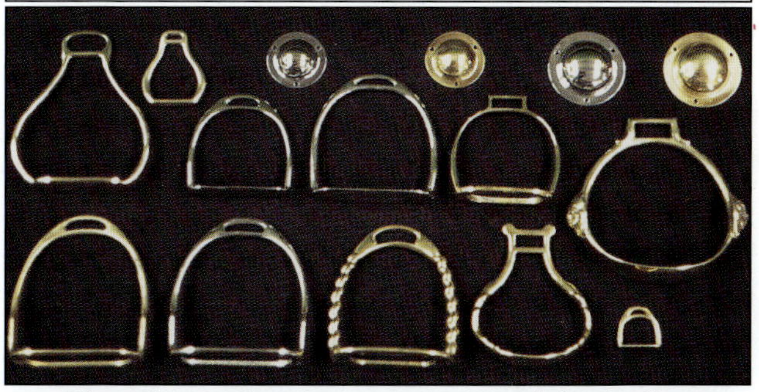

Plate14.5 Rocking horse stirrup irons & bowler hats. Metal fittings may be solid brass, nickel or chrome plated.

Plate 14.6 Nail flaps on over saddle cloths & dummy girth.

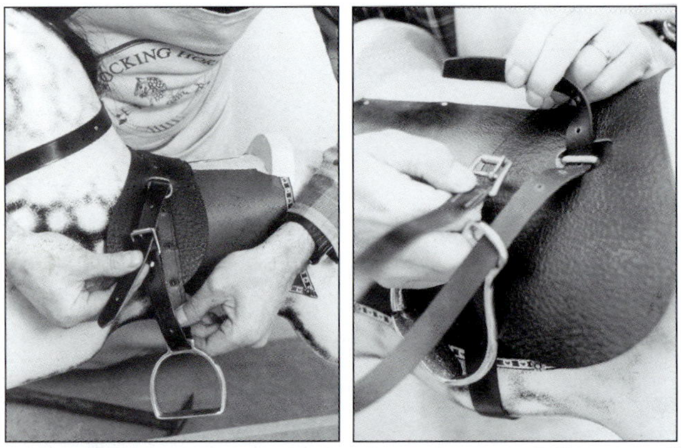

Plates 14.7 & 8 Stirrup leathers hang from Ds (left) on Small horses, stirrup staples (right) on Medium or Large.

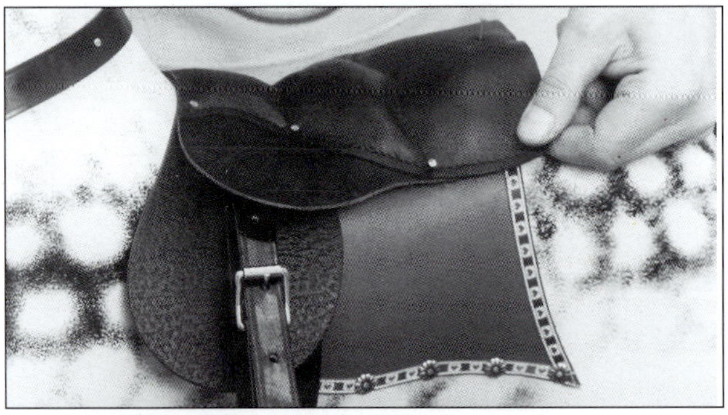

Plate14.9 Pull saddle top tight when nailing in place.

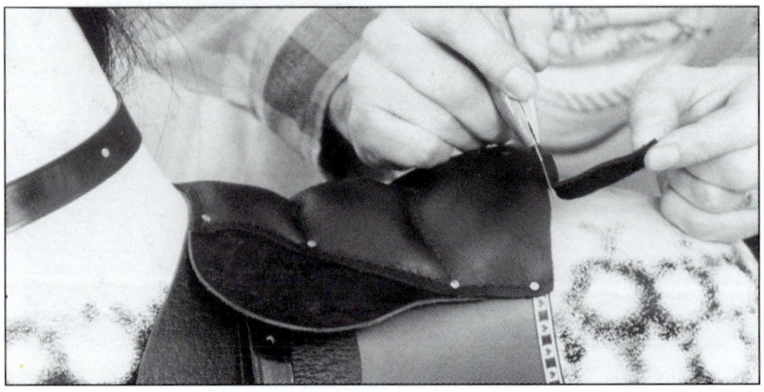

Plate14.10 Trimming off surplus to back of saddle block.

is a short length of strap with a metal D attached to each end. The D strap is nailed onto the horse's back with a D at either side from which the stirrup leathers hang. Half Size horses do not have adjustable stirrup leathers: a length of 1/4in (6) strap with brass stirrups rivetted to it is nailed on in the middle, over the flaps, so the stirrups hang each side.

Place the saddle top in position. Again damp the leather to make it more flexible, and with the front edge aligned with the front of the saddle flap and in the middle, tap in a nail at the stitched corner at each side. Press down firmly on the saddle top and carry on nailing it down along each side. Fixing nails should be evenly spaced at each side.

Adjust the padding, or remove some, so that the top fits back neatly over the top of the saddle block. Any saddle top leather which overhangs the saddle block at the back should be trimmed off with a sharp knife or scissors. The cantle is a length of 3/4in (19mm) wide leather strap, or 3/8in (10) wide for the Half Size horse, nailed over the saddle block from side to side, to hide any roughness and give a neat finish to the back of the saddle.

STRAP-ON SADDLES

Some saddles buckle on with a girth strap. They have a loose saddle blanket which is laid over the horse's back and the saddle is placed on it. The girth strap is taken right round the horse and buckles up tightly each side. Two screws driven through holes in the girth under the belly, leaving the heads proud, help to prevent the girth from slipping round when in use. Although it is an attractive idea to have a removable saddle I do not recommend them strongly since they can never be as secure as the nail-on type. The stirrup leathers on strap-on saddles hang from Ds located under the skirts, and so it is important not to let children put a lot of weight on one stirrup.

A superior version of the girth strap type saddle is sometimes fitted on Medium or Large rocking horses. These saddles are hand made round a wooden tree - the tree being the 'skeleton' of a saddle - just like a miniature real one. Two wooden pegs in the underside of the saddle are made to locate into two holes in the horse's back. The saddle therefore will not slip at all if the girth is

Plate14.11 Nail-on saddle, 'antique' red seat &saddle cloths.

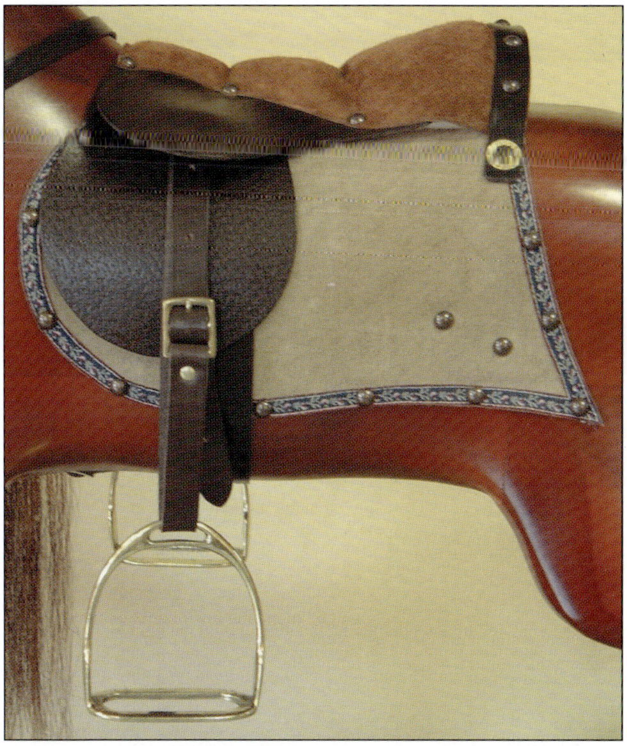

Plate14.12 Nail-on saddle with suede seat & saddlecloths

Plate14.13 Simple buckle-on saddle with girth.

Plate14.14 Saddle on tree,
removable, just like a miniature real one.

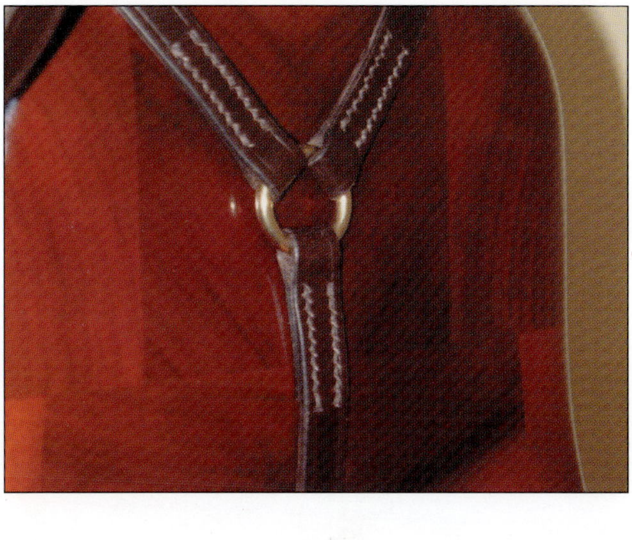

Plate 14.15 (left) Removable martingale,
hand stitched to solid brass ring at centre of chest.

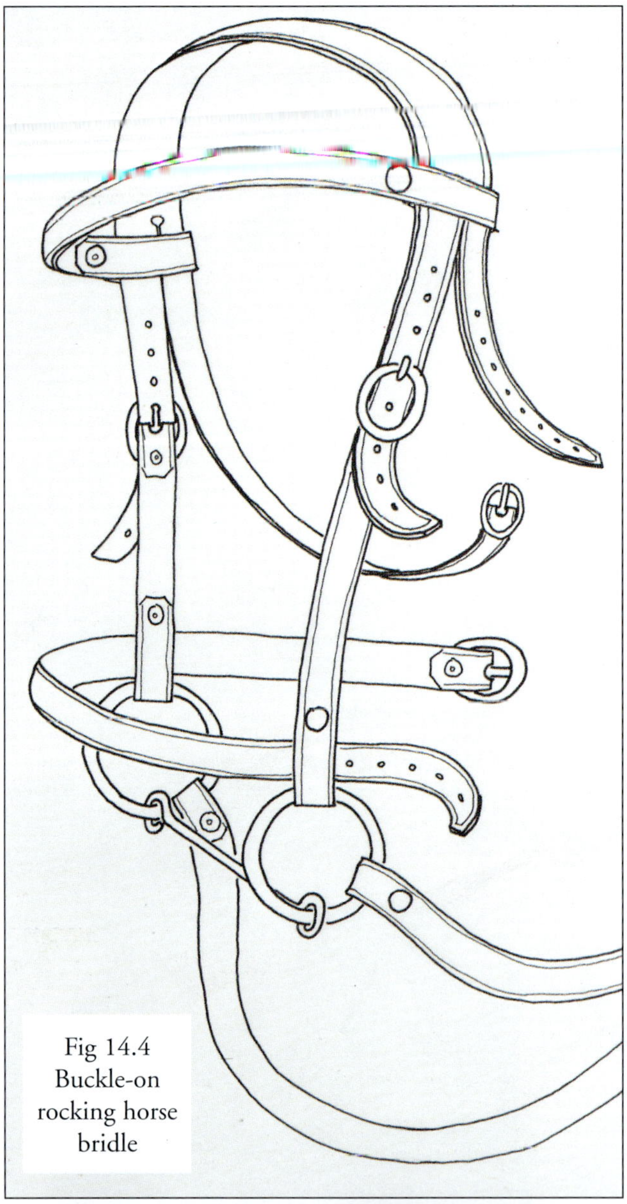

Fig 14.4 Buckle-on rocking horse bridle

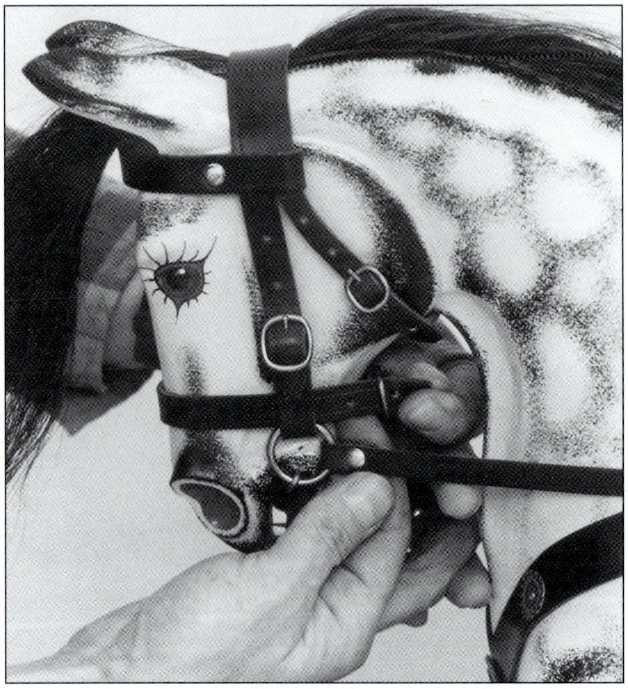

Plate14.16 Buckling bridle onto a Small horse

kept buckled tight, but the saddle can still be removed. Saddles on trees are usually placed over loose saddle blankets made from Melton or sheepskin, edged with coloured braid.

MARTINGALE AND CRUPPER

To form a simple and decorative martingale, a length of leather strapping is taken round the horse's neck and cut off so that the ends meet neatly at the centre of the chest. From this point a further length of strap is taken downward and nailed in just under the horse's belly, out of sight.

Dome nails and brass rosettes are spaced evenly to decorate the strap, and a ribbon rosette is nailed on at the centre of the chest where the straps converge. After the tail has been secured, take a short length of strap, wrap it round the base of the tail and nail together at the top. Another length of strap is nailed on so that it runs from the centre of the saddle block back to the top of the base of the tail. This crupper helps to give the tail a bit of lift, and hides any roughness there may be at the base of the tail.

A removable martingale, rivetted or hand stitched, may be fitted if you are having a removable saddle. This is a loop of leather strap which encircles the neck to a brass or nickel plated ring at the centre of the chest (see Plate 14.15). A further strap runs from the ring down to a smaller loop under the belly round the girth strap.

Leather tack can be kept supple and clean by occasional applications of saddle soap or leather oil.

BRIDLES

Half Size horses are fitted with simple nailed on bridles. The bit is made of brass wire and the reins are rivetted onto the bit rings. The bit is held in place in the mouth by the bridle strap which runs from the mouth right over the top of the head and down to the mouth at the other side, and is folded under and through the rings and nailed in each side. Where the strap goes over the top, just behind the base of the ears, it should conceal the join between the mane and forelock, which should be fixed on first (see mane fixing).The rest of the bridle is made up of short lengths of strapping

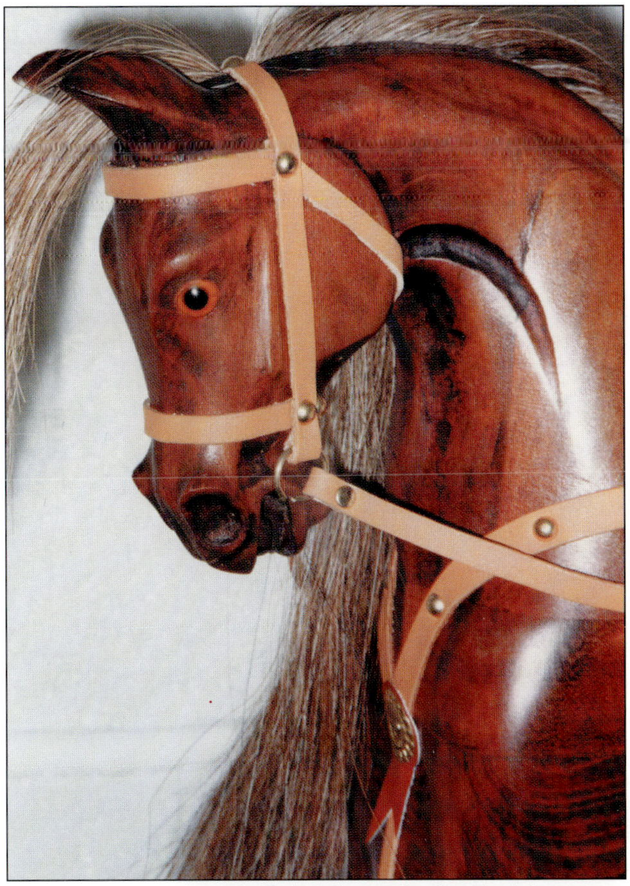

Plates 14.17 & 14.18 Half Size horse bridles are nailed on. Dark brown leather (left) & light tan leather (right)

nailed in position with 1/4in (6) brass dome nails. Damp the leather strap to persuade it to conform to the curves of the head.

Small, Medium and Large horses are usually fitted with bridles made to simply buckle on, and are available with reins attached, with solid brass or nickel plated buckles and bit rings. They are rivetted together, or may be hand stitched. There is a fair amount of adjustment on the buckles and straps to take account of variations in your carved head. In fact it is useful to have the bridle to hand while you are carving the head since if the bridle will not fit it is a good indication that you need to carve more away!

MANES AND TAILS

Half Size horses are usually fitted with real horsehair on hide, because it is easy to fit. The mane is cut from a piece of hide with the hair on, about 1/2in (13) wide and 41/4 to 5in (114 -127) long, nailed (with gimp pins) onto the horse's neck. A small piece of hide, about ½in (13) long, is cut to be fixed at the leading end of the mane so this hair falls forward between the ears to form a forelock. If the hair tends to stick up all over the

Plate14.19 Medium size horse with hand stitched bridle & martingale, real horsehair mane & forelock.

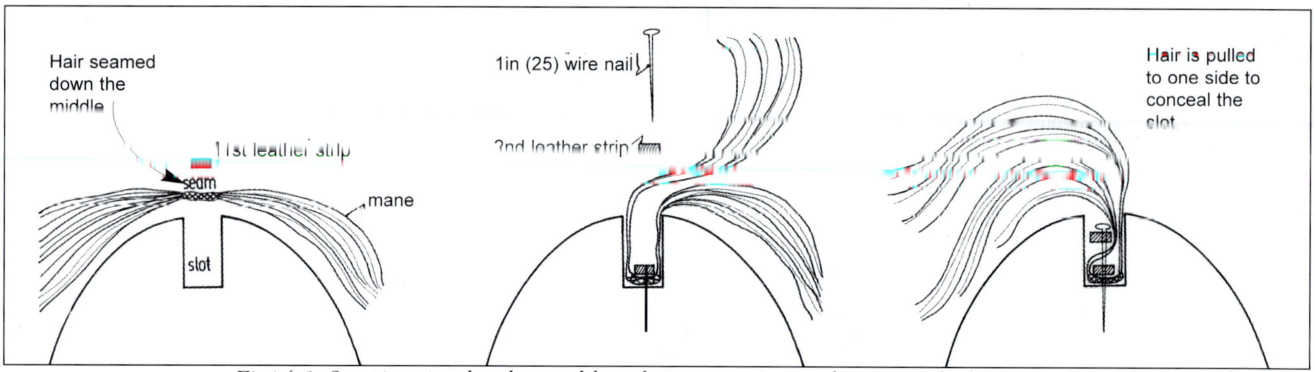

Fig14.5 Securing simulated or real horsehair manes into a slot cut in the horse's neck.

Plate14.20 Fitting seamed mane: inserting 1st leather strip.

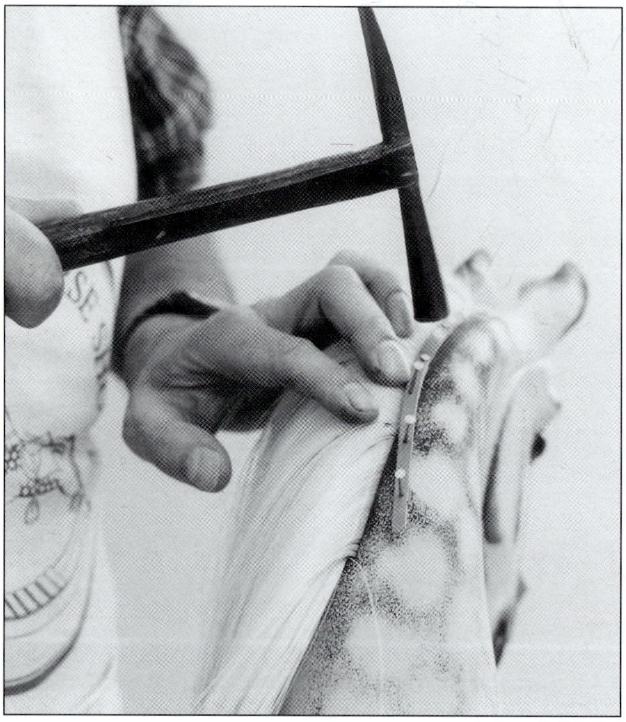

Plate14.21 Fitting seamed mane: nailing in 2nd leather strip.

place, it can be damped and tied down to persuade it to lie and hang correctly, and can then be trimmed to a suitable length.

Hair for Small, Medium and Large horses may be either simulated or real horsehair and the usual seamed type consists of long hair glued and stitched onto a cotton tape. Push the seam of the mane into the slot cut in the horse's neck, using a blunt screwdriver, insert a thin leather strip and nail in place. Three or four nails are sufficient at this stage. Pull the hair to the left and insert a second thin leather strip, nailing it in at about 1in (25) intervals. The mane hair finishes up under the first leather strip and up one side of the second strip, all firmly secured in place with lin (25) round wire nails tapped in with nail punch at about 1in (25) intervals. The hair is then allowed to fall to the right so that it conceals the fixing.

Persuading the hair to go tightly and neatly into the slot can be a bit of an awkward operation, but it is obviously important to fix the mane securely since children will tug at it. A small bunch of the

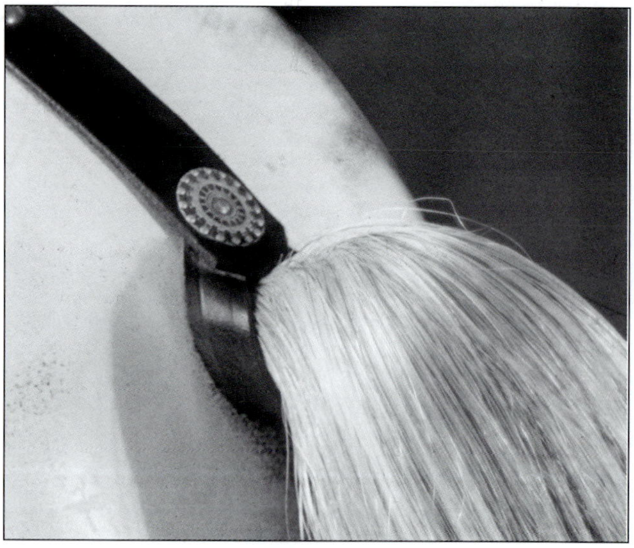

Plate14.22

mane hair is taken forward between the ears to form the forelock.

There is a tendency for the hair to stick up at odd angles. Simulated hair can be persuaded to lie down by blowing warm air over it (not too hot or it will melt) with a hair drier. Horsehair is made to lie down by damping it or rubbing in fabric conditioner and tying it down in position with some strips of cloth or a bandage and leaving overnight.

Real horsehair manes on the hide are sometimes used on new horses and are easier to fit since they do not require a slot in the neck. The hide is usually about an inch (25) or so wide for the mane and is simply nailed onto the neck with 1in (25) wire nails, after damping it to make more pliable. The heads of the nails are tapped into the hide with a nail punch and disappear. Sometimes a shallow rebate, about 1/8in (3) deep is cut just left of centre of the neck, for the edge of the hide to butt up against, concealing it. The top strap of the bridle hides the join between mane and forelock. Good quality manes on hide are always in short supply (who wants the job?), especially the popular greys, and they are usually reserved for the authentic restoration of old rocking horses. There are some other types of mane with different methods of fixing them.

Tails, real horsehair or simulated, are simply fixed by squeezing some glue into the tail hole, inserting the tail and tapping in a small wooden wedge underneath. Finally, the hair can be combed out, trimmed and layered as desired. There will be some hair loss at first but this should soon settle down. Manes and tails should be combed out regularly, particularly simulated hair which has a tendency to get tangled and matted.

Once the horse has been all tacked up to your satisfaction, remove it from the temporary hoof rails and lift onto the stand. Drill the hoof bolt holes on through the hoof rails (or rockers) and insert the bolts. Use 1/4in (6) diameter cup square carriage bolts for Medium and Large horses, 3/16in (5) for Small, and 3/4in (19) woodscrews for the Half Size. Tighten up the nuts and, at last, he (or she if you prefer) is ready to ride!

Plate14.23 Small horse with buckle-on bridle, nail-on saddle, real horsehair mane & tail.

Plate 15.1 A finished horse with thoroughbred head

CHAPTER 15

ALTERNATIVES AND ENHANCEMENTS

There is no perfect rocking horse and there is no end to the scope for varying and enhancing the basic designs. When you have made one or two rocking horses you may like to try some variations and modifications. This chapter aims to give you some ideas to develop - in fact this whole book is only intended to get you started - there are infinite possibilities!

THOROUGHBRED HEADS

I sometimes spot a particularly interesting feature or characteristic on an old rocking horse that comes in for repair or restoration and decide to adapt it and incorporate it into one of my own designs. These thoroughbred heads are based on heads made by a Victorian carver whose work has cropped up occasionally but who remains anonymous. I found the elegantly elongated nose and lift of the head, enhanced by an exaggerated tilt of the head to one side, particularly appealing.

Plate 15.2 Large horse on stand with Thoroughbred head. Stained and lacquered finish with removable saddlery.

A bevel is planed off the head and it is jointed (with dowels) to the neck at an angle in the same manner as for the Medium and Large heads described in Chapter 10. The head carving also proceeds in similar fashion, the head being merely elongated. When we make these thoroughbred horses we work harder to bring out the detailed features of the head and muscling to the neck, as

CUTTING LIST for Thoroughbred heads

	Thickness x width x length	*Thickness x width x length*
	Inches	**Millimetres**
Medium		
Head	2¾ x 7½ x 12½	70 x 190 x 318
Neck	2¾ x 9¾ x 16½	70 x 248 x 419
Eye & ear pieces (both)	½ x 4 x 11	13 x 102 x 279
1st & 2nd neck muscle blocks (all)	1¾ x 8½ x 42	45 x 216 x 1066
Large		
Head	2¾ x 8¾ x 15	70 x 222 x 381
Neck	2¾ x 12¼ x 21	70 x 311 x 533
Eye & ear pieces (both)	½ x 4¼ x 13	13 x 108 x 330
1st & 2nd neck muscle blocks (all)	1¾ x 10¾ x 48	45 x 273 x 1220

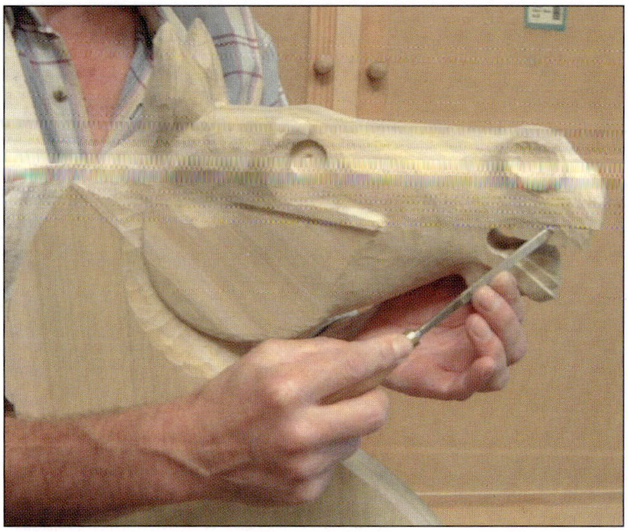

Plate 15.3 Carving teeth on a Thoroughbred head.

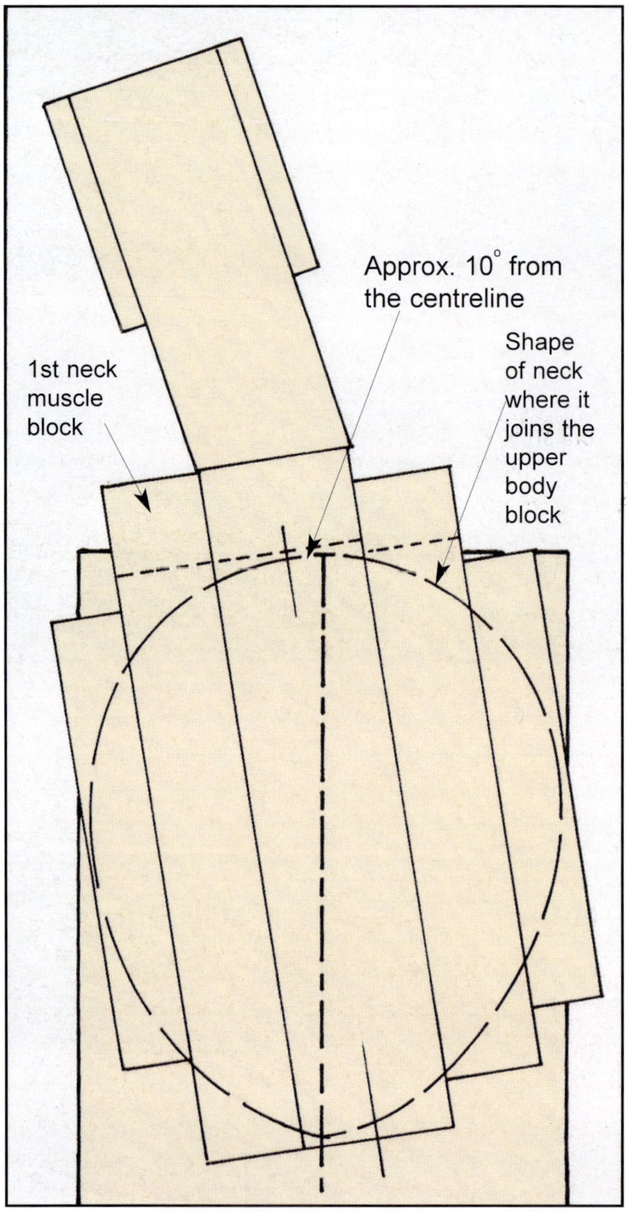

Fig 15.1 The exaggerated angling of the head to the left, with the larger 1st neck muscle block placed on the left. The carving ensures that the base of the neck finishes on the centreline.

you will see from a careful examination of the accompanying pictures, and you may also wish to try to enhance and refine the features.

LOOK MORE TO THE LEFT

The angling of the head to one side can be amplified to good effect by making one of the first neck muscle blocks the same size as the neck, so that when you come to fitting them, the neck can be angled off to one side much further than for the Medium or Large horses in Chapter 10. If the head is made to angle to the left, the larger of the neck muscle blocks is placed on the left. Of course you can angle the head to the right if you prefer.

The second neck muscle blocks are the same size each side. Remember when carving the neck that in spite of the angling of the head to one side the base of the neck should be in the middle, in order for the saddle to sit centrally. The rest of the body, and the legs are made and carved as for the corresponding size of horse, Medium or Large, in Chapter 10.

TENONED LEGS/ ALTERNATIVE BODIES

Those who have had an opportunity to examine many old rocking horses, as I have, will have noticed that a great variety of construction methods have been employed. On many of the quality horses of old the legs were tenoned into mortises chopped into the body. Of course due allowance must be made for the angling of the legs into the body. Some may be tempted to try this method because it may seem to be more like

Plate 15.3 This version of the "thoroughbred " head horse is mounted on clear varnished ash bow rockers

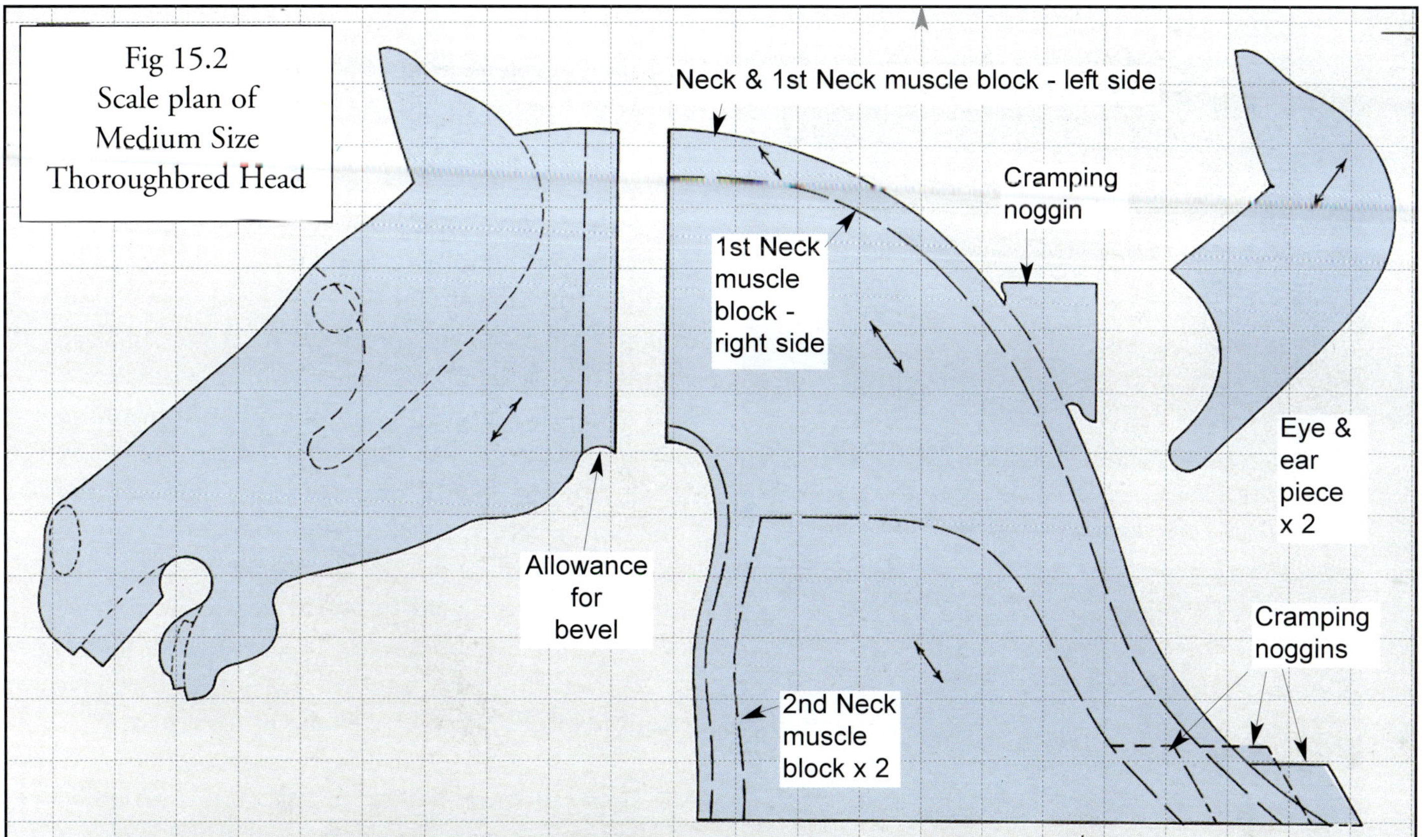

Fig 15.2
Scale plan of
Medium Size
Thoroughbred Head

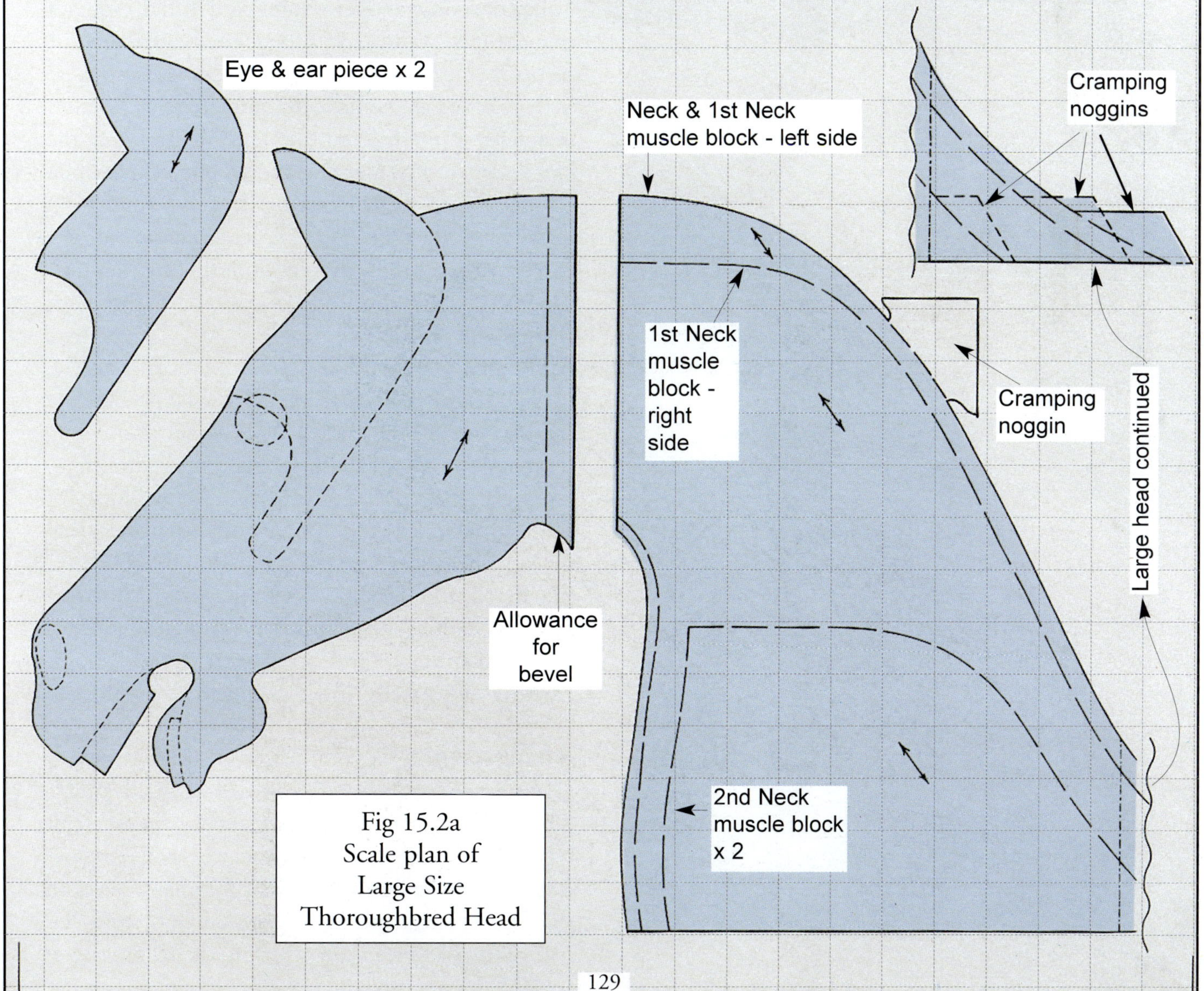

Fig 15.2a
Scale plan of
Large Size
Thoroughbred Head

Plate 15.4 A laminated horse glued up ready to start on the shaping, which involves carving away all the steps.

Plate 15.5 All the carving has been done on one side of this laminated horse. You can see how the steps are carved away to leave smooth curves and contours.

'proper' joinery than the simple butt joints described for all the horses in this book, excepting the carousel style horse in Chapter 16.

On the other hand butt joints do have the advantage of simplicity, and are very strong. I was once in the unusual position of wanting to break up one of my own horses, its head having been smashed in a warehouse when someone dropped a crate on it. I didn't repair the poor thing right away and grew to dislike its broken reproach intensely. So I had it on its side on the floor and was jumping up and down on the legs, trying to break them off, and I couldn't. I am willing to bet that any horse with tenoned legs would have quickly broken under such an assault, and in fact it is frequently the tenoned leg joints that give trouble in old horses that come in for repair.

Studying different makers reveals quite a variety of different body shapes. Some are much squarer than others, some have exaggerated slopes to the rump, some have extra carved elements. Just as with real horses, no two are quite alike. Different makers also use different methods of arranging the blocks when constructing the wooden box which is the basis of all rocking horse bodies, but different body shapes are more a function of the carver's artistry than the method of construction.

LAMINATED HORSES

Laminated plywood has been employed by several manufacturers as well as amateur makers since the 1960s, as a method of construction. The technique involves quite a different approach to assembly and carving from traditional blocks of solid timber, lending itself more to power tool carving with electric angle grinders and Arbortech, the Black and Decker Powerfile, drum and pad sanders. When carved, the ply laminations reveal a very distinctive and striking pattern. People's reaction is generally either to love it or hate it.

Birch ply tends be the better quality - cheaper grades can have unsightly voids - and an advantage of this method of constuction is that the end result will be extremely sturdy. Rocking horse maker Judy Fergusson has specialised for many years in the laminated method of construction, and has had particular success in teaching the technique to

Plate 15.6 A finished Medium Size laminated rocking horse, tack is fitted in the same way as described in Chapter 14.

Plate 15.7 Judy Fergusson at work with a Powerfile.

those who have never carved before (and, perhaps partly because she is one herself, to women). The carving is quite straighforward. As the steps are removed, the carver has a constant guide as the thin laminations are cut into and the patterns of the contours are revealed. Judy is responsible for the laminated horse designs shown here, and although it has not been practicable to include scale plans for laminated rocking horses in this book, actual size plan drawings for patterns are available, with step-by-step instructions and photographs, see Appendix.

TIME CAPSULES

It is an appealing idea to include a little history with your horse, and some makers insert messages for posterity inside the hollow body. Of course these items are unlikely ever to be discovered unless the horse falls apart which, as maker, you probably anticipate will never happen. Also, if you put things inside which move and rattle about (such as marbles), while these may amuse some riders they could well drive others to distraction.

As well as information about the making of the horse, time capsules can contain family photographs and any other items that might be of interest to future generations. We were once able to include photographs of a great-grandmother, a grandmother, a mother, a daughter, a granddaughter, and a great-granddaughter, all of the same family. The earliest of the photographs dated from about 1905, and the same faithful old rocking horse appeared in each picture. In that case the photographs, together with some family letters concerning the horse, were enclosed in a polythene bag which was secured to the underside of the stand beneath a thin piece of plywood screwed on. In that way the archive was out of the way but safe and easily accessible when the horse was tipped to one side. Another good hiding place is underneath a nailed on saddle, where it won't be found until some decades down the line when the horse requires restoration.

Some makers have fitted little trap doors, discretely hidden under the belly, which can be removed to allow small items to be put inside. One maker constructed a sliding drawer the full size of the hollow body cavity. The drawer slides out from the back and because it is under the tail it is not obvious to the casual observer. When the drawer is pushed fully closed a dowel peg on the front underside of the drawer drops into a hole bored right through from under the horse's belly, so the drawer remains shut when the horse is rocked. The front end of the drawer is also held down by a small coil spring. To open the drawer a finger is inserted into the hole under the belly to push up against the dowel peg, releasing the drawer which the spring pushes out a little so that it can be withdrawn: a sizeable compartment which can contain many treasures. Ingenious idea.

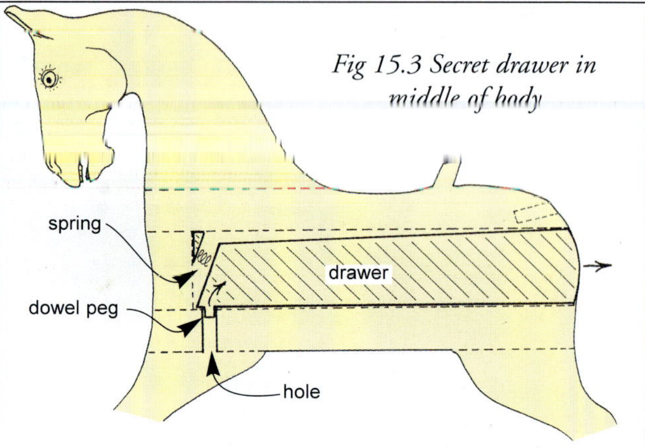

Fig 15.3 Secret drawer in middle of body

OTHER VARIATIONS

I was once asked to make a rocking unicorn for which I devised a soft moulded rubber horn, thinking that a pointed wooden one could be quite a lethal weapon when the horse was rocked.

Also closely related to the horse, the zebra makes an interesting variation, with its distinctive paint pattern and black and white mane and tail. Our version of the zebra is pictured below.

Other makers have produced rocking sheep, cows, goats, dogs, elephants and giraffes, even rocking motorbikes. You name it, someone has probably tried to make it rock.

Plate 15.9 Rocking zebra..

Plate 15.10 Laminated horses. A Medium Size version on a swing iron stand, for children up to about 7 or 8 years or so, and Half Size versions, one on bow rockers and one on a swing iron stand, for dolls to ride.

Plate 15.11 A three seater. Based on a Victorian original, this is a very large horse, but the seats are similar to those used for the little Chair Horse in Chapter 3.

Plate 16.1 The finished carousel from the front...

Plate 16.2 ...and the back.

Plate 16.3 A completed Carousel stylel horse, mounted on bow rockers.

Plate 15.10 Laminated horses. A Medium Size version on a swing iron stand, for children up to about 7 or 8 years or so, and Half Size versions, one on bow rockers and one on a swing iron stand, for dolls to ride.

Plate 15.11 A three seater. Based on a Victorian original, this is a very large horse, but the seats are similar to those used for the little Chair Horse in Chapter 3.

Plate 16.1 The finished carousel from the front...

Plate 16.2 ...and the back.

Plate 16.3 A completed Carousel stylel horse, mounted on bow rockers.

CHAPTER 16

CAROUSEL STYLE
HORSE

This design is based on a style of horse common on small English merry-go-rounds in the early part of the Twentieth Century. The legs are tenoned into the lower body, but overall the body construction has been kept quite straightforward, the head and legs being straight, not turned or splayed, in order to make the carving of the detail, on which the success of the project depends, relatively unproblematic. Nevertheless, this is a more ambitious wood carving project than a rocking horse, and it is presented as an interesting challenge.

Unlike rocking horses, the carousel or merry-go-round style of horse traditionally has the bridle and saddlery, mane and forelock all carved on the horse. Sometimes the tail as well would be carved wood, but more usually it was horse hair. The construction is broadly similar to making a small rocking horse, consisting of blocks of timber bandsawn to shape and glued and pegged together, due allowance being made for the carving of the extra, superficial details of saddlery and mane. The head and legs are cut from thicker timber than for a rocking horse, giving greater scope for shaping these parts, and rendering eye and ear pieces and leg muscle blocks unnecessary.

Before starting, refer back to Chapter 1 since much of the information on tools and timber etc applies to this project. Choose a good carving timber such as tulipwood, basswood or lime. If you are intending mounting the horse on bow rockers, you should leave extra noggins on each hoof, as shown in Fig 16.4, which will aid you in securing the hooves to the cross pieces.

PREPARATION

Mark the patterns out on the timber for the head and neck, neck muscle blocks, and legs, making sure that the direction of grain conforms approximately with the arrows on the drawing. Note where cramping flats or noggins are to be left on the timber before bandsawing out the shapes, and that the legs have tenons attached to them. These are bare faced tenons and are to be set into mortices chopped in the underside of the lower body block. Mortices and tenons are $^3/_4$in (19) thick and $1^1/_4$in (32) deep, 3in (76) long for the front legs, $3^1/_2$in (89) long for the rear legs, in the positions shown on the plan.

Before starting the assembly, drill a $^3/_4$in (19) hole for the supporting pole through both upper and lower body blocks. This hole is 7in (178) from the front of the lower body block, but note that the upper body block is set back by $^3/_{16}$in (5) so the hole is $6^{13}/_{16}$in (173) from the front of the upper body block. After the neck has been fixed on extend this pole hole up through to the top.

CUTTING LIST	*Thickness x width x length*	*Thickness x width x length*
	Inches	**Millimetres**
Head and neck	$2^3/_4$ x 8 x 14	70 x 203 x 356
Neck muscle blocks (1st and 2nd)	$^3/_4$ x $7^3/_4$ x 18	19 x 197 x 457
Upper Body Block	$1^3/_4$ x $5^3/_4$ x $19^3/_4$	45 x 146 x 502
Lower Body Block	$1^3/_4$ x $5^3/_4$ x 20	45 x 146 x 508
Mid Body Blocks (sides) (x 2)	$1^3/_4$ x $3^1/_4$ x 20	45 x 83 x 508
Mid Body Blocks (ends) (x 2)	$1^3/_4$ x $3^1/_4$ x $2^3/_8$	45 x 83 x 60
Back of saddle	$1^3/_4$ x $4^1/_4$ x 5	45 x 108 x 127
Legs (all four)	$1^3/_8$ x $7^3/_4$ x 44	35 x 197 x 1118

Plate 16.4 Fitting leg tenon into mortice in the underside of the lower body block.

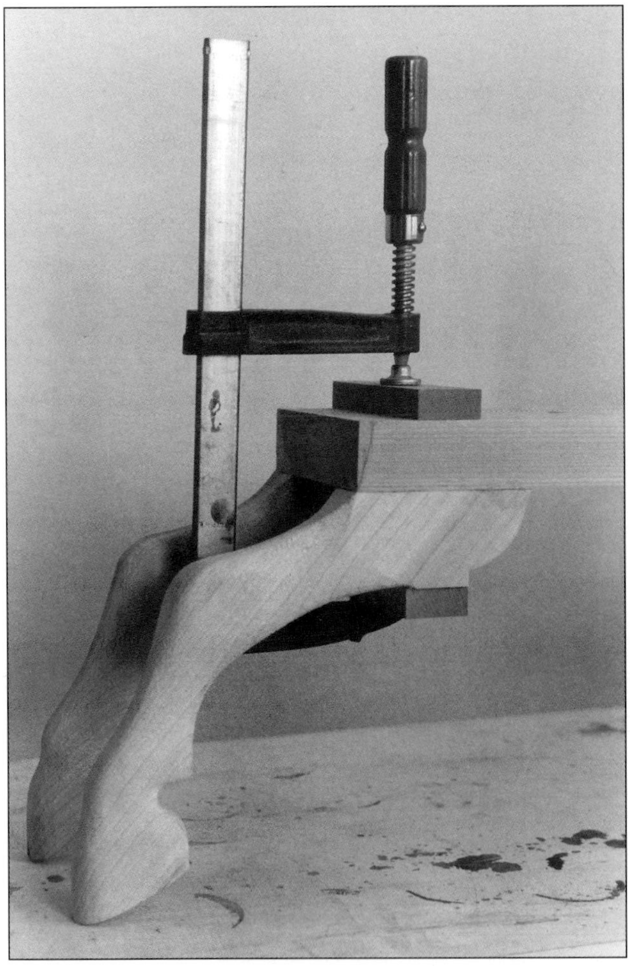

Plate 16.5 Cramping legs to the lower body block.

HOW TO MAKE IT

As with rocking horse making you can do some of the rough carving and shaping of the head and legs prior to assembly, or if you prefer you can do all the assembly and then start to carve. Make sure your leg tenons are a good tight fit into their mortices and glue and cramp them in. Then glue on the middle body blocks, using three fluted dowel pegs along each side, towards the inside edges of the blocks. The neck is glued down centrally onto the upper body block using three fluted dowel pegs and the first and then second neck muscle blocks are glued on at either side.

You will see that the first neck muscle block for the left side is bigger than the other one because the mane will be carved on the left side of the neck. The reason for this is merely an acknowledgement of the tradition: English merry-go-rounds go clockwise and therefore the mane (and the fancier carving) were done on the left side of the horse which was the side on show. On European and American Carousels, which go anti-clockwise the right hand side was more highly decorated. Since the horse we are making here is intended as a decorative artifact, not necessarily to be actually used on a merry-go-round, you can put the mane

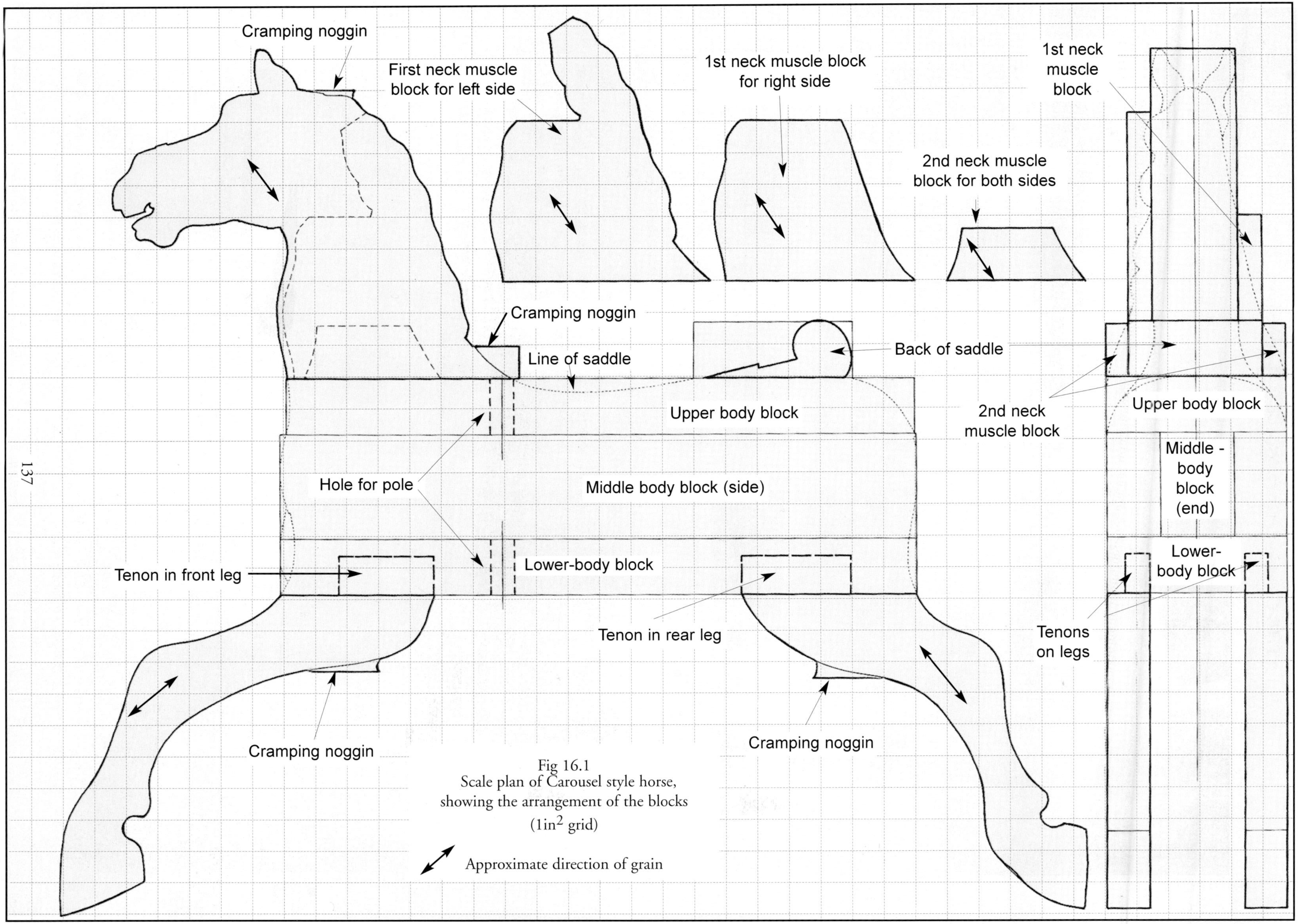

Fig 16.1
Scale plan of Carousel style horse, showing the arrangement of the blocks ($1in^2$ grid)

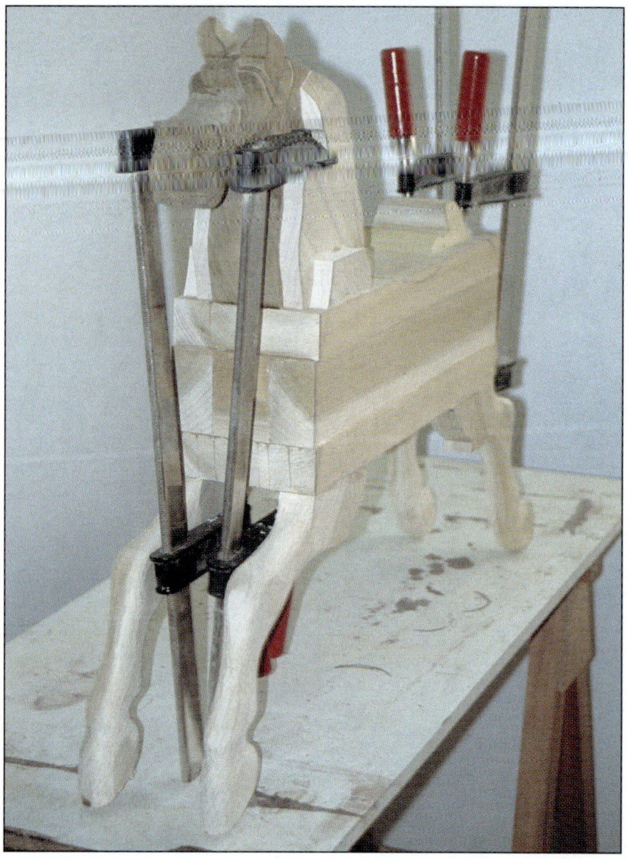

Plate 16.6 Showing how flats on the first neck muscle block aid cramping.

Plate 16.7 The right hand side of the neck - a little carving has already been started on the head.

whichever side you prefer, according to your inclination or nationality.

Glue on the block for the back of the saddle. Plane the tops of the middle body blocks flat, drill for four dowel pegs and glue down the upper body block. That is all there is to the assembly. Pencil in the curve of the saddle and rump, and the outline of the scroll shape at the back of the saddle. With the horse on its side you may be able to bandsaw off the waste along these pencil lines. But if your bandsaw has insufficient depth of cut, the waste will have to be chopped away with a large gouge and mallet. You will then have a profile which looks right in silhouette, but there are lots of corners to remove; the carving can commence.

CARVING

Carve off the corners of the neck muscle blocks so that the neck tapers up from the shoulders, which are rounded over, but leave the mane proud. Turn upside down and shape the lower bulge of the chest between the front legs and the valley between the rear legs, and round and shape the legs, making the legs thinner above and below the knees. Round over the corners of the lower body block. Turn it upright again and round over the saddle and the rump. The back of the saddle is shaped so that it curves smoothly into the back at each side. Pencil in the shapes of the ears - the waste between the ears can be cut away with a coping saw - and taper the head so that at the mouth it is no more than about 2 in (51) wide, but leave the nostrils and the forelock proud.

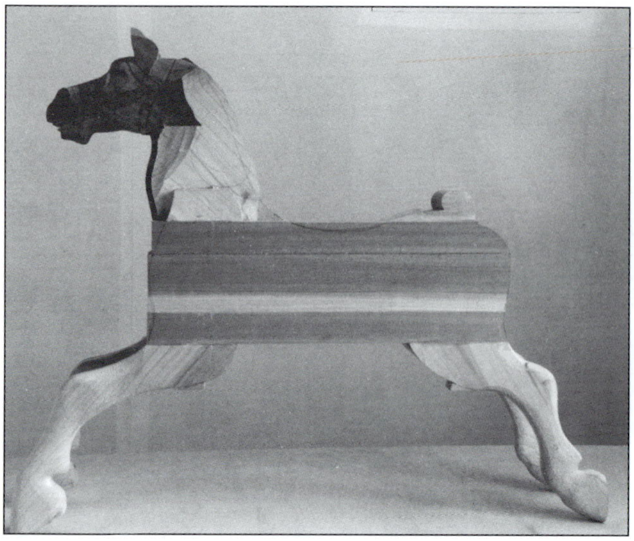

Plate 16.8 With all the blocks assembled the curve of the rump and seat can be bandsawn (or carved) away.

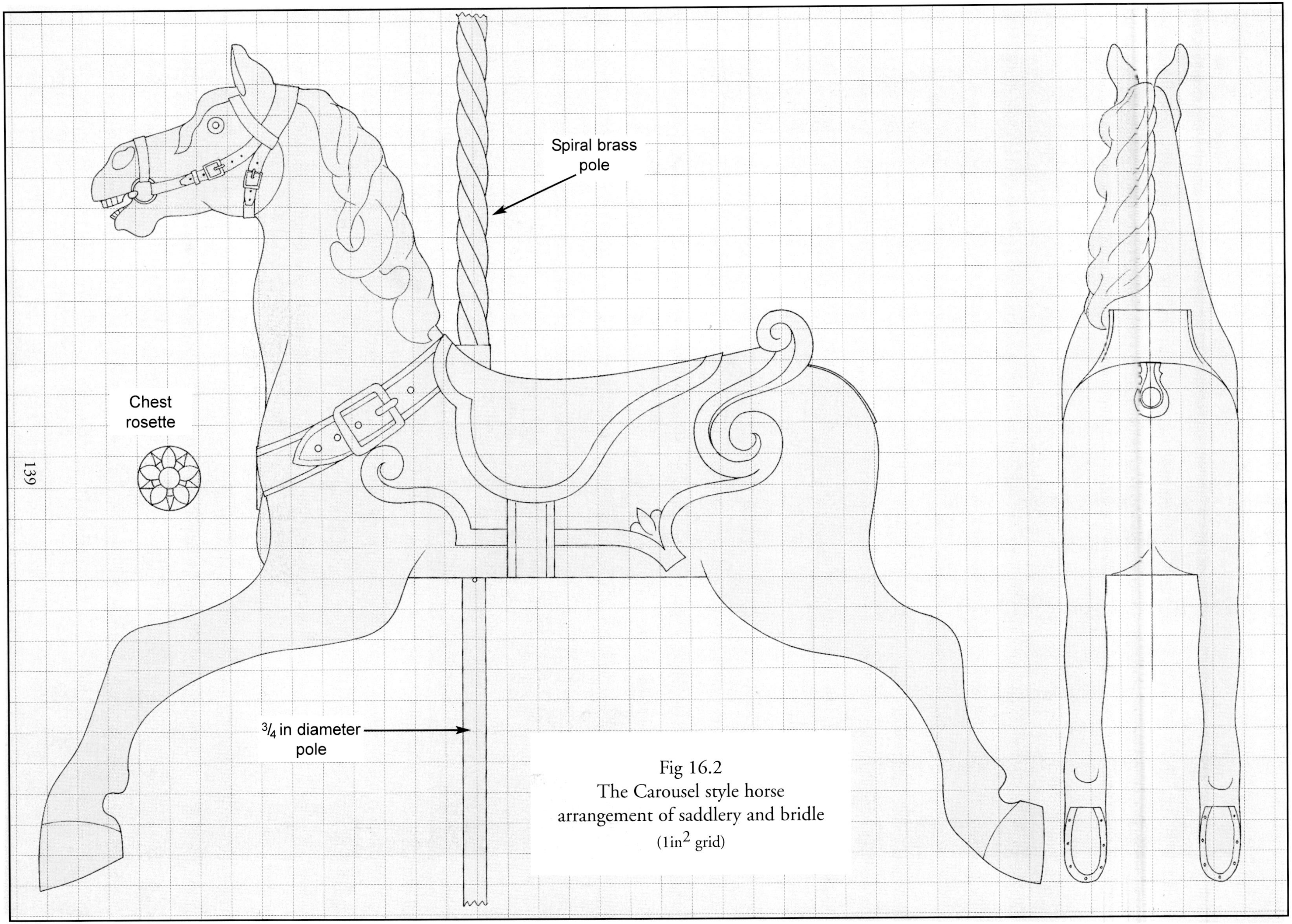

Fig 16.2
The Carousel style horse
arrangement of saddlery and bridle
(1in^2 grid)

Plate 16.9 The body has been rounded so you can make pencil guide marks for the saddlery & start cutting in.

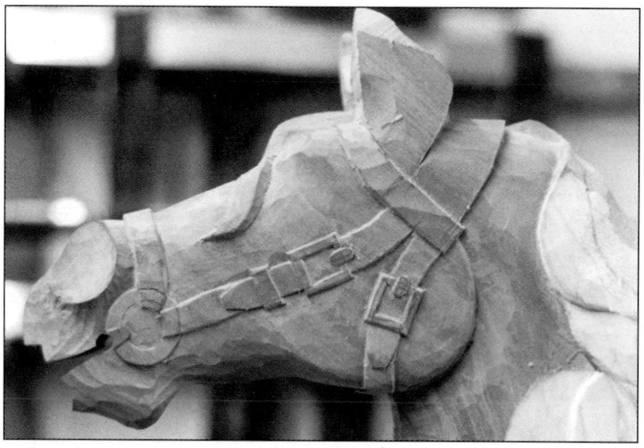

Plate 16.10 Try to ensure that the buckles stand proud of the straps, and the straps stand proud of the surrounding areas..

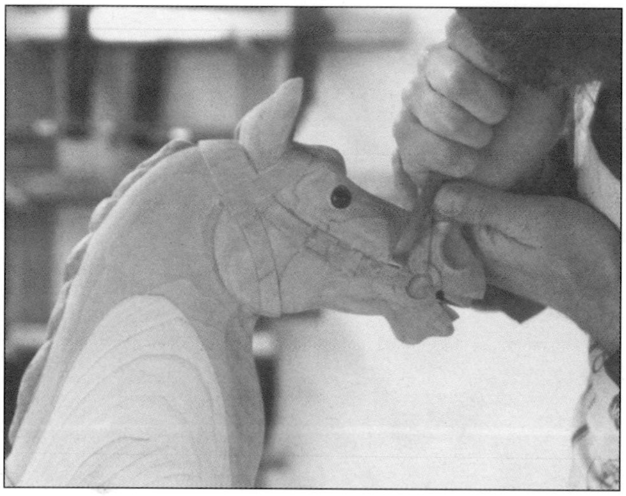

Plate 16.11 Picking out the bridle detail with a straight chisel.

Once you have removed the corners and the shape begins to look more rounded and horse-like, pencil in some guidelines for the saddlery, martingale and bridle, including the buckles. You can then cut along these lines with a straight chisel and carve back the wood on the waste side with a shallow gouge. The 'leatherwork' needs to stand proud of the rest of the horse by $^{1}/_{16}$ to $^{1}/_{8}$in (2-3), and rather more where two or three pieces of 'strap' overlap or cross. By the time you've finished the tack should give every appearance of being put onto the horse, not carved into it. Careful and steady carving is needed to achieve the desired result. In the middle of the chest carve a fancy round rosette, 2in (51) in diameter.

In addition to the six carving gouges listed in Chapter 1, I found I needed three more - a No. 10 - $^{1}/_{16}$in (1.5) and a No. 9 - $^{1}/_{8}$in (3) small deep straight London pattern gouges, and a straight $^{1}/_{4}$in (6) 'V' tool. The small gouges are useful for picking out fine details in the carving and for making the buckle holes and horse shoe nails, and the 'V' tool is used to make incised cuts along pencil guide lines such as the scroll at the back of the saddle, and for the hair. The mane and forelock are shaped to suggest a pleasing flow of hair, curling and interweaving, and the 'V' tool-made cuts following the flow of the hair.

It is intended that the drawings showing the saddlery design on this horse, and the way the mane and forelock are made to curl and wave, should be used as a guide only. You may like to refer to some of the many books dealing specifically with carousel style horses for ideas on how these features, and indeed the overall shape and configuration of the horse can be varied and enhanced. I have tried to keep this design as simple and straightforward as possible to make, whilst retaining the essential features of the carousel-style horse and remaining a fascinating woodworking project. The possibilities for variation are, as always, endless.

The tail hole is 3/4in (19) diameter - note the bit of decorative carving around it, and is drilled right through to the hollow middle. The eyes are 5/8in (16) glass, set into recesses with wood filler. The ears and nostrils are hollowed out a little and the teeth defined with V shaped cuts. It is important

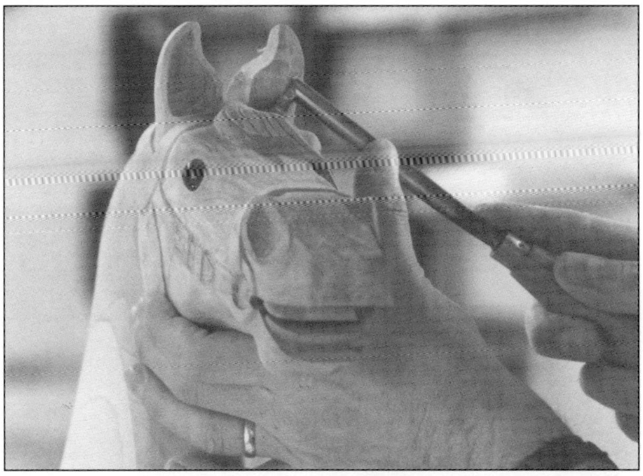

Plate 16.12 Hollowing the ears with glass eyes now in place.

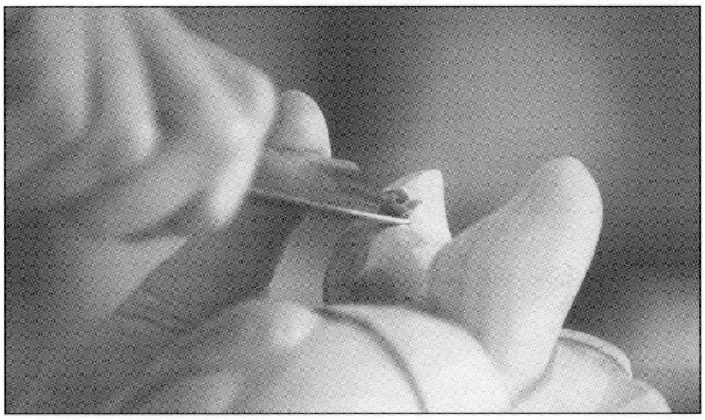

Plate 16.13 Detail of ear carving.

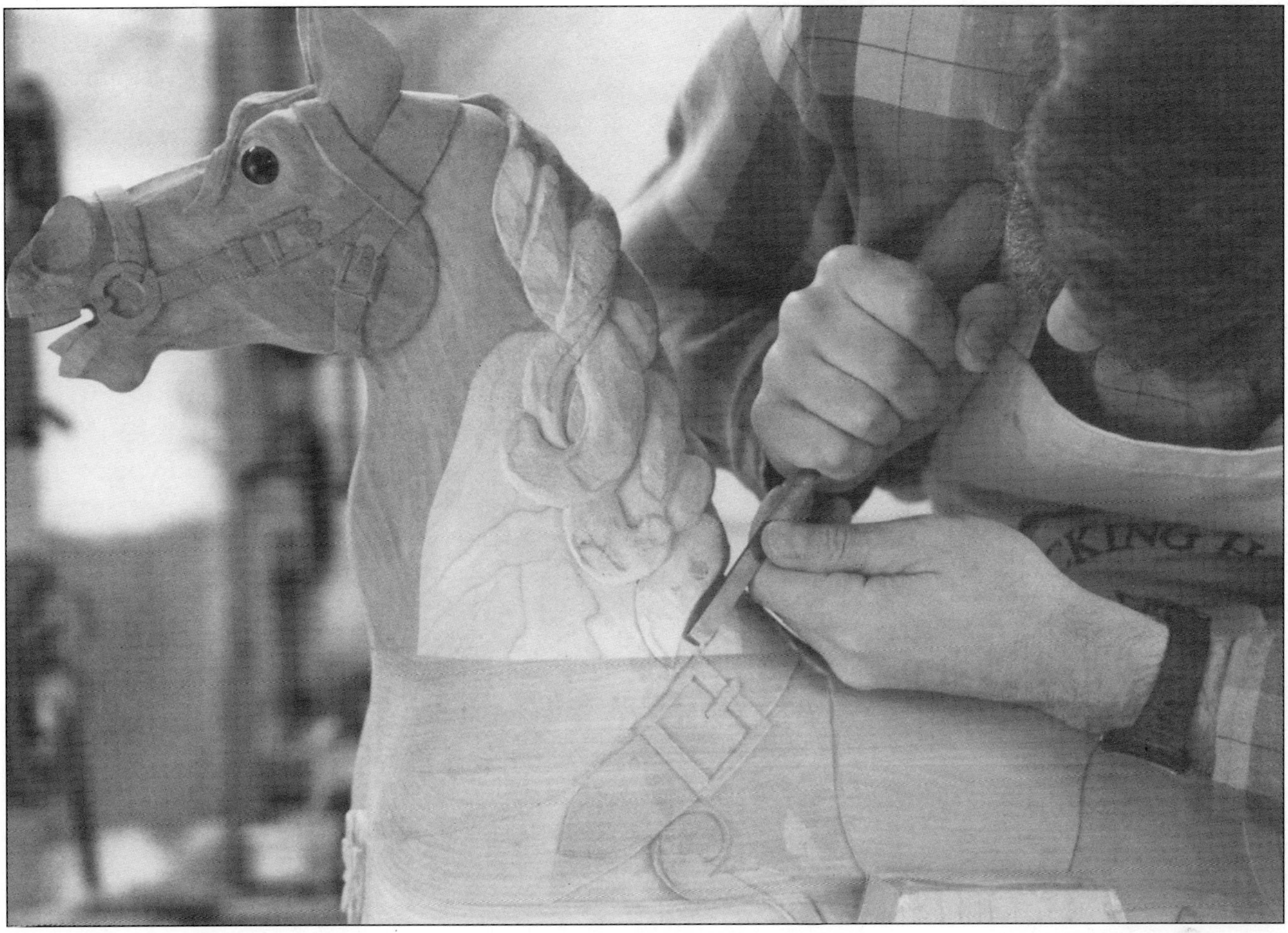

Plate 16.14 Progress is slow but steady.

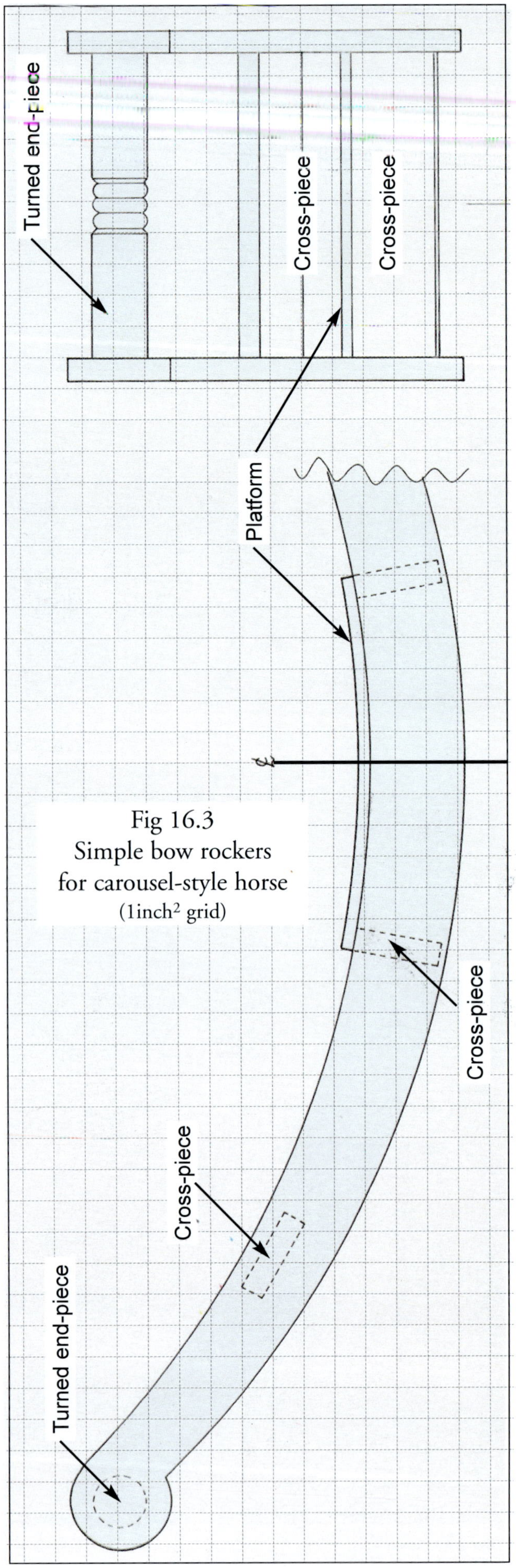

Fig 16.3
Simple bow rockers
for carousel-style horse
(1inch² grid)

to keep your tools sharp, particularly when carving the mane and bridle, because these areas are difficult to sand off and clean cuts with your gouges will require very little or no sanding. In any case when sanding down, take care to keep your carving looking sharp and clean.

In many respects the carousel style horse is similar to the rocking horse. Some of the old time makers made both types, and I regard it as a related species. As a rocking horse maker, I found making this carousel style horse to be a very interesting project; a considerable amount of thought is needed to make the necessary allowances for the thickness and overlap of the various straps, hair and other superficial features. But remember that nothing that happens in woodwork cannot be retrieved or corrected, if you make an error. For example I messed up the chest rosette at my first attempt (my excuse is that it is an awkward area to reach), so I drilled it out with a 2in (51) Forstner bit, and replaced it with another rosette, which I had carved separately to make sure I got it right. Nobody ever noticed.

BOW ROCKER MOUNTING

Since nearly every horse in this book is mounted on rockers, you may wish to make this horse rock as well. The design is unsuitable for mounting on a swing iron stand (there being too little space between the legs), but it is certainly possible to mount it on curved bow rockers, for appearance sake, or for use as a child's plaything.

The bow rocker design in Fig 16.3 and accompanying photographs is quite simple, the rocker sides being parallel. Each of the two sides can be sawn out in one piece, obviating the need for a join in the middle, and both can be cut from 3/4in (19) plywood, 20 x 52in (508 x 1321).

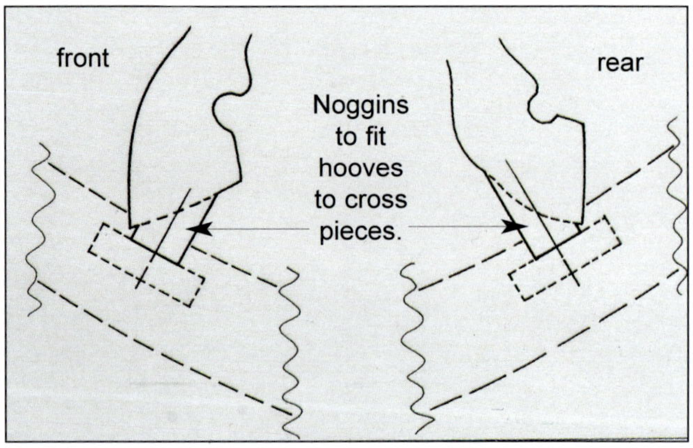

Fig 16.4 Fixing hooves to bow rocker cross pieces.

Plate 16.15 With the carving complete and sanded down, the horse is ready to be painted

Plate 16.16 Making bow rockers for the carousel horse.

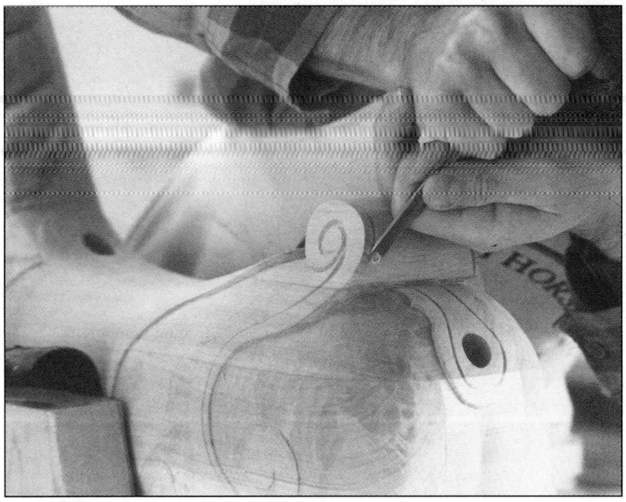

Plate 16.17 Using the V-tool to incise cuts on the saddle block

Plate 16.18 Detail of carving on chest rossette.

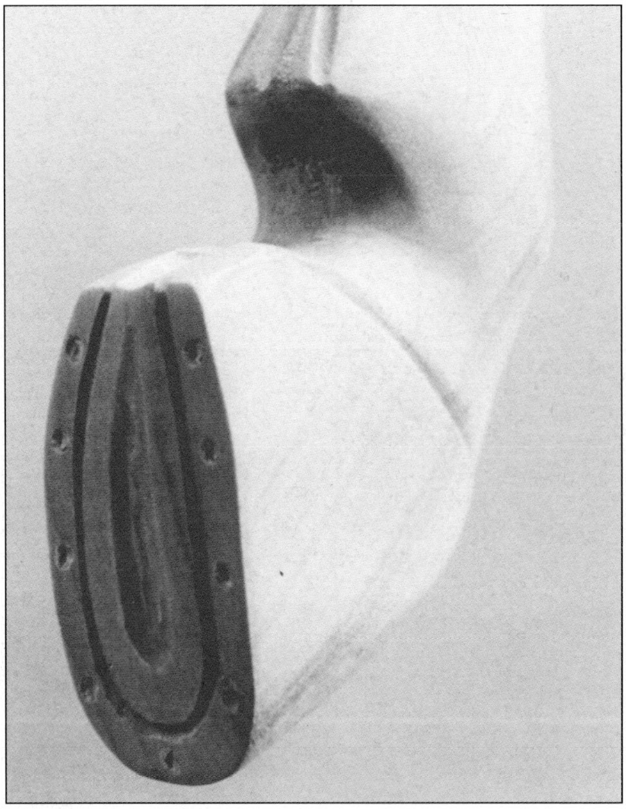

Plate 16.19 Detail of hoof.

There are four cross pieces, each 3/4 x 2 3/4 x 10in (19 x 70 x 254), and two turned ends pieces 1 3/4in (45) in diameter, 10in (254) long. These are glued and secured in position between the rocker sides. The central platform is 1/4in (6) thick plywood, 11 1/2 x 12in (292 x 305), which easily bends round the curve of the rockers and is glued and pinned in place. The hoof noggins are adjusted to sit neatly on to the cross pieces, and the hooves are secured with long screws or screw dowels.

MOUNTING ON A BASE

The horse can be simply mounted on a solid base (in which case the hoof noggins are not needed). The mounting pole, which passes right through the hole previously drilled through the horse, is a length of 3/4in (19) diameter ramin dowel (or metal pipe) 28 in (710) long. Measure 11in (280) from the top end of the pole and drill for a 2in (51) long steel pin on which the horse rests. For the pin, a cut down 4 in (102) nail will serve. The lower end of the pole is inserted into a 3/4in (19) hole drilled 1in (25) deep into a heavy block of timber approximately 1 3/4 x 5 3/4 x 16in (45 x 146 x 406). You may wish to make up one rough base block and pole for mounting the horse on while you paint it, and then another, smarter one, for 'best'. The top of the pole projects a few inches above the saddle and over this can be slotted a length of spiral brass tubing, which has a 3/4in (19) bore, to complete the impression of a carousel horse. I also turned a little decorative finial to neatly finish off the top of the pole.

FINISHING

I was tempted to leave my carousel horse with a natural wood finish, rather than cover all that careful carving with paint, but decided to give it a suitably bright colour scheme reminiscent of that employed by traditional carousel artists. The painting was done with acrylics, for ease of use; first a coat of sanding sealer then three white undercoats rubbed down lightly between coats. The horse, excluding saddlery and mane, was given an antique glaze (see Chapter 13), before painting in the colours. The tail, in this case white horsehair with a bit of black added to echo the painting on the mane, is glued and wedged into its hole, and it is done. A delightful and decorative horse that will certainly enhance your home.

Plate 16.20 The carousel horse nearing completion of the carving.

Plate 17.1 Fine large horse on bows made by F. H. Ayres around 1900, in original condition.

Carr collection

Plate 16.20 *The carousel horse nearing completion of the carving.*

Plate 17.1 Fine large horse on bows made by F. H. Ayres around 1900, in original condition.

Carr collection

CHAPTER 17

RESTORING OLD HORSES

Just because a horse is old does not mean it is a valuable antique. Rocking horses have not attracted the extremely high prices sometimes attained, for example, by collectable dolls. Nevertheless, good examples of fine old rocking horses *are* valuable, and are certainly sought after. There is increasing interest in acquiring old rocking horses. Serious collectors tend to favour horses which retain their original paintwork and tack, even if in a dilapidated state, though the highest prices are obtained for horses in well preserved original condition. If, therefore, you have or acquire an old rocking horse you should think very carefully before stripping off old tack and paintwork, the real patina of which will be irreplaceable.

Old rocking horses do quite often crop up for sale at auctions, in antique shops, and at car boot or garage sales. Bargains can still be found, especially the smaller, simpler horses which need not be disregarded just because they are rather more basic. Prospective purchasers should be warned however, that there are many attractive, carved and old looking horses out there which are in fact cheap modern imports, not the real thing at all. If it seems cheap, be wary.

Plates 17.2, 17.3 & 17.4 (above & right)
This little thing arrived with a broken leg & head, its joints all loose & missing its wheeled platform. Although remnants of the original paintwork & tack survived, the owners opted to have it restored to new condition & then let time take its natural course as it becomes worn again through usage.

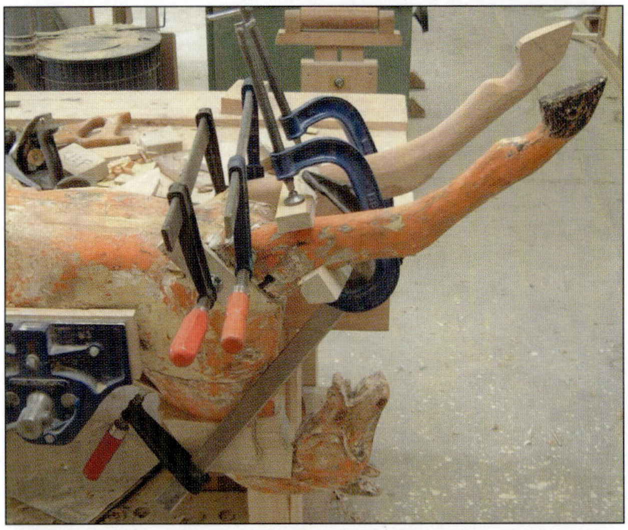

Toy horses often suffer from neglect and abuse. I once had one which appeared to have a terrible case of woodworm, until I realised it had been used as a target for darts practice. Hair falls out, leather perishes and becomes extremely fragile, paintwork chips and is worn away, and the horse may have been re-painted (often very badly). It may have been stored in a damp outhouse (or even outside) so the old animal glue has perished and the joints come adrift; it may suffer from woodworm or rot; wooden parts, especially ears and legs, may be damaged or broken.

Serious consideration should be given before embarking on a project to repair and renovate. A competent restoration by a skilled and experienced professional should not detract from the value of an old rocking horse; in fact it may well enhance its worth (as well as its appearance), but a poorly executed restoration certainly will.

My own view is that a rocking horse is basically a toy for children to play on, and if work is needed to make a battered old horse presentable and safe to ride again, then it should be done. The question is: how much should you do? In recent years I have become increasingly concerned to avoid messing with something which can be so easily ruined. I find I am frequently advising owners who are keen to strip and repaint their rocking horse, to do nothing with it at all. I have talked myself out of a lot of restoration work!

I rarely do any restoration work on the horses that come into my own collection, preferring to leave them in the condition in which they arrived, displaying all the ravages of time and use. Sometimes though, horses come in which are in such an awful state of delapidation that there is no real choice but total repair and renovation.

Plates 17.5, 17.6, 17.7 & 17.8 (left, top to bottom)
This horse had been patched with metal plates nailed over the broken joints, & it fell to pieces when we removed them. It was a mess, but had clearly once been a fine rocking horse, worth fixing. The body was glued & cramped back together, adding new timber where unavoidable. It needed three new legs, a new saddle block & several new muscle blocks. A large section of the old neck which was rotten had to be cut out & a new piece rough shaped, glued & pegged in, & carved. Bottom picture: with all the basic woodwork repairs completed, mounted up on new ash bow rockers, its original rockers having been lost.

CHAPTER 17

Restoring Old Horses

Just because a horse is old does not mean it is a valuable antique. Rocking horses have not attracted the extremely high prices sometimes attained, for example, by collectable dolls. Nevertheless, good examples of fine old rocking horses *are* valuable, and are certainly sought after. There is increasing interest in acquiring old rocking horses. Serious collectors tend to favour horses which retain their original paintwork and tack, even if in a dilapidated state, though the highest prices are obtained for horses in well preserved original condition. If, therefore, you have or acquire an old rocking horse you should think very carefully before stripping off old tack and paintwork, the real patina of which will be irreplaceable.

Old rocking horses do quite often crop up for sale at auctions, in antiquc shops, and at car boot or garage sales. Bargains can still be found, especially the smaller, simpler horses which need not be disregarded just because they are rather more basic. Prospective purchasers should be warned however, that there are many attractive, carved and old looking horses out there which are in fact cheap modern imports, not the real thing at all. If it seems cheap, be wary.

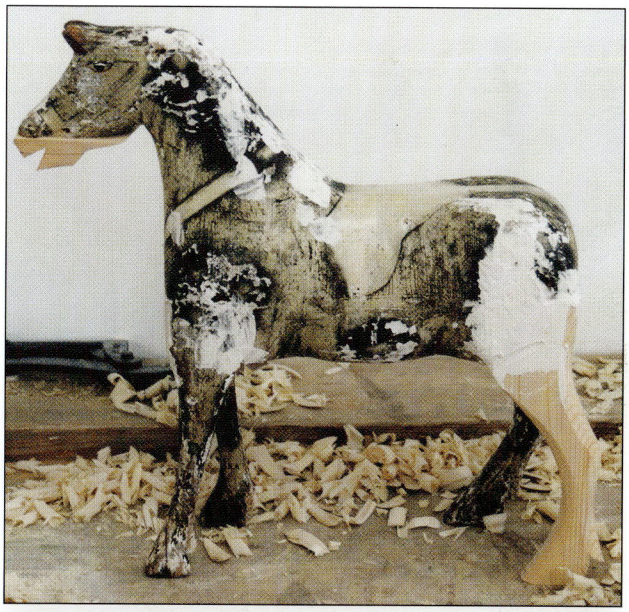

Plates 17.2, 17.3 & 17.4 (above & right)
This little thing arrived with a broken leg & head, its joints all loose & missing its wheeled platform. Although remnants of the original paintwork & tack survived, the owners opted to have it restored to new condition & then let time take its natural course as it becomes worn again through usage.

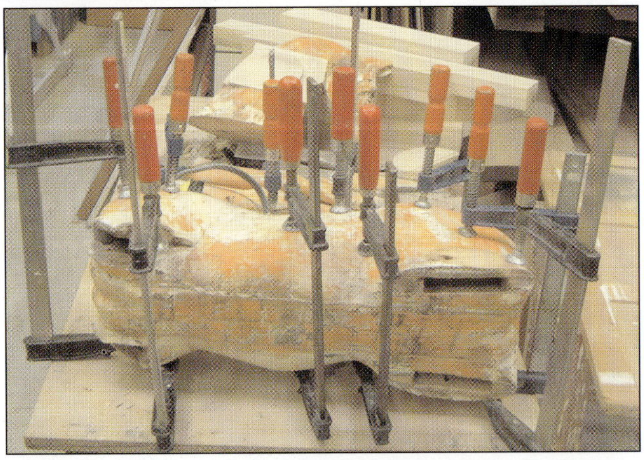

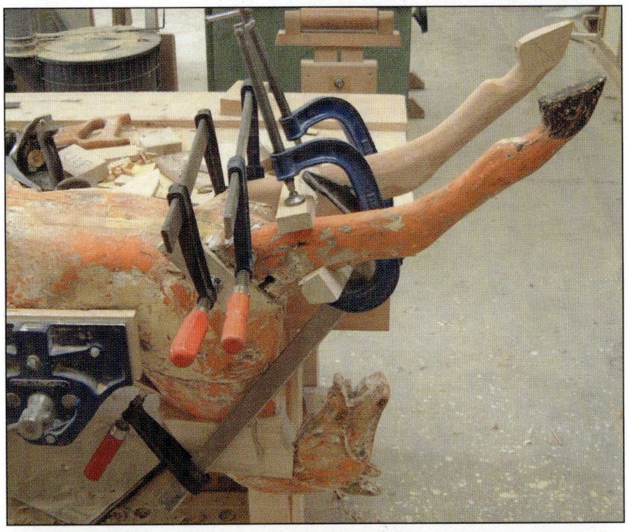

Toy horses often suffer from neglect and abuse. I once had one which appeared to have a terrible case of woodworm, until I realised it had been used as a target for darts practice. Hair falls out, leather perishes and becomes extremely fragile, paintwork chips and is worn away, and the horse may have been re-painted (often very badly). It may have been stored in a damp outhouse (or even outside) so the old animal glue has perished and the joints come adrift; it may suffer from woodworm or rot; wooden parts, especially ears and legs, may be damaged or broken.

Serious consideration should be given before embarking on a project to repair and renovate. A competent restoration by a skilled and experienced professional should not detract from the value of an old rocking horse; in fact it may well enhance its worth (as well as its appearance), but a poorly executed restoration certainly will.

My own view is that a rocking horse is basically a toy for children to play on, and if work is needed to make a battered old horse presentable and safe to ride again, then it should be done. The question is: how much should you do? In recent years I have become increasingly concerned to avoid messing with something which can be so easily ruined. I find I am frequently advising owners who are keen to strip and repaint their rocking horse, to do nothing with it at all. I have talked myself out of a lot of restoration work!

I rarely do any restoration work on the horses that come into my own collection, preferring to leave them in the condition in which they arrived, displaying all the ravages of time and use. Sometimes though, horses come in which are in such an awful state of delapidation that there is no real choice but total repair and renovation.

Plates 17.5, 17.6, 17.7 & 17.8 (left, top to bottom)
This horse had been patched with metal plates nailed over the broken joints, & it fell to pieces when we removed them. It was a mess, but had clearly once been a fine rocking horse, worth fixing. The body was glued & cramped back together, adding new timber where unavoidable. It needed three new legs, a new saddle block & several new muscle blocks. A large section of the old neck which was rotten had to be cut out & a new piece rough shaped, glued & pegged in, & carved. Bottom picture: with all the basic woodwork repairs completed, mounted up on new ash bow rockers, its original rockers having been lost.

Plates 17.9 & 17.10 (below & right)
This beautiful Victorian horse was completely restored after being discovered in a barn. It had broken ears, legs & rockers - & it was painted purple all over!
It would not originally have had a buckle-on bridle like the one fitted, but I couldn't bring myself to bang any nails into that fine old head, which was the inspiration for the thoroughbred heads described in Chapter 15.

Dew collection

Plate17.11 The same horse as in Plate 17.8. The blemishes have been filled, a pair of glass eyes fitted, & it has been given several coats of gesso & sanded smooth, ready to start painting.

Dew collection

Plate17.12 This small horse has a rounded body, but it is the painting more than the carving that makes it attractive.

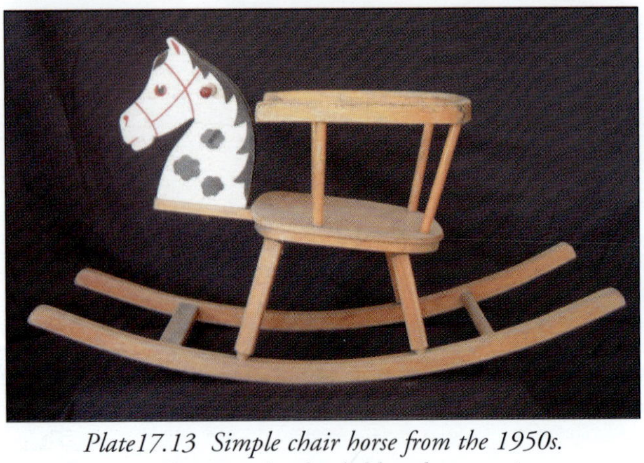

Dew collection

Plate17.13 Simple chair horse from the 1950s. The painted cut-out head is held on by two wing nuts

No wooden rocking horse is completely beyond repair, though it is true that the cost involved may be beyond its economic worth, especially with the smaller, simpler styles of horse. But if it is a well loved family plaything then sympathetic restoration is called for, both to make the horse strong again and safe to ride, and to enhance its appearance.

Before you do anything else, take photographs of the horse from various angles, for help and reference later on. Then try to make an assessment of what is needed. If woodworm is present, this should be treated straightaway with a proprietary woodworm killer squirted into the holes - bearing in mind that the holes are flight holes; the damage has already been done but there may still be more worm in there, which need to be eradicated. Clean sawdust in or around the holes is a sign of active woodworm. When examining the horse, pay particular attention to the undersides of the hoof rails and stand, these areas tend not to have been painted or varnished, so are where woodworm tends to be most evident.

If woodworm infestation, damage or rot is severe and has destroyed the structural strength of the timber, the affected part will have to be removed and replaced with new timber, cut and jointed in, and carved to match the old. Sometimes woodwork repairs are minor and easily accomplished, but sometimes the restoration of a very battered and neglected old horse can turn into a major three dimensional jigsaw puzzle which may involve considerably more work and time than the construction of a new horse. But if the horse is basically a fine example of a historic horse, an heirloom, then the effort and cost are worthwhile.

Once the woodwork is repaired and sound, the remainder of the old paintwork can be removed. We prefer to use a hot air paint stripper and scrapers for this, rather than chemical paint removers. Do not send the horse to be 'dipped and stripped' as this can seriously damage the joints. With the basic structural integrity restored, the painting, dappling and fitting of new tack follows broadly similar methods to those employed for a new horse (see Chapters 13 and 14), though naturally every maker has their own particular style of paintwork and saddlery which, to be authentic, can be reproduced.

A total renovation may be unnecessary. If the horse suffers only from minor degradation of paintwork, scuff marks or cracking, this can be rectified by some judicious touching up. New tack and hair can be fitted if the original is perished beyond repair, or is missing. Such work need not be beyond a reasonably competent amateur.

To restore an old horse accurately to something like its original glory requires a careful study of the particular methods and styles of the old makers. Good professional restorers can recreate the individual dappling style and tack of the various old time makers, but it is beyond the scope of this chapter to examine these, though some examples are given in the accompanying photographs.

Saddle shapes and styles vary enormously, and range from the basic (a piece of material nailed on)

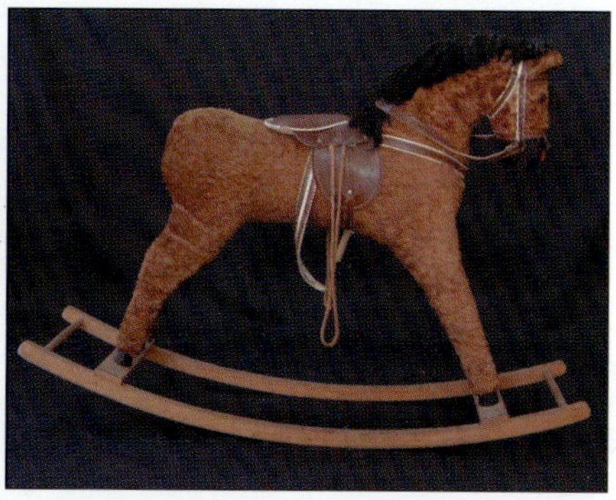

Plate17.14 (left) Painted hessian covered walking horse, with wooden head & legs. Plate 17.15 (centre) Fur fabric covered horse with plastic nose, convertible to push-along toy on its wheeled platform. Plate 17.16 Cheap modern fur fabric covered rocker.

Dew collection

Plate17.17 Skin covered convertible horse, made in Germany in the 1920s. The leatherwork is rather perished, but it's all still there!

Plate 17.18 Mobo tin horse. Made with different paint patterns & mountings, this example on tubular metal bows.

Plate17.19 Simple plywood box construction horse.

Plate17.20 Similarly simple box construction, this one has a bit more shape to the head & neck, & a well padded saddle.

to the realistic. If you have the remains of the original saddle, this can be copied. Some old horses have no saddle block but they can still be fitted with a nail-on type of saddle by removing some of the padding and fixing the back of the saddle tight down to the horse's back. Also, before nailing down the back of the saddle, a length of strapping is tucked underneath the saddle top in the middle to form the crupper. We sometimes fit an old rocking horse with a removable bridle rather than the more common old practice of nailing on the bridle and reins, because children like to be able to remove the bridle in their play, and it saves having to hammer more nails into the old head.

Almost all old rocking horses were fitted with horsehair manes on hide - in other words a strip of hide with the hair still attached to it - and this type may still be obtained. The hide is wetted to soften it and is simply nailed on down the horse's neck with 1in (25) wire nails. The nail heads are punched in and bury themselves out of sight in the hide. A smaller piece of hide is nailed on at the front of the mane, with the hair going forwards between the ears, to form the forelock. Smaller, cheaper horses, may be fitted with synthetic manes and tails, sometimes made of rope or wool.

Sometimes delightful relics are to be found inside the hollow bodies of old wooden horses. Over the years we have retrieved quite a collection of pens, cigarette cards, marbles, dice, hair pins, dried peas, a sandalwood needle case, anything small enough to poke through the tail or pommel holes. Sometimes these throw an interesting light on the history of the horse. Inside one rocking horse which belonged to a school we found an old class list and managed to trace one of the names on the list. Now an elderly gentleman, he could vividly remember the experience of being allowed to ride the rocking horse as a treat during his first week at school many decades before.

We have sometimes found pieces of newspaper used as padding under the saddle, which can help date a rocking horse; either when it was made or previously restored. Often interesting aspects of a horse's history can be learned from its owner or past owners. One old horse contained a large

Dew collection - on loan from Mr & Mrs Smith

Plate 17.21 Excellent example of a Lines 'Bronco' horse, made in 1915 & in absolutely original condition.

Plate17.22 A very simple horse made by Collinsons of Liverpool. Unusual, because such simple horses rarely survive.

Dew collection

Plate17.23 A typical Collinson dapple grey dating from the 1970s. Remarkably consistent style for many years, though on the later ones the carving is more basic, the dappling brasher.

Dew collection

Plate17.24 All wood Collinson horse covered with fur fabric.

quantity of dried rice! It transpired that the lady owner, now in her late seventies, had hated rice as a little girl, so whenever rice was on the menu she would wait until her mother's back was turned and get rid of it into the rocking horse.

Some old rocking horses have two round holes just above the stirrup staples. These were for pommels, shaped hardwood covered in thin leather, with round pegs. They ensured a secure seat for tiny children (who could hook their legs over them), and little girls could practise riding side-saddle. Since they were removable they are frequently lost and most restorers do not bother to replace them, they just fill (or leave) the holes, and fit the new saddle over the top. However, new pommels can be fitted if you wish. You will need to cut round holes in the saddle flaps and/or skirts in the appropriate positions to align with the holes in the horse. Sometimes a small leather flap is nailed on close to the pommel hole to conceal it when the pommels are not in use.

STANDS AND ROCKERS

Stands and rockers were often originally varnished and may only require a good clean and polish. Sometimes stands have transfers or painted stencils with the name of the maker, retailer, or the patent date, and you should try not to obliterate these. A mixture of vinegar, white spirit and linseed oil will, when rubbed gently, remove dirt without damaging old paint or varnish. If the stand or rockers were originally painted - often green - they can be either cleaned, or stripped and varnished. On stands, the swing irons and brackets will need to be removed, cleaned and probably repainted, and the bearing strips renewed if worn down.

As a rocking horse gets older, he may be loved, abused, battered, bruised and broken, but every few decades he can be fixed up and given a new lease of life, for new generations of children to enjoy. In this way a rocking horse can live forever!

FURTHER INFORMATION and ADVICE

More information on historic makers can be found in 'The Rocking Horse - A History of Moving Toy Horses' by Patricia Mullens, undoubtedly the best reference work on the subject (unfortunately now out of print, but should be obtainable from libraries), and back copies of 'The Rocking Horse & Toy Magazine', available from the address in the Appendix. Or ask a professional restorer; advice is usually freely given.

Plate17.25 Pre 2nd World War example of a typical dapple grey made by Collinsons. Rectangular posts & bold dappling.

Dew collection

Plate17.27 Leeway horse with its distinctive sprayed dappling, chamfered square posts & typically bright saddlery.

Plate17.28 Close-up of the Leeway head with its round nostrils pointing down &, in spite of its age, plenty of hair.

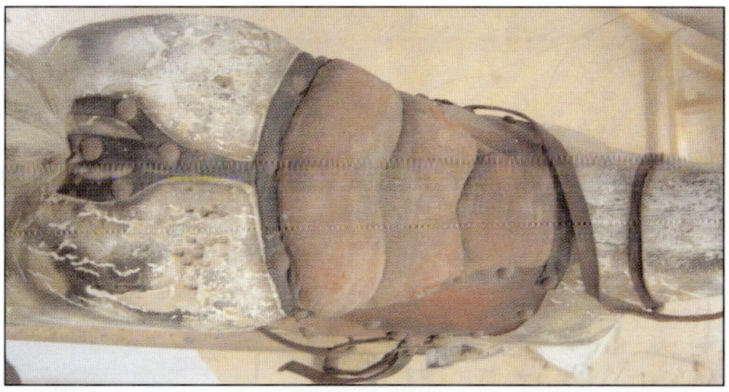

Plate17.26 Typical Collinson saddle, with corduroy seat, leatherette skirts & saddlecloth, stirrup leathers nailed on.

Dew collection

Plate17.29 A large Haddon fibreglass horse often used in schools, this one with a secure seat for small children.

Plate17.30 This fibreglass 'Ragamuffin' horse, made in the late 1970s, is based on a spring mounted wooden Victorian horse.

Carr collection

Plate17.31 Lines rocking horse in original condition. Ayres horses are generally considered the best, Lines come a close second.

Courtesy of Pam & Stuart MacPherson

Plate17.32 Ayres horse on rare steel sprung swing iron stand.

Dew collection

Plate17.33 (& opposite) Large Ayres swivel head horse dating from the late 1880s. Note the leather covered saddle pommel.

Plate17.34 Fully restored large Ayres horse. A rare animal, the head swivels to left and right when the reins are pulled, returning to look forwards by means of a large coil spring hidden in the base of the neck. The join is concealed under a wide leather band.

Appendix

ACTUAL SIZE PLANS

To save you the bother of enlarging the scale drawings in this book, full size plans are available for each design, supplied complete with step by step instructions and pictures.

Actual size plans and instructions are also available for laminated rocking horse designs and the carver's chops.

VIDEO

A professionally produced video entitled "Making Rocking Horses" is available, in which Anthony Dew demonstrates all stages of making a fully carved Victorian style rocking horse, including the assembly, carving, finishing, dappling and mounting.

TIMBER PACKS

Packs of selected high quality kiln dried timber are available, machined to size and with all the initial preparation done, up to the point where you can start on the assembly and carving of each project. Timber Packs for horses are normally supplied in tulipwood, and include all the parts of the horse bandsawn to shape, with some of the angled joints pre-cut. Timber Packs for stands and bow rockers are normally supplied in ash, and include ready turned posts or end pieces.

TOOLS & EQUIPMENT

Carving gouges, sharpening equipment and carver's mallets are available, as well as power carving accessories and sanders, adhesive, woodfillers, Surforms and Microplanes, spokeshaves, drawknives and other tools, paint and gesso packs. Ready made carver's chops can also be supplied.

ACCESSORIES & FITTINGS

The most comprehensive range of high quality accessories and fittings - glass eyes, leather bridles and saddles, horsehair or synthetic manes and tails, stirrup irons, swing irons etc are available, either in Accessory Sets containing everything needed to complete a project to perfection, or separately. There is a choice of colour combinations for hair and leather, and metal brackets, buckles, bowler hats and stirrup irons are available in polished solid brass, or chrome or nickel plated.

RENOVATION KITS

A unique service for battered old horses in which leather bridles and saddlery are made to measure in a style and size to suit a particular old horse. Leather can be supplied with a special "antique" finish. Renovation Kits include manes and tails and all the accessories and fittings needed to enable you to re-tack your old horse, with instructions.

RESTORATION SERVICE

The Rocking Horse Shop offers a complete Restoration Service, and can recommend other suitably qualified restorers.

NEW ROCKING HORSES

At The Rocking Horse Shop beautiful new hand crafted rocking horses are continually being carved, and may be made to commission. The shop also stocks a number of rocking horses from other makers.

OLD ROCKING HORSES

The Rocking Horse Shop is home to Anthony Dew's collection of over a hundred rocking horses and other toys. The collection is open to the public and aims to show some of the great variety of sizes, styles and types which makers have produced over the years. Several of the horses in the collection have been gifted or are on loan and, if you have an old rocking horse that needs a new home, Anthony welcomes new additions.

Please write or phone for a brochure, or see website for more information.

The Rocking Horse Shop
Fangfoss
York
YO41 5JH
ENGLAND
Telephone: 0044 (0) 1759 368737
www.rockinghorse.co.uk

THE GUILD OF ROCKING HORSE MAKERS

The purpose of The Guild of Rocking Horse Makers is to promote and encourage the traditional craft of Making Rocking Horses.

Any person who has actually made a Rocking Horse can apply to become a Member of the Guild. Everyone else - restorer, enthusiast, or just interested - can join the Guild as a Friend.

The Guild publishes regular newsletters with features and articles of interest to rocking horse makers, restorers and enthusiasts, and has a dedicated website. Each new member receives a special badge and certificate of achievement, signed by Guild President Anthony Dew.

The Guild website provides a forum where Guild members and Friends can exchange information and news on all aspects of the craft. There are also various Guild benefits including discounts on tools and equipment, insurance, a regular prize draw and invitations to Guild events.

Further details from:

The Guild of Rocking Horse Makers
c/o The Rocking Horse Shop
Fangfoss
York
YO41 5JH
ENGLAND
Telephone 0044 (0) 1759 368737

Access to Guild website through:
www.rockinghorse.co.uk

ACKNOWLEDGEMENTS

Many people have helped and encouraged me in the preparartion of this book,
and I would like to thank:

All the staff at The Rocking Horse Shop,
especially Jane Cook and Sheila Whitaker,
Barrie, Barbara, Julie, Rosie, Jenny and Sam Lawley.

Rocking horse makers Sam Glass and Pam & Stuart MacPherson.
Sue Austen for the miniature and Judy Fergusson for the laminated rocking horses.
Jimi Ogden and his father, who found the 1st World War pictures.
Joe & Catherine Carr.

Lynn Dew, Jacky Exelby, Pat and Bryn Allen, Kate and Pat Dew,
and my parents for their unfailing help & support.

Photographers Dr Alan Robson, David Golledge.
John & Kwan fromGledhill Design, Rob from Bestprint,
Paul & Angie from Craftsman magazine
Wrightsons photolab.

Amber Cruickshank, Francesca Billingham and all the other children
who have ridden my rocking horses and who are such excellent critics.

And all my other friends, rocking horse enthusiasts and Members of The Guild of Rocking Horse
Makers who, over the years, have offered so much useful advice and information.

NOTE for MAKERS

As stated in the opening pages, this book supercedes my previous ones and, although some of the designs have been published before, I have taken the opportunity afforded by writing this new book to introduce many modifications and improvements to them. In some cases these make the version of the design in this book incompatible with previously published versions. On publication of this book, the actual size plans supplied by The Rocking Horse Shop will be modified to accord with the designs in this book. Confusion may arise if makers attempt to use a previously published plan in conjunction with the designs in this book. Keep it straightforward and work to one plan, preferably the most up-to-date one.

Good luck with your project!

INDEX

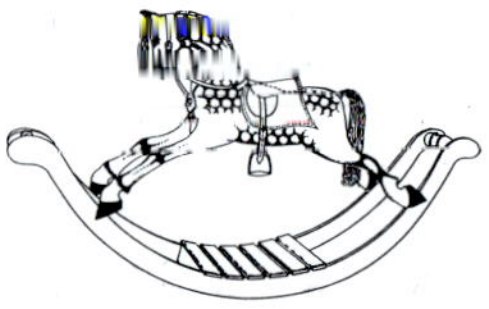